Bible Quotes are Word English Bible (WEB) except where noted.

Follow the Firstborn
Sown in Weakness and Shame
Raised in Power and Glory

JON FARMER

Copyright © 2025 Jon Farmer

All Rights Reserved. No part of this book may be reproduced, stored in a retrieval system, or transmitted, in any form or by any means, electronic, mechanical, photocopying, recording, or otherwise, without the written permission of the author.

Scripture quotations are taken from the Word English Bible (WEB) unless otherwise noted.

Scripture quotations marked NKJV are from the NEW KING JAMES VERSION®. Copyright© 1982 by Thomas Nelson, Inc. Used by permission. All rights reserved.

Scripture quotations marked KJV are from The Authorized (King James) Version. Reproduced by permission of the Crown's patentee, Cambridge University Press.

Scripture quotations marked NRSV are from The New Revised Standard Version of the Bible, copyright © 1946, 1952, and 1971 National Council of the Churches of Christ in the United States of America. Used by permission. All rights reserved worldwide.

The subtitle of this book is taken from 1 Corinthians Chapter 15

Printed in the United States of America

ISBN 979-8-9893593-6-3

Bible Quotes are Word English Bible (WEB) except where noted.

"Jon's training and mentorship into our ministry staff have proven tremendously impactful. He has a deep love for God's Word and a passion for sharing its truths. His ability to teach Scripture with clarity and depth – and with both kindness and boldness - sets him apart as a gifted communicator and servant of Christ."

> Hoon Ju, Director, Christian Youth Revival Retreat

"We are so glad to have Jon streaming live from Mon Christian Gifts regularly! Jon has the unique ability to show the tender heart of God in his loving and passionate approach while bringing forth the gospel and highlighting the importance, urgency and immense power behind it, all while making it fascinatingly interesting by not shying away from but embracing the more difficult and seemingly strange parts, while staying true to the word of God."

> Jared Burnett, Mon Christian Gifts, Raleigh, NC

"In a teaching event on the Blood Covenant of Christ and its implications for Marriages, just one of Jon's simple comments radically impacted my marriage for the better."

> Anonymous

"Jon loves the Word of God. He goes deeply into the Word, and his relationship with God and His word is phenomenal. Jon is an inspiration to us all."

> Faith McMillan, Associate Pastor for Counseling Services, Bethel City Church, , Morrisville, NC

"The hungry believer is immediately invited into a place of amazing victory, increased authority, deeper intimacy and great confidence as New Creations in Christ. Follow the Firstborn is uniquely graced to tear off the veil of unbelief and abolish average 'Christian living' through a brilliant scriptural exposition of our inheritance in Christ, its realities and our capabilities as sons and daughters of GOD.

Follow the Firstborn is an enjoyable read and an incredible resource! Jon has systematically presented new biblical truth in a cohesive manner, unlocking dozens of 'mysterious' passages, awakening joy and bringing to light the virtually limitless grace of God available to believers (see Ephesians 1) convincingly, with clarity.

In particular Jon shows that, what the early converts were watching for and then "believed in" was simply the overcoming power of "Christ in You" that is available NOW on a life-exchange basis. The result is excitement and hope, because we see that the plan of God is indeed to make us like Him, and we see that the "free indeed" Christ spoke of is still there!

Jon is a "jump-starter." Jon's strong teaching gift awakens listeners to their Sonship and dominion in CHRIST. For years I have enjoyed watching as Jon has discipled, equipped, empowered and released GOD's people into these new covenant realities through intensive equipping and training.

Jon is very much in love with the Word of God and has a remarkable command of the scriptures. Jon has become unwilling to hold the form of religion but deny the power of God. Instead of "theologizing" failures, he overcomes the resistance of status quo and unbelief and inspires others around him to do the same."

> Marcus Plating, Lead Pastor, Bethel City Church, Morrisville, NC

Bible Quotes are Word English Bible (WEB) except where noted.

FOREWORD

Beginning in 2018, a sequence of discoveries brought me to realize that there were several amazing promises of God that were *for this life* - that I "left on the table". There are a few soldiers of God – Lake, Blake, and Bercot that brought these to my attention. These discoveries provide an important background for *Follow the Firstborn*.

Through the writings of John G. Lake I discovered that the *Kingdom of God* and *Dominion* form the **most pervasive unifying story line of the Bible**, and that the life Christ call us to is the life of the loyal soldier. I am grateful to Lake for that!

Shortly after discovering Lake, I found John G. Lake Ministries and Curry R. Blake. I am deeply grateful to brother Blake not only for his diligently scriptural teachings, but for his ongoing personal demonstration of the life Christ demonstrated and taught - as He said "follow me".

I had been studying for *decades* to reconcile all the "seemingly irreconcilable" scripture passages that we see in English Bible translations. I had made great breakthroughs by the time I started this book series about four years ago. But as I got into this book, I found myself to be *more concerned than ever* to get my essential salvation doctrines *fully accurate* in meaning, *plain* in terms, and *adequately precise*.

But then in great timing - for me, that is, I discovered and devoured the works of David Bercot on the written scripture interpretations of early church leaders; and also books by Matthew Bates on the underlying "Allegiance" nature of "saving faith. The depth of scholarship of these two brothers - combined with their obvious love for God - have allowed me to rest assured I have gotten the core gospel essentials right.

With this foundation, I present Follow the Firstborn in hopes that you the reader will awaken to precious elements of the transformative power of God that many believers, like I myself had "left on the table" for so many years.

DEDICATION

I dedicate this Book to the Lord Jesus Christ, who is "the Lover of my Soul"; He grants us freedom, dignity, strength, mercy, and joyful anticipation of the coming Kingdom!

Contents

PART 0: INTRODUCTION 4
    The Poster Helps Keep "The Forest" in View 11
    Like a Book With Kingdom as its "Covers" 16
    Christ the Firstborn The Supreme King of Glory 20
        Said "Follow Me" Having Overcome Sin and Death 21
    Grace is the Second Mankind "Planted" by God 22
        He Tends His Garden Loving, Nurturing, and Providing . 23
    Poster-Flow Narratives At Progressing Levels of Detail 26
        "Drive-By" Narrative: A *Few Sentences* Per Panel 27
    Poster-Flow Narrative About a *Half-Minute* per Panel 30
    Poster-Flow Narrative A *Few Minutes* Per Panel 36
    Maintaining Vision: Keeping the Big Picture In View 46
        Showing His Glory: Both the Forest and the Trees 47
    Two-Page Spreads: Scriptures Left, Comments Right 48
        See the Invitation; A Hundred Different Ways 49
    Do You Desire "Rest"? God offers *Restoration* 50
        Of "That Which Was Lost" But ... *What Was Lost?* 51
    Bear Again The Image of God; No Shame! 52
        Embrace His Promise And Partake of His Nature! 53
    Let's Be Honest About the Need to Persevere 54
        Scriptures are Plain And Stakes Could Not be Higher 55
    Some Valid Definitions That Resolve Contradictions 56
    Pistis: Allegiance, Loyalty, Fidelity, Faithfulness 58
        Faith in Action is Faithfulness and Fidelity 59
PART 1: THE MISSING PIECES 60
    Clearing the FOG The Forgiveness-Only Gospel 64

Raised in Power and Glory

Bible Quotes are Word English Bible (WEB) except where noted.

  To See God's Call To Holiness, Glory, and Dominion 65
 The Way of Holiness The Redeemed Shall Walk There 68
  A "Highway" No Ravenous Beast Shall Be There 69
 Spirit vs. Soul vs. Body: What *Am* I? 70
  Your Spirit is "You" and You're No Longer a Sinner 71
PART 2: HIDDEN IN PLAIN SIGHT 72
 Foundation & Pillars Upon God's Love & Forbearance 76
  He Who Loves Christ Follows Him into *Strength* 77
 By the Love of God: All We Need is Provided 80
  Yes, It's Mystical! As the Word of God Explains 81
 Cover Photo "Pillars" Form a "Backbone" of the Bible 82
  The First Adam Corrupted; The Second Adam Purifies ... 83
 Foundation: God's Steadfast Love & Forbearance 86
  He is Absolutely *Just* ... Yet He is Also *Merciful* 87
 Pillar: The New Covenant Promised, Ratified, Fulfilled 88
  Unites Us with God In a Solemn *Blood Covenant* 89
 Not Just "Secure" But Secure *In Christ* 90
  To Be "In Christ" Is to Live to Do His Will...................... 91
 The New Covenant Sacrifices & Exchange of Gifts...................... 92
  For Both Sides God Provided the Sacrifice 93
 Pillar: The Second Man The "Mankind *Do-Over*"! 96
  Are We Still Sinners? Not if We are Born Again 97
 Pillar: Dominion & Inheritance.. 100
  Life as a Son of God Is Hope, Peace, and Joy................. 101
 In this Age: First Fruits In Spirit, Soul, and Body 102
  Not the Ultimate But the Earnest 103
PART 3: DOMINION GIVEN ... *FORFEITED; STILL AWAITING* 106
 The Beginning: All Things Under Our Feet 108
  A Profound Expression of God's Love 109
 We Gave It Away Seeking Personal Dominion 110
  Who Will Be Satisfied To Rule With & *Under* Christ? .. 111
  Sown in Weakness and Shame

The Dominion Intent Stands Through the Ages 114
    Gospel of the Kingdom: Invitation to Dominion 115
A Cloud of Witnesses Sons Being Brought to Glory 118
    Glory is "Winning" But the Opponent is Not Man 119
Dominion: For Him Who ... *"Overcomes"?* 120
    The "Do-Over" Under Wonderful Conditions 121
Christ Shall Reign And in Him, We Shall Reign 122
    To Him Who Conquers Glory, Honor, Immortality 123
Restoration of All Things Peace, Joy, Glory, and Honor 124
    Everything that Creeps... Would You Crush Them? 125
The Kingdom of God Allows *Violence*? 126
    To Be Again Crowned With Glory & Honor 127
PART 4: NEW COVENANT PROMISE & ARRIVAL 128
PART 4A: A NEW SPIRIT AND A NEW HEART 130
    Forgiveness + ... Desire + Power = Free Indeed 131
The Days are Coming I Will Make a *New* Covenant 132
    Forgiveness of Sins: Merely the *Foyer* of the *Palace* 133
New Heart, New Spirit; Freedom, Provision, Belonging 134
    An Inner Constitution Possessing the Mind of Christ 135
    The Shedding *Of Innocent* Blood was Required 137
He Bore Our Sickness and Carried Our Pains 138
    He Will See the Fruit of His Travail and Be Satisfied 139
The Spirit of God Poured Out for All Mankind 140
    We Should Hunger for It It is Intended for Us All 141
PART 4B: THE ARRIVAL OF WHAT WAS PROMISED 142
We will Love Him, Make Our Home with Him 144
    Surrender into Union with God Through Christ 145
This High Priest Did what "The Law" Could Not 150
    Restoring Desire & Power To Do What is Right 151
PART 5: CHRIST THE SECOND MAN MADE THE WAY 153
The Last Adam, The Second Mankind 156
Raised in Power and Glory

Bible Quotes are Word English Bible (WEB) except where noted.

Sown in Weakness, Shame Raised in Power & Glory 157
I Give You as a Covenant To Restore What was Lost 158
Even Christ Embraced ... *Hope of What is Promised* 159
To Crown Mankind with ... *Glory and Honor?* 162
Glorify: To Bring Glory to Another 163
To Bring Many Sons To Companionship and Glory 166
Not Ashamed To Call Us His Brothers and Sisters! 167
Christ *Became* Sin Then was Raised in Glory 168
What's There to "See"? More than "Sins Forgiven" 169
Christ: The Bread of Life Let's Be *Nourished* by Him! 172
Be Nourished The Sacrificial Lamb of God 173
The Hour Has Come For Union – *"One as We are One"* 176
Fully at Peace, But with Staggering Implications 177
Reuniting Us with God Completing the Mission 180
"We" Were Raised To "My Father & Your Father" 181
Finally, With Us in Him "Seated" ... Where? 182
Far Above Every Name The Ultimate Kindness 183
Ambush Completed Rulers are Coming to Nothing 184
On Our Behalf, The Greatest Victory of All Time 185
Christ Went Before Us 186
Finally, to Send That Which Was Promised 187
PART 6: OUR INITIAL SURRENDER - ENTERING INTO HIM 188
Getting Right with God Stakes Could Not Be Higher 189
A Turn of Allegiance To Seek the Kingdom of God 190
See His Glory and Make the Trade 191
If Any Man Would Come After Me 194
Let Him! Jesus Has Said It Plainly 195
The Way to Glory Passes through Self-Denial 196
Self-Will Resists! But His Death Made a Way 197
The Way is Now Open to Escape & Partake 198
Greatest Promise *Never Heard In Most Churches* 199

Sown in Weakness and Shame

The Important Opening Of Peter's Pentecost Sermon 200
    The King of Glory … Calls for Your Allegiance 201
In Hope, I Forsake Sin To Follow the Firstborn 202
    Baptism is Surrender A True Pledge of Allegiance 203
I Am Recreated In My *Innermost Being* 204
    The Last Adam, The Second Mankind 205
Freed From Sin To Turn from it & Serve God 208
    Bearing Fruit of Holiness and Its End … *Eternal Life* ... 209
I Ask & Receive Power to Overcome the Enemy 212
    Christ *in You* Restoring that which Was Lost 213
Craving Righteousness Desiring to Be … *a Son of God* 214
    Hungry for … *This*? If So, You *Shall* be *Filled* 215

PART 7: ABIDING IN HIM, BECOMING LIKE HIM 216

Let Go and Let God? Good! … if *Rightly Understood* 220
    Passivity is Deadly! Saving Faith Is Allegiance 221
    Abandon Self-Will Follow Him to His Kingdom 223
Abide in My Love By Keeping My Commands 226
    But This is Possible … Only in Dying to Self-Will 227
We Persevere To … Glory, Honor, and Immortality 230
    He Makes Us Free Providing Incentives and Power 231
I Put on the New Man Overcoming Sin by *His Power* 232
    When He Appears *We'll* Appear *with Him* in *Glory* 233
I Confirm … My Election with All Diligence 234
    How Long Will Theologians Spoon-Feed Us? 235
No Eye has Seen What God has Prepared … 238
    But God Has Revealed Them By His Spirit 239
1st Mankind Sees 2nd: Two Possible Responses 240
    An Issue of Dominion: *Who* Shall Reign Forever? 241
Walk According to Spirit … and Live 242
    The Life of a True Follower: "No Condemnation" 243
He Perfected Man Our Conscience Finally at Peace 244

Bible Quotes are Word English Bible (WEB) except where noted.

To Be His People Living by His Life In Us	245
Some Jews were Jealous! But *God* Sees and Chooses	246
Not by Bloodline Nor Rituals, Empire, or Society	247
Becoming Like Him This Hope Does Not Disappoint	248
No Fear As He Is, So are We in This World	249
A Mature Son of God I Overcome, and Yes - I Tread	250
Advancing the Kingdom On Earth as it is in Heaven	251
Until the Day With Christ as He Returns	252
But there is a Treading For This Age	253
Freed by His Death As Us Not Only *Buried* with Him	256
But In the Unseen, We Were Also *Raised* with Him	257
Part 3 Revisited: The Body of Christ, Growing	258
Shall We Join Them? The Remnant in White Robes	259
PART 8: THE ROMANS CENTER-LANE	**260**
Two Mankinds, Two Lineages, Two Laws	266
The Romans Center Lane: In "Three-Up" Format	267
Romans 1, 2, 3 For Obedience to the Faith	268
Romans 4, 5, 6 … Fixing Shame of What We Are	269
Romans 7, 8 No More Sinner by Constitution	272
As a Salvation Matter: Put Sin to Death by His Spirit	273
Chapters 4-8 In One-paragraph Summaries	274
PART 9: THE WAY OF HOLINESS Cover Photo Analogy	**275**
PART 10: SECOND MANKIND GOSPEL SUMMARIES	**279**
The "STEP OUT" Acrostic	289
Put On Righteousness Overcome, Unload, and Tread	292
Looking Ahead in Hope To Dominion Restored	293
Will You Ascend? Gain *Clean Hands* & *Pure Heart*	294
All That We Need: No More Guilt, No More Shame	295
Kingdom & Dominion Water of Life, Tree of Life	296
To Him Who Conquers: Glory, Honor, Immortality	297
The Apostle's Creed: The Early Church's Summary	298

Sown in Weakness and Shame

  Christ Made the Way Forgiveness, Resurrection, Life ... 299
 The Full-Grace Witness: The Power of Our Testimony 300
 The Act of Witnessing Must Flow from the Fact 302
  People Seek The Meeting of Their Needs 303
 Announce the Offer Keeping Promises & Terms in View 306
  As Simple as Possible but No Simpler 307
 The New Covenant: Benefits & Terms 310
 A Time to "Major" In the Gospel of the *Kingdom* 314
  It Makes Us Free ... If we *Know* It and *Walk* in It 315
 Gospel Narrative In "We and You" Points-of-View 318
 Simple Truth Makes you "Theologian-proof" 326
  Application We are Invited to Live that Life 327
 New Covenant Impacts for Sound Teaching 330
  Final Salvation: By Simply Utilizing the Gift 331
CONCLUSION 342
 See His Glory And Hunger for Righteousness 344
  Bear His Image And Fulfill the Commission 345
 Narration Of a Changed Way of Thinking 346
  Healthy Motives Not Only Allowed, but Required 347
 The True Church As the Age Draws to a Close 348
  Kingdom Demonstrations With the Enemy on Notice ... 349
 Full Salvation: Entering Followed by Abiding 352
  He is Calling; You'll Be More than Satisfied 353
Questions for Study 354

ACKNOWLEDGMENTS

I am deeply grateful to my review team at Bethel City Church - for their beautiful lives and friendship! - and for their prayerful and constructive feedback: Marcus Plating, Faith McMillian, Ed and Wendy Kraft, Brian and Celia Nguyen, Robert and Jen Waldrop, Jared and Monica Burnett, and M'Shiela Hawthorne.
I especially thank Dena Snead for her excellent editing assistance.

I thank John G. Lake (1870-1935) for his "Hundredfold Consecration" in action and his testimony that woke me up.
I thank Curry R. Blake for his demonstration of obeying the gospel and living from Heaven to Earth.
I thank Pastor Marcus Plating for believing and proclaiming the whole Word of God without compromise, rightly divided, and in context; and for the warrior-trainer that he is.
I thank Bible historian David Bercot for showing in his "Historic Faith Commentary Series" what the Early church leaders unanimously believed regarding free will and predestination for the first 3 centuries A.D. until Augustine entered.

I am especially grateful to my amazing wife Mary, for her unfailing patience and support in this long season of writing.

Bible Quotes are Word English Bible (WEB) except where noted.

Follow the Firstborn

Sown in Weakness and Shame; Raised in Power and Glory

JON FARMER

Bible Quotes are Word English Bible (WEB) except where noted.

PART 0: INTRODUCTION

*"What Do I Wish to Become?
One of <u>These</u>, or One of <u>Those</u>?"*

This is the question that determines our eternal destiny.

The *Second Man Now* Series seeks to bring back into view what popular Christianity, by and large, has **buried**. That thing is the *New Covenant* itself; It is the news that Christ came to be fruitful and multiply *Himself* – sons and daughters of the living God; We are to be that fruit (Read John 12:24 carefully).

This is not just interesting but misguided "mysticism". It is the key that unlocks the numerous passages that are so foreboding on their own that they never see the light of day in the typical modern evangelical church. As examples, please open a Bible and read Romans 2:7 or 1 John 2:17.

They seem "legalistic" – even **totally contrary to "Grace"**:

> *Romans 2:7 to those who by patiently doing good seek for glory and honor and immortality, he will give eternal life;*

> *1 John 2:17 And the world and its desire are passing away, but those who do the will of God live forever.*

The solution is not to find a church that ignores these or explains them away with mind-numbing contradictory theology – there is far too much at stake. The solution is to find out, from the Bible itself, how to become the being that has the power to do what is right and to experience it as a light burden.

Let's be honest – we see most of the church (lowercase c) defeated and powerless, as if Christ came to create a multitude of sinners settling for "forgiveness now and Heaven someday". The truth of this matter is that we are to see ourselves being transformed to bear the image of God – in both love and strength, we must not settle for forgiveness of past sins (Rom 3:27). The Word of God tells us that we can be confident on the day of judgement when we can say along with the Apostle whom Jesus loved:

> As He is, <u>*so are we in this World*</u> (1 John 4:17).

It seems to me that, those that believe they have received just "forgiveness and heaven-bound" cannot possibly be okay with it – because nobody is content with enslavement, loneliness, shame, and defeat *in this life*. I was there for decades living in that state. I led men's ministry the way everyone did it, then I discovered what the scriptures plainly said about freedom in Romans 6 and everything changed. And I had never heard it ... "in church".

To be clear – we *cannot* love people as Christ loved them *unless and until* we come to surrender ourselves into Christ, to obey His command to love – *by His own righteousness living in us and operating through us*. And it is far from passive. Presumption and neglect lead to death, and not just physical. Along with the glory passages that motivate our rightful surrender, I will bring out the warning passages as well.

Again, if we are honest – and there is no time left for games – we see that Holiness (righteousness in the *soul*) is *neither optional nor automatic*. Fortunately, however, His divine power has given us everything we need for life (the life of God) and godliness (2 Peter 1:4).

Intended Audience

My landing page is Secondmannow.net. I am creating it as a larger orientation to the *Second Man Now* Series. Of course, every living human can benefit from obtaining the life of God living through them. But here, I want to speak especially to those that have had long exposure to the over-simplified "Forgiveness-Only Gospel" (FOG) that does not bring to you – in this life – the means of overcoming the work of the enemy.

If you have gained your concept of Christianity in the Western World, particularly in the Americas, and you are less than 60 years old, then you have probably been indoctrinated into the "Forgiveness-Only Gospel". However, once you see the truth concerning the *glorious creature that He invites you to become*, you will experience a very different way of seeing everything else.

Christ came to make us like Himself – always by replacement and growth; by planting, germinating, and appearing. It is my prime desire to tell you all about it, straight from the scriptures that have been hidden in plain sight.

This book will tell you the true and powerful Gospel of Christ, in which He saves mankind from "sin", not just "sins".

This book is for jump-starting in you the mind-renewal that activates true and effective faith; embracing and living from the mind of Christ that is already in you (if you are born again; 1 Cor 2:16).

Bible Quotes are Word English Bible (WEB) except where noted.

Purposes – and a One-Minute Gospel

My purpose in writing is to describe a feast that *is there waiting for you*:

- I intend to announce to the *unbeliever* the comprehensiveness of that feast.
- To announce to the dry, disillusioned seminary-trained theologian; that God actually meant what the Lord Jesus demonstrated, taught, trained, and commissioned before He said "follow me"; Christ demands that we surrender to obey His commands, but by His power and by His "Life".
- To wake up, shake up, "pop-Christianity" – both the saved and the unsaved in it – to embrace and realize all the aspects of "Grace" – not just forgiveness.

Nevertheless, At the outset, I will state a one-minute gospel very *succinctly but not inaccurately:*

> Mankind by default is alienated from God and disconnected from His "Life", and we on our own can do nothing about it.
>
> By the love of God, by the sacrifice of Jesus Christ, and by the power of His Spirit:
>
> If we will publicly acknowledge our selfishness and forsake it and actively live by His power, then God will *give us both the desire and the power to live a life pleasing to Him*. He does this by making His home in us and guiding us.
>
> If we make this surrender and maintain it as He demands, then we will escape the corruption of lust, greed, and pride, and we will partake of the Nature of God. We will not become "divine", but we will *partake* in His nature. Massive freedom will emerge in this life as we stay the course. We persevere – seeking after glory, honor, and immortality – because by His power He pioneered the way and gave us everything we need for the journey.
>
> There will be an unmistakable appearance of God's own holiness in us, and its reward is "life through the ages"; We will reign on the Earth, with and under Christ, forever.
>
> Christ is *still* working for us as our just and faithful high priest and as the lover of our soul. You can experience His loving presence and the victory-joy of His mind in this age, in this life.

It is for your spouse and children as well.

In the scriptures we see that Christ promised all these things. Millions of people through the ages discovered them to be real and true. Above all, they discovered the companionship of God and would not trade it for anything.

Because I have been gazing into the "New Covenant" and the "Second Mankind" themes intensively for about three years now, I was able to write the above version in about thirty minutes. I can state it easily and boldly because I broke fully out of the FOG – the forgiveness-only gospel. I hope and expect that you will as well!

In sharing this reconstituted gospel, my hope is that every reader see the outrageous but true promise that Christ has <u>*made the way for us to become like Him*</u>. My job is to speak the truth of the promises and the conditions that we see in the scriptures, and watch for the appearance of hunger for the righteousness that is *of God* – a hunger for transformation.

The book brings to the foreground the profound aspects of grace that are most ignored by popular Christianity. At the end of this book, I will present a "reconstituted" Gospel from different *perspectives*, for different *time constraints,* and for different *audiences*. But the heart of it is the same in every case (the foundation and pillars).

Reversing the Deadly Mindset

If your church tradition has convinced you that you are still "just a sinner saved by grace", then I hope to show you irrefutably from the scriptures that this is a deadly trap of the enemy that keeps people from ever finding actual deliverance from the condemnation of the enemy. Such teaching is the way the enemy can continue to control even those that have accepted the atoning work of Christ.

I have literally seen – and looked in the eye – the "spirit of religion" that disables the church by this lie. But He whom the Son sets free is free indeed (Matthew 6) and overcomes the enemy (Rev 2 and Rev 22).

The Authority of the Scriptures

I refer to *Bible* passages as the Word of God. I do this without hesitation because the truth contained in them has turned my heart to surrender to my Maker, who is Good. He has radically changed me – in just a few years – through these words. They are alive!

I understand that, to a reader that is just "exploring", such things may be very hard to believe; But I testify that the Spirit of God stands ready to wake you to amazing things (1 Cor 2:9). As the Spirit of God stirs in you, you will doubt the

Bible Quotes are Word English Bible (WEB) except where noted.

Authority of the Bible less and less. If, in response to the love of God you surrender your life to Him, you will become radically changed and consciously connected with Christ and the Father and the Spirit of God.

As you are filled with the Spirit of God (this is the New Covenant itself), what first looked like nonsense will become for you the most precious promises offered to mankind. But they are conditional upon our surrender.

By college and training and career experience, I am the consummate "analyst", and being "real" is absolutely imperative for an analyst. But *not all that is real is visible*, and not all that is real *can be recognized by mere human observation and rationality*.

With regard to the "authority" of scripture, I admit that man does not have even one provably-original manuscript, and that even our translations are imperfect; Nevertheless, I testify that the Truth that will make you free is still plainly visible in the types and shadows of the Old Testament and in the plain words the New Testament. When you see the connections and consistencies among the vision passages, *you see it all* **resonate** in a way man could not manufacture.

Sadly, as I noted, these powerful truths have been very, very effectively buried by much of the church; This is due to systematic *infiltration* at the highest levels and due to *deception* at the middle levels, and *unawareness* among the masses – including many, many teachers that have been spoon-fed a small version of grace that doesn't actually produce overcomers.

But thanks to God, the Spirit of God makes the glory of God shine to us – makes the truth resonate within us and changes us.

The Mind Renewal Index (MRI)

In this book and its accompanying poster, you will find about 100 key scriptures. They are all shown in the poster, and they appear on the openings of parts (sections) and chapters.

These passages are not only among those that are most systematically buried by most of the modern church world; they are among the most powerful passages that go to the renewing of your mind (Eph. 4:23 and Roman 12:3).

Without a doubt, mind-renewal is an ongoing process in this life; Nevertheless, there are radical breakthroughs that can propel us into huge gains. For example, there are truths about conversion itself that radically change us in an instant. I don't mean "in a moment", but in an instant.

MRI - Individual

Furthermore, since there are about 100 of them, I suggest that we can get a rough picture of our mind-renewal "progress" by doing a scan of the passages and ask ourself how many of those 100 we have embraced in your heart – which means "in our *will*". In other words, "of the 100, how many of them have moved us to action?"

MRI – Pastor/Preacher/Teacher

Has the Dominion theme dominated your teaching? What percentage of these key passages have you mentioned to your congregations? The teachings of the Early Church were focused on "allegiance" that we all owe to the King that had just showed up. Justification meant not "getting right with God", but also "staying right with God" in the form of obedience. No early church leaders writings (until Augustine) show "justification to be merely a "got-saved" event.

MRI – Church

Likewise, we can use the same measure to assess and improve the life-transforming potential of a church. Pastors – many, many of you are burned out from trying to fix the problems of believers in your congregation, and you just don't have much fuel left for it (if any).

I know for sure – because I have seen this in effective operation firsthand – that if we will bring back and affirm the most radical promises of the New Covenant and the true and full Gospel, then we will discover the "times of refreshing" (Acts 3:18) we need. I experienced a radical explosive growth in my faith in the course of just a few months when I discovered the Kingdom backbone, and so many truths fell into place.

As a wonderful additional effect, I loved the Dominion Gospel - the true and complete Gospel; I now share it naturally and with sincere zeal for advancement of the Kingdom of God. I these four years of studying the gospel and learning to state it precisely, my evangelistic "conversion rate" went from nearly zero to about 30%.

Bypass the Theologians

I have escaped the corruption of the World-system and am partaking in the very nature of God; I know from personal experienced that the most radical promises of God have survived intact in the honest translations. Some systematic distortions are present, but still, the core problem is that Pastors avoid them.

I have tasted of the Heavenly gift – which is *Christ in Me* – and the powers of the age to come (Hebrews 6); I have tasted the goodness of God that far

Bible Quotes are Word English Bible (WEB) except where noted.

exceeds forgiveness alone. What interests me is the fact that God invites you, the reader, to follow Christ as well! The Spirit (God revealing Himself to you) and the Bride (all those of the Second Mankind) say "come join us!" (Rev 22).

Many Gospel Statements

Throughout this book I provide statements of the Gospel – perhaps 25! I state it from different perspectives; at different levels of detail; different levels of technicality; for different attention spans; for different audiences.

I also add in the various elements of salvation where they belong. In particular, when there is need to show the differences between the Old Covenant and the New Covenant.

In the final section of the book, I provide some much-expanded Gospel statements. I believe we all need to be able to state the Gospel in the time we have to the audience we face.

JON FARMER   FOLLOW THE FIRSTBORN

The Poster
Helps Keep "The Forest" in View

Over the course of two years – well beyond 1000 hours – I curated and arranged "the Poster" (below). It is free for download from secondmannow.net). To create that poster, I started with the ten or so passages that most *dramatically* changed my spiritual life but most of which *were never mentioned in the "Evangelical" churches I had attended*. I continually refined it (and still refine it) to produce that collection of passages that would tell the whole story of the grace of God and how that **power** – again, not just forgiveness as pop Christianity teaches – is administered to Man.

How is it that *the power of God is in <u>so absent from so much</u> of mainstream Protestant Evangelical teaching*? It baffled me and frustrated me for forty years. But now I see it plain as day. You will see it as well. The Second Mankind is an affront to the First Mankind. So, so many want a savior that does not require a renouncement of what they are and what they have invested in. It's the "sunken investment" fallacy of investing.

The gospel that makes that little adjustment – eliminating that stumbling point – *sells much better*.

Now, back to the "Poster" discussion.

I had to fit these panels and passages in a four-by-eight-foot area that could be read from fifteen feet away (by good eyes); and I had to arrange them in a pattern that would tell the complete and unified story of salvation. Only about fifty passages could fit, even using compact, terse excerpts – allowing for the headings that I added to tell the story fluidly and coherently. Like a museum curator, I refined the selections continually, always looking for the best floorplan and the best artifacts that would fit the facility; and I refined the walkways so that the visitor could keep the entire story in view.

At the deepest level I have sought to help the visitors to see better where Christ went and invites us to follow.

Poster Panels Correspond to Book Parts

For every panel in the free poster (downloadable from secondmannow.net) there is a "part" in this book. I urge you, for the season of your reading this book, that you keep the electronic poster accessible for frequent reference.

Bible Quotes are Word English Bible (WEB) except where noted.

The poster is quite a tool for teaching. I organized these passages into a very intentional arrangement and have given them very carefully formulated headings.

On secondmannow.net I also provide downloadable images of individual panels for panel-level lessons.

In summary, I developed this book and this poster together to solve these various communication problems, spending well over 1000 hours in 2023 and 2024 on the Poster alone. These hours do not count "prayer times", although the poster-development and writing required constant fellowshipping with God as I worked.

Now, as I "teach" – and as my trainees teach – we all keep the *New Covenant, the Second Mankind, the Kingdom* squarely in view while we study any given Bible book, topic, or passage.

If you download the poster and display it on your biggest PC monitor or cast it to your TV, then as you read this book the poster will greatly help you to not "lose the forest for the trees"; you will better see the Word of God as an integrated whole, and the beauty of the invitation of Christ – to become like Him – will become very clear. Your hunger will grow as He intended! Here is a screen shot of just a prototype version of the Poster (though it has an outdated title panel):

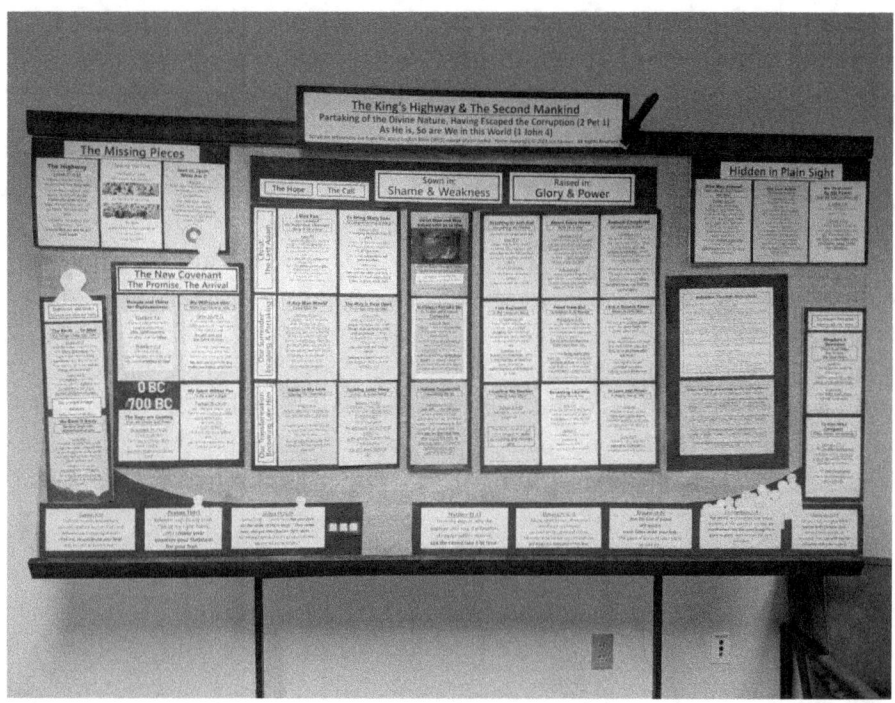

Concurrently as I write this section – near the end of the project – I have worked on telling the Gospel using <u>restored *New Covenant terms*</u> in time spans ranging from one minute to thirty minutes.

"Sequential" Limitations of Books and Lectures

In those two years I was also leading JGLM study groups (see JGLM.org). The JGLM teaching modules are excellent! You can find them on YouTube by searching for "Curry Blake New Man". Brother Curry's teaching modules are excellent not only because he systematically focuses on the transformative power of God and the Gospel of the Kingdom, but because he lives his life as a true ambassador of that Kingdom and exercises the power of it. He is a consummate teacher, and his Dominion Bible Institute (DBI, two-year Bible School) is excellent.

However, even though the videos and workbooks include many key passages, *all books and all videos – including Curry's – are inherently sequential.* So, this material suffered from the same limitation that all excellent books and videos suffer from: ***You never get to physically see the forest as you physically inspect the trees***. Brother Curry does his best to connect dots as he goes, but <u>*only a picture*</u> overcomes the limitations of sequential communication modes.

Bible Quotes are Word English Bible (WEB) except where noted.

Therefore, I sought to arrange the material in a manner that manifests *the "architecture" of the forest*. An "architecture" manifests the highest-level organizing themes and principles of a complex system, making it manageable to the mind (my definition).

Since my discovery of John G. Lake's biographies (not JGLM yet at that time), I found myself "falling in love" with *all* the New Creation scriptures. But I was frustrated by one thing at the end of every JGLM "New Man" study group semester. Everybody advanced spiritually by their exposure to the truth of the Word of God; Nevertheless, I noticed that very few students could state the terms of salvation in way that goes beyond the terms of "Romans Road" "just accept forgiveness from Christ" teaching. Even here, lest anyone think I just spoke heresy – *forgiveness of past sins is indeed solely by the sacrifice of the innocent blood of Christ*! But this is not the whole truth and we must stop omitting the requirement for - and the wonderful means of - growing in actual holiness by the provisions of God.

Grace is not only mercy, also liberation power; and God expects us to make use of it. The overwhelming body of scriptures show that this active perseverance *is a salvation matter*.

So, I saw that even though many students indeed understood that holiness and dominion were the objectives of God, they could not integrate those truths into a coherent gospel statement. In my assessment, about half of protestant evangelicals have been conditioned by a *"reduced-grace narrative"* – *exactly as I had been* for so many years. As a result, our gospel summaries still tend to omit critical elements that are quite easy to restore, if only we can stop reducing the grace of God to *forgiveness alone*.

I am writing in hopes that believers will become better able to state the Gospel of the Kingdom naturally in their own words, awakening in the hearer a *hunger* for strength, freedom, dignity, and joy. I want believers to manifest the combination of love and power that Christ demonstrated, taught, trained, and commissioned.

Our testimony will then be more than "I got saved"! We will get the "backbone" of scriptures right. At the grand scale, if the church will – as the early church did - embrace the "everything we need for life and godliness" (2 Peter 1), the Church itself will find its backbone once again. It will surely happen, but how many will discover this invitation while they are still living and breathing, and before their children leave the chruch?

So – the poster *spatially* organizes about seventy passages, strategically selected, grouped, and placed. Naturally, since the "New Covenant", "New

Birth", "New Man", "New Creation", "First Man", and "Second Man" etc. are the most important elements of the Gospel (Gal 6:15), I began with passages that go directly to these truths. I then built carefully outwards from them. Anyone that does this will find that – surprise! – the true and complete Gospel is supernatural and revolutionary through and through.

Christ reconstitutes man from his innermost being, making him free indeed (John 8); Fills him with His Spirit (Acts 2). Then Christ calls that man to then use this freedom and power to put on the character of Christ in his soul (2 Pet 1:3-4). Anybody that simply reads the New Testament honestly – without the lens of the "forgiveness-only gospel" (FOG) – will find this to be plainly and repeatedly stated in the gospels, epistles (the letters), and most pointedly in Revelation chapter 2. You cannot miss it.

Of course, we cannot come to a point of life-exchange (of Son of Man for Son of God) without seeing the hope of what will grow out if we plant that seed.

The poster seeks to drive that message – and that hope – home. I venture a guess that anybody that attempts to curate a set of 100 core passages, will find *"all" the same themes*, even if they only end up with *50% of the same particular passages*.

Repetition is Intentional

In *Follow the Firstborn*, you will find several passages brought repeatedly across sections and even within sections; 2 Peter 1:3-4 and 1 John 4:17 are good examples. I repeat passages for the following reasons:

1. The repeated passages are among the very most important for true salvation and a life of victory over the World, the flesh, and the devil. They absolutely bear repeating!
2. Many of the repeated passages have been ***omitted*** from preaching and teaching hundreds or thousands of times in many churches. You can handle a few dozen repetitions in this book to help dismantle the errors and unbelief that false teaching has built up.
3. Repetition "gets the truth of God it into your DNA" – especially if you say it aloud and personalize it. If you are a son or daughter of God, you have the right to take the truth and state it personally (Philemon 1:6).
4. If you are using the book for mediating, and you have jumped straight from the table of contents to an interior section without reading the material that precedes that section, then you will not have in mind the required context to enable you to fully grasp – and fully appreciate – the material you have jumped into.

Raised in Power and Glory

Bible Quotes are Word English Bible (WEB) except where noted.

Like a Book With Kingdom as its "Covers"

The Gospel itself is "this Gospel *of the Kingdom*" (Mt 24;14). A King's "domain" is the scope of His authority. Dominion is sovereignty or control. Good, you are believing this so far, but amazingly, God sovereignly granted – even commanded – dominion on the Earth to *man*. No believer can ever, ever have any victory without accepting this.

> Genesis 1:26-28 God said, "Let's make man in our image, after our likeness. *Let them have dominion* over the fish of the sea, and over the birds of the sky, and over the livestock, and over all the earth, *and over every creeping thing* that creeps on the earth." God created man in his own image. In God's image he created him; male and female he created them. God blessed them. God said to them, "Be fruitful, multiply, fill the earth, and subdue it. Have *dominion* over the fish of the sea, over the birds of the sky, and *over every living thing that moves on the earth*."

The dominion theme goes to the most "gaping" void left by the popular gospel. It needs to be filled carefully. If we do not replace the "poor sinner" consciousness, then we will continue to live as poor victims of the deceiver.

God made man to enjoy companionship with Himself. He delegated power and authority to him and assigned the Earth to him. There was work to do; and a creeping enemy to subdue; but it was not a problem. This First Adam enjoyed glory, honor, and immortality.

However, in a move of selfish pride and independence, he broke away to live for himself, to serve himself. He severed himself from the Life of God and Death entered. The entire lineage was infected.

Yet God never gave up on His desire for Man to reign on Earth. This is why we have the Dominion theme running from end to end and "enveloping" the other panels. As we will see so clearly from the Word of God, the road to **dominion** goes straight through **surrender**. Not *passivity*, but a transfer of **allegiance to the true King**.

The Book Covers are "Glory"

As you stand back and look at the poster, please imagine it represents an open Bible lying on the table. Imagine the covers are gilded in gold, representing glory on the left and right – both at the *start* of human history and *at the final eternal state*.

Between them is every imaginable picture of battle. There are many ways to lose – as Ancient Israel demonstrates (and modern unbelievers demonstrate), but there is exactly one way to win. We actually win over the true enemy if we will actually surrender to the One True God.

When I say "win" *I do not mean just "get forgiven" or "get saved"!* I mean "win". Christians must once again:

(a) manifest a goodness that is truly unselfish – AND
(b) have power over the creeping things – evil spirits

What we now call Christianity lives still as the First Adam and lacks both; As a result, the world simply has no interest in it.

But the Second Man, the Last Adam personifies both. So again, your Bible Covers are both "golden", and they are both calling you to glory, honor, and immortality.

The interior Panels show us the Way Christ made for us to enter and enjoy the lineage and heritage and privileges of the Second Mankind.

The center left insert shows the prophets announcing the New Covenant that was coming, along with the plain statement of Jesus that the "way" was Himself.

The center panels (the three tiers) show:

1. Center Top: Christ, in hope, went where we needed to go, as the Second Mankind – the firstborn from the dead. As a seed, He did not want to remain *alone* (John 12:24); He wanted to bring many sons to glory (Heb 2); and he did just that (John 17).
2. Center Middle: We voluntarily renounce what we are so that we become what He is. We plant the seed, because we are tired of being what we are, and we are tired of being alone.
3. Center Bottom: having taken up our cross, we actively "follow Him". This is a salvation matter (John 15:11 and many others). We have received the abundance of grace and the gift of righteousness, so we persevere by His power, and we have an advocate if we fail in weakness.

Different ones among us have "tended our gardens" in varying degrees of diligence, and will receive varying rewards for "what we did with what we knew". But if we have surrendered into Christ and remained in Him – by His power – we are saved.

Bible Quotes are Word English Bible (WEB) except where noted.

Notice that, at the lower right corner of the central panel, people of various glory (*doxa* – manifest presence and image of God) we are deposited into the "great cloud of witnesses" at the end of their earthly lives; into the bottom-right "L"-shaped segment of the dominion "tray"; the "spine" of the dominion book cover. They are joining the **overcomers** that have gone before them and they await the resurrection of the very "body" of the Second Man.

"First fruits"

In the bible, "first fruits" refers to the first harvest of a season of farming it was given back to God (to His work in the temple or tabernacle) recognizing He was the source of it. In the New Testament, several benefits for this age are referred to as "first fruits"; They are "early, partial installments" of things that will come in full force in the Ages to come.

God the Father planted Christ and Christ was *willing* because He looked forward to the fruit of the travail of His soul. Christ was the first fruit of those born from among the dead, the Second Mankind. The rest of that harvest is … "us"!

> *(1 Corinthians 15:20) But now Christ has been raised from the dead.* ***He became the first fruits*** *of those who are asleep.*

> *(Romans 8:29) For whom he foreknew, he also predestined to be conformed to the image of his Son, that he might be* ***the firstborn among many brothers****.*

The Holy Spirit – the very presence of God the Father and the Lord Jesus dwelling in us is – is described as the first fruits of the Spirit (2 Cor 5:5).

Putting the Enemy on Notice

God has chosen to put the enemy on notice by the powers of the age to come being manifest in His people.

> *(1 Corinthians 2:7-8) We speak ... a wisdom not of this world, nor of the rulers of this world,* ***who are coming to nothing****. But we speak God's wisdom in a mystery, the* ***wisdom that has been hidden****, which God foreordained before the worlds* ***for our glory****, which none of the rulers of this world* ***has*** *known. For* ***had they known it, they wouldn't have crucified the Lord of glory****.*

We eagerly await the full glory of the "celestial body" that we will enjoy forever. It compares to the mortal body ***like a tree compares to a seed*** (1 Cor 15). We are called to "plant ourselves as a seed" so to speak, *dying to selfishness in this age*. This is "denying ourselves, losing our lives so that we might find them" (at 16:24). Yet even in this age we are privileged to "***taste of the Heavenly gift***" (the indwelling Spirit of God and His righteousness) and the "***powers of the age to come***" (Heb 6).

Millions of churchgoers have never been taught that God has promised them. You will see these promises in *Follow the Firstborn*, and I hope you will go after them!

God intends for His people to learn to overcome the real enemy by the power of God. There is such a thing as the *joy of battle*, especially with a vision of the Kingdom that will be given to us!

Bible Quotes are Word English Bible (WEB) except where noted.

Christ the Firstborn
The Supreme King of Glory

*... that you may **walk worthily** of the Lord, to please him in all respects, **bearing fruit in every good work**, and increasing in the knowledge of God; **strengthened with all power**, according to the might of his glory, for all endurance and **perseverance** with joy; giving thanks to the Father, who **made us fit to be partakers** of the inheritance of the saints in light; **who delivered us out of the power of darkness, and translated us into the Kingdom of the Son of his love**; in whom we have our redemption, the forgiveness of our sins;*

*15 who is the **image of the invisible God, the firstborn of all creation**. For by him all things were created, in the heavens and on the earth, things visible and things invisible, whether thrones or dominions or principalities or powers; all things have been created through him, and for him. **He is before all things**, and in him all things are held together.*

*He is the head of the body, the assembly, who is the beginning, **the firstborn from the dead**; that in all things he might have the preeminence. For all the fullness was pleased to dwell in him; (Colossians 1:10-19)*

Sown in Weakness and Shame

Said "Follow Me"
Having Overcome Sin and Death

Who is this that has called us to follow Him? Please gaze with me at this King:

We're to Bear Fruit that Pleases God, by His Strength

The grace of God provides everything we need to live lives pleasing to Him. Christ on Earth in the flesh, lived this life of goodness and victory not because He was God - though He certainly was – but because even having set aside His God-powers, He became a man in whom the fulness of God was pleased to dwell (Phil 2:6). By His life of obedience, He succeeded where the first Adam failed. Each of us that *entrusts ourselves into Him* is transferred out of the powers that have oppressed us and lovingly transferred us into the Kingdom of this King.

The Image of God; Firstborn of All Creation

Christ in His identity as God was never created, but He entered the life of man, becoming man, by human birth. But instead of absorbing the evil of the world system (Greek *cosmos*), He displayed for us not just supreme kindness, but both the goodness and power of God *that God had intended for mankind* from the beginning. This is "glory", as in "Christ in you, the hope of glory" (Col 1:27).

And the Firstborn from the Dead

Jesus Christ demonstrated "Life" – the Life *of God* (Geek *Zoe*) and offered it to man. This is so far beyond forgiveness alone! Everywhere He walked, He – *and those He trained* – showed the will of God to be that we be "free indeed" *in this present age* (Titus 2:11: Matt 10). We are called to be born again (John 3:3) of the same Father as the Firstborn (Heb 2:11). Indeed, if we surrender into Him and abide in Him, we shall be like Him (1 John 3:3; 1 John 4:17).

Here we have our first puzzle-piece-drop (PPD). Revelation chapters 1 and 2 are actively buried by some traditions, but if you see the Firstborn calls you to overcome evil by His indwelling life, the chapters make perfect sense. Here are two small clips, but you will be blessed by reading these chapters in full:

> *and from Jesus Christ, the faithful witness, the firstborn of the dead, and the ruler of the kings of the earth. To him who loves us, and washed us from our sins by his blood;* (Rev 1:5) ... *He who has an ear, let him hear what the Spirit says to the assemblies. To him who overcomes I will give to eat from the tree of life, which is in the Paradise of my God.*
> (Revelation 2:7)

Grace is the Second
Mankind "Planted" by God

Huh? Planted? Consider that Christ in fact "planted" himself! As we shall see, we "must" overcome an enemy, and the Word of God tells us exactly How, and the Lord Jesus Christ demonstrated how. If you love Him He will show you!

> *(John 12:24-25) Most certainly I tell you, unless a grain of wheat falls into the earth and dies, it remains by itself alone. But if it dies, it bears much fruit. 25 He who loves his life will lose it. He who hates his life in this world will keep it to eternal life.*

To many, the requirement to "overcome" might appear to be a contradiction with "Salvation is by grace through faith" but the Bible states plainly that Eternal Life is "for him who overcomes". What gives?

The key lies in the difference between the New and Old Covenants.

Under the Old Covenant, the Law of Moses worked to show sin for what it was, and its penalties also functioned as a deterrent. It was like a taskmaster to constrain sin to a degree. But no rule-system could turn a corrupted species into a good one.

> *Matthew 12:33 "Either make the tree good, and its fruit good, or make the tree corrupt, and its fruit corrupt; for the tree is known by its fruit."*

Under the New Covenant – **if we have entrusted our lives into Christ** then not only are we **recreated as beings in whom the fulness of God is pleased to dwell**; Upon request – as *Sons* – we are **filled with the same power** that raised Christ from the dead.

He Tends His Garden
Loving, Nurturing, and Providing

God has made us in His image, and even in fallen state man possesses the capacity to choose, even if it comes to a moment of desperate life-exchange. God has no desire to be loved by beings programmed to "simulate" love.

"Grace" Includes Love, Power, and Freedom

The enemy does all in His power to paint God as the cruelest of beings, unilaterally, arbitrarily appointing about 6 billion people to eternal torment. Millions of precious souls – perhaps you are one of them – have been born into such tradition, but such teaching arose from the "gnostics" (not "agnostic") and was carried into the Roman church mainstream by Augustine in the fifth century; resurrected by Martin Luther (an Augustinian monk) and John Calvin in the Reformation.

The absolution of all responsibility sounds like grace, but it is not of God and is not Christianity. The grace of God brings us into true freedom and true love.

> *Where the Spirit of the Lord is, there is freedom (2 Cor 3:17)*

> *If the Son therefore shall make you free, you shall be free indeed. (John 8:36)*

I realize of course that to some this is an extremely sensitive topic. For some of us it means rejecting the beliefs of family and friends and perhaps generations of ancestors. The truth is in fact considered "heresy" in some traditions:

> *God provides everything we need; He then expects us to use our new freedom and power to overcome sin and increasingly live as He commands. And this is not just for rewards – it is a salvation issue.*

God is Glorified When Truly Free People Choose Him.

Many imagine that this is impossibly difficult, against the idea of grace, or incredibly unpleasant, but:

a) There is initial event of our conversion and rebirth, which is triggered by our response to the sacrifice of the innocent blood of Christ; But these are just components of the salvation process. As soon as we accept this, the sooner we will see hundreds of passages fall into place. Anda wonderful boldness will come upon us.

Bible Quotes are Word English Bible (WEB) except where noted.
b) The power that God provides is more than enough;
c) The hope that God provides – partaking in the divine nature and inheriting all things – is of enormously effective if we will set our hearts and minds on them;
d) There is an amazing dignity that we experience even as is merely begins to take hold – and an amping up of that hope just mentioned;
e) We have the benefit of His mercy when we fail.
f) Our joy appears as we quickly see ourselves being changed – reversing the work of the enemy on our own souls over the years – and experiencing true *refreshment*;
g) Our joy grows even more as we taste "the heavenly gift" – the presence of the indwelling God – and the powers of the age to come.

You might think I am exaggerating, but as we shall see throughout *Follow the Firstborn*, these things are plainly stated by Christ in the Gospels and by the Epistle-writers (letter-writers) as throughout the New Testament.

He Offers to Be a Father
And to Make Us Like Himself

But without the breaking of the power of sin, and the indwelling of the presence and power of God, all you have is "religion" – which inevitably brings misery and self-condemnation. But by the power of God that He accomplished through Christ, we have been given the *right (John 1:12)* – and the *means (John 14:5)* – to *become* one of the Second Mankind (1 Cor 15).

Bible Quotes are Word English Bible (WEB) except where noted.

Poster-Flow Narratives
At Progressing Levels of Detail

It is SO difficult to resist drilling down into each of these areas – because each is very exciting and there is so much to unpack! Nevertheless, **we must get the forest clear** (the big picture) before we go too deeply into groves (panels) and trees (frames) and their branches (passages & commentary).

I will narrate the "poster-flow" at a few increasing levels of detail. My purpose is that you can get the "forest" clearly in mind before we drill down at all into the scripture passages.

I will progress through these levels:

1. A few sentences per panel;
2. About a half-minute per panel; and
3. A few minutes per panel.

Okay, some of these sentences are … long sentences; Someday I will shake the hand of whoever invented the comma, and give a hug to whoever invented the semicolon!

In these narratives, I will not be sharing many scripture references – I will be merely "story-telling". Again, my hope is that throughout the entire balance of the book, you will know the "story" of the Gospel. This way, you will be very prepared to evaluate – as we get into the meat of the book – whether I have proven that the God of the bible is actually offering to make you like Christ – in both goodness and power.

"Drive-By" Narrative:
A *Few Sentences* Per Panel

Poster Title: The Second Mankind and The Way of Holiness

You will notice that the "poster" title does not match the book title; this is because I finalized the book title after the physical poster had been photographed in very high resolution. Nevertheless of course, there are very close parallels between "the Way" and following!

The Gospel is the invitation to actually become one of the Second Mankind. It's an invitation to escape the power of sin so that we can stop hurting each other; to receive into ourselves His very life for our living; to receive adoption as Sons of God; We have escaped the judgement as a natural consequence of it. We will not be destroyed but will enjoy the Life of God through the ages.

Subtitle: Sown in Weakness and Shame; Raised in Power and Glory

In gardening we plant this dead little seed in hope of what will appear – if we will patiently tend the garden. Likewise, in a true conversion we renounce the deadness of what we are, in hope of what we shall become.

The Missing Pieces

To a great extent, the enemy has infiltrated some of the largest seminaries and has removed teaching that suggests that God brings the power to overcome the enemy. Why is that?

Hidden in Plain Sight

Numerous passages tell of the way that we escape sin and partake in the nature of God. But if we grow up a church culture that insists on honoring weakness, then we will never see them.

Dominion Given but Forfeited

God created man – the First Adam, the First Mankind – with no consciousness of sin and with perfect, unashamed, fellowship with Himself. He crowned us with glory and honor – even creating us in His own image, and all things were <u>**under our feet**</u>, but in our arrogance, we opted for selfish independence, and we were cut off from the life of God.

Bible Quotes are Word English Bible (WEB) except where noted.

But God's Plan of Dominion for Man Stands Forever

The theme of dominion – ***domination over the enemy*** – on Earth – is all over the entire Bible. It is there, from cover to cover; and God is not giving up on that vision.

Under Our Feet Again – as He Commanded

The work of Christ was to "restore *that* which was lost", not merely "save those that were condemned". So, He made a way not only for the forgiveness of "*what we **done***" – but also for the restoration of *what we **are***.

Dominion Restored to Him Who Overcomes

In Revelation 2, we see eight times that the fully manifest wonders of the Kingdom of God are given "to him who overcomes". This is still "the gift of God" because He has given us everything, we need for life and godliness" (2 Peter 1:3).

Nobody doesn't want freedom, strength, and dignity, but what we needed was nothing less than a *redo of Mankind – and that's what He has provided!*

The New Covenant: The Promise, The Arrival

In about 700 B.C., the prophets told plainly of the New Covenant that was coming, in which God would undo the destruction of the enemy – with all benefits built upon our reunion with Him, His Spirit dwelling inside us, and a replaced heart. This is the power and the desire to do what is right! In John 14, Christ plainly explains that He has accomplished exactly those things; The promise has arrived!

Christ, the Second Man and the Last Adam

The Father invited His Only Son to be the ultimate "reset" of Mankind – to enter into our fallen world and be the Firstborn from the dead, to go where we need to be, and to give us the power to follow.

To win back what was forfeited, God had to actually become a man – the "Second Man" and the "Last Adam" (1 Cor 15) – and succeed in His humility and obedience exactly where the first Adam failed in his pride and rebellion – and then literally die "as us" and be raised with us…

Our Surrender: Escaping and Partaking

The Good News is that Christ invited us to follow Him into that dominion and that glory – the unspoken but manifest presence of God – even in this World, in this age. The terms are that we surrender our rebellion and practice obeying

His command to love as He loved (John 13, John 14, John 15); but we indeed become "like Him".

Our Transformation: Becoming Like Him

With the gift of *Christ's own righteousness in us*, we have "everything we need for life and godliness" – and we have the merciful "Advocate" – Jesus Christ the righteous" (1 Jn 2). So, we use our "free-indeed" to put sin to death and gain its reward, eternal life (Rom 2:7 and 6:22); We also "taste the heavenly gift and the powers of the age to come" (Heb 6)!

A Very Short Gospel Statement with That Focus

At many points in this book I share the Gospel, expanded using terms you might not have heard before, in the context of the truth that has just been presented. As we shall see there is so much more than just getting forgiven and going to Heaven!

At some points I will be speaking only of what the Good News *itself* is; while at other points I will be focusing on the *response* that God is looking for from us.

The Gospel - *the Good News itself* - is that God has sent His Son, in human flesh, to demonstrate His love and goodness, and also His absolute power over that of the enemy. He announced the awaited Kingdom that would never end, and invited us to become both sons and citizens, with unspeakably wonderful privileges. We are invited to *share in His Nature*.

The cost is life-exchange: the doing of our own will and the going of our own way. The central privileges are the death of the selfish innermost nature, the birth into the second mankind; the indwelling and conscious companionship of God Himself, and the authority to continue the work that He taught, demonstrated, and commissioned.

Bible Quotes are Word English Bible (WEB) except where noted.

Poster-Flow Narrative
About a _Half-Minute_ per Panel

Suppose we have somebody's ear because we have been genuinely kind to them, or because their pain went away at our command. Now we can give some more detail, because we have whetted their appetite.

(Remember – the poster headings provide an important framework or our understanding, but we would not provide them unless we are explaining the Poster – as I am now).

Poster Title: The Second Mankind and The Way of Holiness

The Gospel is the invitation to actually become the Second Mankind, which is not only a restored mankind that is "set apart" from the coming judgement. Even more, it is God calling for us to be reunited with Him, and to have the power to joyfully serve Him.

Poster Subtitle: Partaking of the Divine Nature, Having Escaped the Corruption

2 Peter 1:4 here explains the two parts of the "way". By identifying with (accepting them as _our own_) the death and resurrection of Christ, we find that we _escape the compelling power of sin_ and _partake in His Nature_. Not to "become divine", but nevertheless to partake of His nature. All the benefits of the Grace of God flow out of these as we unlearn the mentality of natural limits, and renew our minds.

Book Subtitle: Sown in Weakness and Shame; Raised in Power and Glory

Everybody knows how gardening basically works. There is this thing called a seed; It is void of all beauty and is as dead as dead can be. That must be our opinion of ourselves if we are ready for conversion.

Repentance and conversion happen if – and only if – we see what God offers us to become, and we choose to bury our selfish independence – in hope of becoming the far more glorious living thing.

The Missing Pieces

The scriptures that present the essential _and accurate_ way to become a Son of God have been all but buried by popular church culture. Trying to get as many people to nod to John 3:16, then walk an aisle and repeat a prayer. What God requires is a *surrender of the **will***, not just a twinge of recognition that *If God is there then I might be in trouble* and "should get my ticket punched".

A true salvation will never be anything less than a life exchange. We must restore the missing pieces. As Einstein has said, (and you'll see me repeat it throughout the book):

> "Make it as simple as possible, but no simpler."

Hidden in Plain Sight

There are a few hundred radical, outrageous, mystical, and even cosmic passages right there in plain sight in the New Testament alone. But if we grow up in church, never reading the scriptures for ourselves, without tradition-tinted glasses, then *we see only what we have been told* is there; If we do recognize what looks like a serious contradiction in the scriptures, we trust the theologians that assure us that it's just a language issue; or maybe we are in a tradition that simply says that our leader's interpretation is infallible so don't worry about it. All this makes us sleepy or confused; or it gives us a headache; or we just put it on the coffee table.

Consider an honest "seeker" – maybe your teenager that has to make some critical decisions on how they will live when they leave the home of their upbringing. He or she, when faced by seeming blatant contradictions – might simply cross Christianity off their list of concerns. We will see in this book how we could win these souls simply by presenting a more accurate and complete statement of how salvation works - and what is at stake both positively and negatively; both *in this life* and in the ages to come.

Dominion Given but Forfeited

We shall see that Dominion – or "The Kingdom of God" - is the cover-to-cover uniting theme of the Bible – not just "getting saved". Even the teenager would embrace the Kingdom Vision if he or she knew it were there and saw evidence of the power of God … in a church or in a Christian anywhere.

God created man – the First Adam, the First Mankind – with no consciousness of sin and with perfect, unashamed, fellowship with Himself. He crowned us with glory and honor. He created us in His own image. As Dutch Sheets has said, "when creation saw Adam, it saw God and obeyed".

We reigned *with* and *under* God, and all things were **<u>under our feet</u>**, even the creeping things.

Raised in Power and Glory

But we were baited into a move of pride and selfish independence. We forfeited the companionship of God and were **no longer image-bearers**. Sin and death entered.

But God's Plan of Dominion for Man Stands Forever

The theme of dominion – **domination over the enemy** – on Earth – is all over the entire Bible. It is there, from cover to cover.

As it turns out, 90% of the Bible speaks directly or indirectly about *battles* and *wins* and *losses*; Even after the fall of man, there are constant reminders of God's plan for man to have "all things under our feet".

There are "Old Testament saints" and "New Testament saints". They are the ones that looked forward or backward to the work of Christ and abandoned their own way to follow Christ. They all saw His glory in one form or another, and said – "I want that".

They only needed to lay down their self-will, self-righteousness, and *independence*.

Under Our Feet Again – as He Commanded

The work of Christ was to "restore that which was lost", not merely "save those that were lost". Glory is victory, and Christ is even now, "bringing many Sons to that glory". So, He made a way not only for the *clean hands* – forgiveness for "*what we done*" – but also for the *pure heart* – the ultimate and complete fix for *what we **are***.

He instituted the Lineage of the Second Mankind. He is the Firstborn from among the dead, and He calls us to follow Him. This means to plant the seed in weakness and shame. We will be raised in power and glory. Nobody would plant the seed of their lives and not intend to tend the garden (unless they are under passivity teaching).

If we tend it, we will mature; and we will undo the works of the enemy, internally and externally. We will "overcome".

Dominion Restored to Him Who Overcomes

In Revelation 2, we see eight times that the fully manifest wonders of the Kingdom of God are given "to him who overcomes". But how can this be "saved by grace through faith"?!

The answer has two parts:

1. "He has **given us everything we need** for _life_ and _godliness_"; and

2. Faith, faithfulness, allegiance, and fidelity are all the same Greek word *pistis*. The Pistis of saving faith is the *package* of these ingredients! Not mere "fact-faith".

If we've grown up under a *passive* "get-saved" model of salvation (in which we discover that fortunately God programmed us to trust and obey Him), then the sooner we *study the scriptures for ourselves* the sooner we will experience one of the greatest breakthroughs of our lives. The passages collected into this book should demolish the stronghold of passivity. Any tradition that breeds this passivity *is not Christianity*.

So, we see that Dominion of Man on Earth always was, and always will be, the plan of God in His kindness toward man. But to win back what was forfeited, God had to actually become a man – the "Second Man" and the "Last Adam" (1 Cor 15) – and succeed in His humility and obedience exactly where the first Adam failed in his pride and rebellion.

The New Covenant: The Promise, The Arrival

In about 700 B.C., the prophets – most notably Ezekiel, Jeremiah, and Isaiah – told plainly of the New Covenant that was coming, in which God would undo the destruction of the enemy – with all benefits built upon our reunion with Him, His Spirit dwelling inside us, and a replaced heart.

Up to then, man only saw God either "coming upon" man on occasion, or, with Moses, God being "with" man. But we have the amazing promise: God's own Spirit "inside" us.

For the proud and independent, the reaction would be: "who would want that? ... Oh – I'll take just that amnesty part!". But for the humble there was nothing more liberating than being in the constant fellowship of the most High God, and the dignity of "clean hands and a pure heart" (Ps 24).

In John 14, Christ plainly explains that He has accomplished exactly those things; The promise has arrived! Much of popular Christianity has chosen to go with just the "amnesty" and proclaim, "just a poor sinner saved by grace". But we can honor God better than that. Blessed are those who hunger and thirst for righteousness, for they shall be filled (Matt 5:6). The offer stands, for a limited time.

Christ, the Second Man and the Last Adam

The Father invited His Only Son to be the ultimate "reset" of Mankind – to enter into our fallen world and be the Firstborn from the dead. As the head of the fallen human race the first Adam led us into rebellion and death – yes this is mystical, but somehow – we all were born in the enemy camp. It seems unfair

Bible Quotes are Word English Bible (WEB) except where noted.

at first, until we find that we are freely invited to be reconciled and born into the restoration of freedom and strength.

We are invited to be literally filled with the Life of God, and to enjoy having Christ live on the earth through us. So, He went before us as a pioneer, through self-denial, death, burial, resurrection, ascension, and seating in authority. And all along the way, He put the enemy on notice of the coming New World Order. He came to bring many sons to glory (Heb 2). Had the rulers known that a swarm of these beings was coming, they would never have crucified Him.

Our Surrender: Escaping and Partaking

The Good News is that Christ invited us to follow Him into that dominion and that glory (Greek *doxa* – the unspoken but manifest presence of God), even in this World, in this age (John 14:12). The terms are that we surrender our rebellion and practice obeying His command to love as He loved (John 13, John 14, John 15).

This truth might be hard to accept for one that has been churched under false or incomplete teaching, but there is no salvation without a surrender to forsake sin and do the will of God.

John G Lake said:

> "If a man is in Christ, he is God's son, man's servant, and the devil's master."

Please remember, nobody becomes a Son of God or gains authority over devils unless he or she will become the servant of mankind. Man is no longer your enemy, and in fact never was.

But if we will die to self-will and selfish independence, then God will restore us; That is what baptism declares. We will no longer be ashamed and alone. He will satisfy us – quite literally – with His life and presence in us (Ezek 36:25); It is the "gift of righteousness" (Rom 5:17).

It is the power to overcome! What shall we do with it?

Our Transformation: Becoming Like Him

With the gift of Christ's own righteousness in us, we have "everything we need for life and godliness". We have escaped the power of sin (when we identify with His death – we *feel it break!*), and we are partaking in the divine nature – born of Him and filled with His Spirit; We hear His voice.

Though it will not be admitted in many circles, scriptures tell us plainly that we must use our "free-indeed" to *put sin to death*. This is the *inward* dominion we all had hoped the Gospel included; But very few Christians have been taught and trained on exactly how to walk in it.

It is battle but it is "winning battle. Then, as our shame and fear disappear, we can increasingly pray the prayer of faith without doubting or wavering, and receive the thing we ask for. Even the demons become subject to us (Luke 10:19).

We are the "overcomers" of Revelation chapter 2. We reign in life (Rom 5:12) in this age (Titus 2), and we "taste the heavenly gift and the powers of the age to come" (Heb 6). So, we see that we *overcome by God's grace*.

Again, as Einstein has said,

> **"Make it as simple as possible, but no simpler."**

Raised in Power and Glory

Bible Quotes are Word English Bible (WEB) except where noted.

Poster-Flow Narrative
A *Few Minutes* Per Panel

In the segments that follow, I expand the gospel at the level of about *a few minutes* per panel.

Title: The Second Mankind and The Way of Holiness

The first mankind is enslaved by his love of the things of this world, which is going to pass away. He is rebellious in his innermost constitution; He *is a sinner* by nature; What we have done is the evidence, but the problem is what we are.

In short, He who does the will of the Lord endures forever but the first mankind cannot do it. This, and this alone, is the fundamental problem humans face.

We cannot learn to do the will of God by improvements; Only replacement will do. In order to be set apart, passing out of condemnation, we must first be recreated into the Second Mankind. Christ is the firstborn of that Lineage – the Second Man; the Last Adam; To be "In Christ is to be doing His will, and gladly". This is how Christ alone is "The Way" to be set apart ("Holy").

Poster Subtitle: Partaking of the Divine Nature, Having Escaped the Corruption

Christ has made a way for us to escape the compulsive power of sin and to partake in His Nature. Not to "become divine", but nevertheless to partake of that nature. All the benefits of the Grace of God flow out of it.

This is from 2 Peter 1:4. In my opinion, it is the most complete and precise statement of the gospel we have in a single verse – in the entire Bible. Yet so many Christian traditions have buried it, in favor of *just* "get forgiven". It is no wonder that most Christians are living defeated lives. It doesn't have to be that way.

Sown in Weakness and Shame; Raised in Power and Glory

For the Book, I am using this different subtitle, which closely reflects that same truth from the Poster. The poster subtitle states "what" we need, while the Book subtitle states the "Way" the need is met by the *power* of *God*, yet by *our* act of *surrender*.

We are invited to become one of the Second mankind, but it is available only by life-exchange; No amount of theology gets us around the requirement to surrender our self-will. The Bible likens this "way" to that of a seed. If – and only if – it is planted and the garden is well-tended, it will germinate; it will set roots; and will appear in the expected final form that is different than the seed.

The Way to be reborn into the lineage of Christ is to despise ourselves; admit that the problem is what we are; renounce it; and put it to death. What then grows is a being that has both the desire and the power to do the will of God. We actively do all this by the provision and power of God ("grace" is all this, not just forgiveness).

The Missing Pieces

Today, many Christian traditions no longer think and speak in these terms, and some never did. The "gospel" has been reduced to FOG (the forgiveness-only gospel). The typical person in such a tradition tries to read the Bible but cannot understand why "forgiveness" passages are "few-and-far-between". It is a like puzzle – fragmented and scattered on their kitchen table; they see it day after day making no real sense and generating no excitement. Very little is appearing in the puzzle; and there is no breakthrough in the challenges of their lives. Something – something beyond forgiveness – is *missing*.

In this sense, we are certainly still in "the dark ages".

Hidden in Plain Sight

But as we approach the return of Christ, the Second Mankind is already appearing in thousands of people that have escaped the corruption and are partaking in the Nature of God – "not becoming God"! – but certainly *partaking* in His nature, just as the scriptures plainly say. These of the Second Mankind are the people that had seen the nature of God in a human and wanted it badly enough to trade their lives in for it.

I addition to these persons, there are millions of others that are truly surrendered and have truly been born-again; yet are *unaware of what they are*. More specifically, they are unaware of the gifts and powers that exist *precisely for doing the will of God*.

The fact is the core truths – the "backbone" of the Gospel and the "Centerline pieces" of that puzzle – are right there as they have been for a long time. I have gathered about 70 of them into this book and its accompanying poster.

I could be bitter about the fact that I have had forty years of "churching", much of which had *systematically omitted several of the most important pieces*. But they were there for me to discover for myself if I had not been so lazy. The fact is, I was *worse than lazy*. Deep down, what I really wanted was to "get saved and still go my own way" – *in the name of grace itself* – I preferred the

Raised in Power and Glory

Bible Quotes are Word English Bible (WEB) except where noted.

oversimplification that was being offered. So, I bought into it. Life was a losing battle, but I tried to stay grateful for "getting saved". It didn't work very well.

Then I discovered the life and exploits of John Lake, who simply believed and obeyed the gospel with all he had, and changed South Africa forever in five years. Instead of reducing the Bible to "great thoughts for mere humans"[1] he did the same foolish, crazy, outrageous thing the early church did; He didn't just believe facts and live in defeat. Rather, he entrusted himself into Christ, _and acted on the authority that had been granted to him._

In the midst of this personal awakening, I had a life-changing 7-second dream. I saw the heaven-version of my daughter, woke up, and said simply **"I want that"**. I had **zero** doubt. I went back to sleep.

The next morning, I learned I had instantly gotten the first burst of a constructive miracle in my daughter's eye. In a new kind of faith became mine; it was more than the faith of the centurion (_he_ only represented a _human_ empire).

I found John G. Lake Ministries and got my mind renewal underway. I was gaining the consciousness-mind of Christ, not merely attending Bible studies. I got trained and ordained; and life changed. Now my passion is that some more people might discover that same breakthrough. So, I write, I preach, I teach, and I train.

In this poster and book combo, I have curated and arranged a manageable set of key passages that should lift anybody out of the small-grace FOG. My intent is that you will see in them _Christ in you, the Hope of Glory_; and make the trade now, while there is time.

You will taste the Heavenly gift and the powers of the age to come, and you will have everything you need for life and godliness (2 Peter 1:3). As soon as you surrender into Christ, you will see the first tender shoot of the good tree. You will know the Father sees it (He tells you); You will know the Lord Jesus is merciful when you fail; and your fear will be … gone.

The missing pieces were always there, and _they are there for you_!

Dominion Given but Forfeited

God created man – the First Adam, the First Mankind – with no consciousness of sin and with perfect, unashamed, fellowship with Himself. He crowned us with glory and honor. He created us in His own (_their_ own) image. As Dutch

---

[1] We're not mere humans (1 Cor 3:1-3).

Sheets has said, "when creation saw Adam, it saw God and obeyed". The Gospel of Luke shows the first Adam as having been a "Son of God".

Thus, He placed all things **_under our feet_**, having given us everything we need – both power and authority – for subduing even the creeping things. The only thing we were not to dominate and subdue was "other humans"!

We enjoyed perfect fellowship and perfect dominion… until we were deceived. We took the bait of an offer of independent supremacy over God Himself. The first Adam Made himself – and his lineage – an enemy of God. Sin entered, along with its consequences, which are sickness and death.

We were no longer image-bearers. Creation did not obey; and the enemy of course did not obey. Glory, power, immortality gave way to weakness, shame, and death.

Selfish independence was, and is, the sin that underlies all other sins.

But God's Plan of Dominion for Man Stands Forever

Salvation is **_rescue and restoration_** *from all aspects of captivity and oppression.* If that's a "palace", then forgiveness is the entry way; the *foyer* to that palace. But the church has made forgiveness out to be the only benefit of the work of Christ that we get to enjoy in this life, in this age. It is not.

Unlike the theme of forgiveness, which occurs in types and shadows in various in a few dozen Old Testament chapters, we find that the theme of dominion – **_domination over the enemy_** – on Earth – is all over the entire Bible.

A dear friend of mine commented as follows during a mind-renewal class:

> "Why in most churches do the children go downstairs on Sunday – learn of all the Old Testament *heroes and battles and victories*, but we adults stay *upstairs* and hear *none* of that good stuff?"

God's fellowship with mankind is the highest gift He has given. His granting of dominion on Earth to mankind – is His highest public expression of His kindness toward man – and this is **_in the face of the enemy_**. That's **_"glory"_**.

As it turns out, 90% of the Bible speaks directly or indirectly about *battles* and *wins* and *losses*; There are numerous promises and reminders of God's plan for man to have "all things under our feet". The first Great commission was a command to subdue the enemy, and every other great commission in the Bible is simply God giving man another try… If man would only stop demanding self-righteousness and *independence*.

Bible Quotes are Word English Bible (WEB) except where noted.

Under Our Feet Again – as He Commanded

God's promises stand forever, but so do His Justice and Mercy. The work of Christ was to "restore that which was lost". Christ did in fact accomplish that, and He did so in a way that satisfied both the "mercy" of God and the "justice" of God.

Glory is victory, and Christ is even now, "bringing many Sons to that glory". But there are actually two aspects of victory and glory, and they are interdependent. Psalm 24 asks: "Who shall ascend the hill of the Lord?" (that's access to the throne room of God, and dominion) and answers it: "He who has clean hands and a pure heart". Christ made a way not only for the *clean hands* – forgiveness for "*what we **done***" – but also for the *pure heart* – the fix for *what we **are***.

He instituted the Lineage of the Second Mankind. He is the Firstborn from among the dead, and He calls us to follow Him.

By His power at work in us, the sin in us is no longer "what we are"! we can finally put it to death, and we must do so. *This is the **inward** battle*. Until and unless we do this, we live in shame and fear and cannot ask anything in unwavering faith.

But once we identify with the death of Christ and are born again through surrender (the seed thing), we can overcome sin and renew our minds. Instead of cowering before the unseen enemy, we begin commanding and receiving.

Dominion Restored to Him Who Overcomes

In Revelation 2, we see eight times that the fully manifest wonders of the Kingdom of God are given… But it does not say it is given merely to those that are "forgiven". Rather, it says that these are given "to him who overcomes". If we reread the New Testament in light of this, we see amazing consistency emerge, and there is no more "fog".

But how can this be "saved by grace through faith"?!

The answer has two parts, but some of us must be willing to embrace the truth even after decades of wrong teaching, and at the cost of *breaking with centuries of family tradition or religious tradition*.

1. "He has given us everything we need for life and godliness". At the heart of grace are the *breaking of the power of sin* and the *partaking in the nature of God* (2 Peter 1:3-4). Grace is, in fact, the ability to do what God requires of us, but it is by *His own righteousness*; by His own … *Life*;

2. "faith" (Greek *pistis*) is the same word as *allegiance* and faithfulness. Overcomers are those that deny themselves (Mankind 1.0) to be transferred into the Second Mankind, ... and faithfully follow the Firstborn by His own power.
3. As the Second Mankind with the New Heart (Ezek 36), we do not *practice sin*; but we can in this life, fail in *weakness*; Every plant emerges as a tender shoot. So – as part of "everything we need" – we have an advocate, Jesus Christ the righteous (1 John 1:9-10; 1 John 2:1). Before Him we can confess our sins and receive not only forgiveness, but *cleansing*. If we learn to confess reflexively, and be restored quickly, then we no longer even carry consciousness of sin or its judgement (Heb 10:2).

That's freedom! We must not neglect so great a salvation!

The New Covenant: The Promise, The Arrival

The "New Covenant" is the Way of Reunion with God. It is a "Blood Covenant", the most solemn and absolute mutual commitment mankind could enter. All ancient cultures understood them, although today Western Christian culture has erased the concept. It is essential to the mind-renewal into authority and victory! I highly recommend two books on this:

- *The Blood Covenant: The Hidden Truth Revealed at the Lord's Table* by E.W. Kenyon
- *The Power of the Blood Covenant* by Malcolm Smith

God works through Hope that induces investment. Again, it is the mind of the gardener. In the middle of the Babylonian exile – the most hopeless-looking defeat of Israel, God promised there would come a restoration of fellowship and the reversal of all damage done by their rebellion.

All prophets told aspects of it, but Ezekiel, Jeremiah, and Isaiah spoke most directly of this "New Covenant". Ezekial and Jeremiah announced it, and Isaiah expounded on it. Isaiah chapters (roughly) 40-60 speak of the double realization – of Israel's release of captivity and also the glorious freedom of the New Covenant.

Marvelously, this reunion would be so complete that it would include the very indwelling of the Spirit of God inside us, to live in us and through us. We would belong to God and God would belong to us.

Now – remember that the cover-to-cover intention of God toward man was and is ... **restored relationship** and **subsequent dominion – all in a Kingdom that shall never end**. This New Covenant was the center of the ambush plan that

Bible Quotes are Word English Bible (WEB) except where noted.

would bring man back to dominion (1 Cor 2:8). Glory is *winning*; and the Mystery hidden though the ages is "Christ in you, the hope of *glory*" (Col 1:27).

Furthermore, we would be given a new heart; a teachable one, that would desire to do what is right, that could love unselfishly.

God would give us both the power (His life in us) and the desire (a new and teachable heart) to do what is right (Titus 2:11).

Now I want all to see without a doubt that Christ was the fulfillment of that Covenant. At "The last supper" – the Feast of the Passover, Christ puts into effect **"The *New* Covenant *in my* blood"**. In John 14 Christ plainly affirmed the indwelling of Father, Son, and Holy Spirit; He plainly and repeatedly states that this reunion of God and Man is now available to *all who obey His commands*.

In the middle of the chapter is an astonishing promise (John 14:12); This internal reunion and restoration is linked to the ultimate external dominion Dear reader, please verify this for yourself; ask the Lord to tell you if these things are true!

To be "In Christ" is to be united with God Himself and united with His in His goodness toward man; This in turn is the beginning – the "first fruits" – of *all things under our feet*.

Sown in Shame and Weakness, Raised in Glory and Power

(Here we are about to get into the central three panels of the poster.)

Salvation is not merely "taught" by Christ; It is entirely demonstrated by Him. He is both the pioneer and perfector of our faith. As pioneer he is the first, clearing the way. As perfector, He is the Adam of the Lineage that overcomes.

Now, note that Christ demonstrated every single element of our response. His most repeated phrase was "follow me"; Will we?

If we embrace the hope, then our faith and love will spring from it (Col 1:3). There are now these three panels that come next:

- Christ, the Last Adam
- Our Surrender: Escaping and Partaking
- Our Transformation: Becoming Like Him

They all follow the same pattern; All three have a required response to a call, and that response gets its power by hope. If we respond to the hope that is set before us, then we shall – in due time, with patience, reap the expected harvest.

Such is the dynamic of a hopeful, confident *gardener*, except for one minor difference: Christ sows the seed of Himself (John 12:24) and calls us to do the same. It is not that He did so we don't have to; Rather He does so and demonstrates the joyful result of glory and dominion – both inward (Heb 5:8) and outward (Total domination of the enemy).

He leads us to tend the garden of our soul. You might ask, "How?". It is by the power of the Life that is born when we entrust our life to Him.

Christ, the Second Man and the Last Adam

The Father invited His Only Son to be the Firstborn from the dead (John 1, John 12:24, Col 1, Heb 2). That invitation appears directly in Isaiah 49. Christ's death on our behalf is described directly in Isaiah 53 – 700 years before He was manifested in the flesh).

Please notice the pattern of Hope, Response, and Results. Christ the Pioneer, meaning that *He went exactly where He wants us to follow*.

With that hope – of bringing *many* sons to glory, Jesu responded to His calling.

He denied Himself (at His baptism He *renounced the going of His own way*); He took up His cross (accepted death to self-will, putting down temptation); and He followed the Father (He did what He saw the Father doing).

He did all these things, not "so we don't have to" (as popular Christianity insists), but so that we "can" follow Him everywhere we needed to go! From walking the Earth to burial; to resurrection to the surface of the Earth, and most importantly – to Union with the Father with the Authority over every name and with the privilege of sending His Spirit into man.

Our Surrender: Escaping and Partaking

As we saw directly from Christ's words in John 14, the benefits of the New Covenant, including *defeating the enemy by the power of God* (John 14:12), are ours if – and only if – we "have His commands and keep them". The truth might be hard to accept for one that has been churched under false teaching, but there is no salvation without a surrender to forsake sin and do the will of God.

But by His divine power God has given us everything we need, including the hope that it takes to induce us to plant the seed (2 Pet 1:3-4)! In other words, if we "follow Him" in His own surrender to do the will of God. Then we will be raised with Him and seated where He is. We will be "bilocated" – walking and acting on the Earth while at the same time seated in the heavenly places – in Authority – with Christ and in Union with the Father. To the degree that we renew our minds to this truth, we overcome the enemy. God is honored when

His people win, but most of what we call Christianity is oblivious to this truth, living in prolonged defeat and shame.

It does not have to be this way! Let us take our cue from the apostle Peter in Acts chapters two and three, and state the Gospel that is true to the Prophets and to Christ Himself.

We must not let pride of our tradition keep us from doing the right thing here. Literally everything is on the line; We must not hesitate – we will be surrounded with brothers and sisters and engulfed in the love of our maker. Then those around us will notice that something has changed in us – and they will see the very same invitation.

Plant the seed that is your *life* – and it will die and germinate. You will still exist, but you will be living the life of Christ by the power of God. You will be free indeed.

If we will forsake sin, believing the promise that God will not only forgive us – but also give His Spirit to those who obey him" (Acts 5:32) and ask for that Spirit (Luke 11:13) … then He does exactly that.

You can make this exchange *now*. If you can see that God is offering to make you a new kind of being that has nothing to be ashamed of and nothing to fear, then you don't need anyone to say "repeat after me". You will accept Christ's death as your own in order to have His life as your own. That's "baptism". Come on in – the water is fine!

Our Transformation: Becoming Like Him

If we have denied ourselves, and traded in the life of the old mankind for the new mankind, and asked for His indwelling Spirit, then we have, in fact, "everything we need for life and godliness". We are then living by motivation of Romans 2:7:

> "But to those who by perseverance in doing good seek after glory, honor, and immortality, He rewards them with eternal life".

If we know our union with God, and are trusting in Christ our advocate, and are using our freedom to put sin to death, then we finally make progress in *inward* dominion. As our shame and fear disappear, we can increasingly pray the prayer of faith without doubting or wavering and receive the thing we ask for. Even the demons become subject to us (Luke 10:19).

As Lake has said,

> "If a man is in Christ, He is God's son, man's servant, and the devils master."

These are the "saints", the "overcomers" of Revelation chapter 2.

Through the centuries, each soul must decide whether to serve God or themselves. Those that make the trade receive the "abundance of Grace and the gift of righteousness" (not just forgiveness). They reign in life (Rom 5:12) in this age (Titus 2:11-14). They will join the great cloud of witnesses until the return of Christ, participate in His millennial reign, and enjoy the restoration of all things in the World to come (Rev 21-22).

Bible Quotes are Word English Bible (WEB) except where noted.

Maintaining Vision:
Keeping the Big Picture In View

I have just given an overview of the gospel at the level of "poster panels". Now – in this accompanying "book", of course, I am not limited by the real-estate of the poster. There is plenty of room for gazing at individual "trees". I provide:

- expansion of the terse excerpts into regular paragraph contexts.
- corroborating passages.
- commentary, including pre-caps and recaps.

This section and those that follow present the scriptures organized around about a hundred core passages. It is my hope and expectation that this sequence of material – with the poster on your wall or a nearby screen – will bring the glory of the Kingdom of God "into view"; and that they present to you the *invitation* to that Kingdom. You likely know of other such passages. They all awaken "hope" – the Hope that will not disappoint (Rom 5:5). They awaken hunger that will not settle until it is satisfied.

They are pictures of things that absolutely await us if we surrender into Christ and patiently follow Him by practicing obeying His command to love.

These promises – even the profoundly supernatural ones – are too good to not be true! They are quickly marked off as "misinformation" in some circles but they bring intense joy to those that see them and act on them, and soon taste them in experience. They renew the mind to see what mankind was supposed to enjoy – and to be – forever.

The passages depict the "Life of God" and *so do His people*! They depict glory, honor, and immortality that we obtain "by persevering in doing good" (Rom 2). To some readers, this will sound like it cannot possibly be "grace"!! – but the key to resolving the seeming contradiction is to understand what the New Covenant tells us directly (as we will see in Ezekiel 36).

> The good news itself is that when we exchange our lives for the life of Christ, His death becomes our freedom and *His life in us (in the spirit) germinates and becomes our righteousness (in the soul)*.
>
> If we grasp this, then our Bible makes sense. If we don't, then it doesn't.

If you will be satisfied to reign *with* Christ *and under Him*, still *far above any other name that is named*, then will you make the trade – from your life of the First Mankind to the Life of the Second Mankind?

Showing His Glory:
Both the Forest and the Trees

(Matthew 5:6) Blessed are those who hunger and thirst after <u>righteousness</u>, For they shall be <u>filled</u>.

This book brings into view about 200 key passages from the Word of God. They are among the most mind-blowing radical passages of the Bible, and most of them are curiously absent from all preaching and teaching in most of today's American churches. For three years I have organized these promises of God so that nobody can visit them in this arrangement and still fail to see:

1. That God is calling them to freedom, glory, honor, and immortality; and to *a Kingdom*.
2. That the power of God has provided for us everything we need for it. There is effort required, but it is certainly not "earning".

Poster Panels and Book Sections

I present the passages not only in a very intentional sequence, but also in very intentional groupings. The book *sections* correspond to poster *panels*. In the poster you will see that the passages are carefully ordered and positioned. In particular, the poster's centered 3-tier panel is laid out to show columns for ***call, hope, response, and results***.

As you work through these scriptures, please stay attuned to what tier you are on and what heading you are under. If you keep these in mind, then you will be in a good position to *apply the promises of God correctly* and experience the major breakthroughs that are there for you. You will be equipped to overcome the enemy – inwardly and outwardly.

Build Your Favorite Passages Set as You Go

To me, 2 Cor 5:21 and 2 Peter 1:3-4 are excellent passages to keep in the back of your mind (but not too far back). Eventually you will identify a key five, then a key ten that the rest knit into. And the FOG will be cleared from your mind forever. For all who are hungry for the Life of God, The Holy Spirit stands ready to bring the Word of God alive to you.

Bible Quotes are Word English Bible (WEB) except where noted.

Two-Page Spreads:
Scriptures Left, Comments Right

The layout of the entire book is built around "two-page spreads", with "key scriptures immediately followed by commentary". The paperback and hard cover books keep the scriptures on the left and the commentary on the right – so that you do not have to turn a page to refer back and forth. Some eBook readers will do this as well, but even phone-based readers will at least have them close together.

To Study this material, you may therefore select a passage heading and consider it *in light of the section it is in*. As we shall see, the very worst two distortions of God's Word in popular Christianity are:

1. That God "arbitrarily chooses" of who will be saved and who will not – implying amazing cruelty as God's character and nature – the worst possible news! and
2. The oversimplification of the salvation process; the notion that once (a) happens to you, that's it. You can go your own way (even though that is the definition of sin as we shall see) and you will still inherit eternal life

Many Know There Must Be More

In America, the most popular "gospel" presentations can be summarized as "forgiveness now and going to Heaven someday". If God were really that small, then I would move on to try other gods. And that is exactly what most people do – both Christians and non-Christians.

When You See the Truth, Boldness Happens

The primary requirement for becoming and effective witness, teacher, or preacher is simply to see the glory of God clearly and correctly; and seeing the offer of God in Christ clearly and correctly. This is precisely why the fishermen were so quickly transformed into World-changers; More precisely, they became effective ambassadors for the Kingdom that is to Come; They were "In Christ" because they were no longer speaking their own ideas; trying to outshine each other with their human glory; and acting like "mere mortals":

> *(1 Corinthians 3:3 NKJV) for you are still carnal. For where there are envy, strife, and divisions among you, are you not carnal and behaving like mere men?*

See the Invitation; A Hundred Different Ways

There are thousands of Books on Christianity, ranging from theology to personal spirituality, all with scripture references. This book – and the entire *Second Man Now* Series – is very different in that I am bringing forward *specifically themes and passages entirely buried by numerous churches today*: Kingdom, Dominion, The Second Mankind, and Grace *to Overcome*.

"The Kingdom of God" and "Dominion"

As it turns out, God's first desire is for us to be born of the Second Mankind and reunited with Him… forever!!! But if we truly believe in the Word of God, then this doesn't mean 'Once-saved-always-saved". Rather, it means there are people who will not only see the kindness of God and humble themselves; Once they are set "free indeed" (and we will see what this means) they love Him enough to remain in Him.

Second to our reunion with Him, God's principal expression of kindness to man is that by that union, man would enjoy not only the very real inward freedom to live above the power of sin, but *also to fulfill his original assignment on the earth* – which was to "bear His image"; to "be fruitful and multiply (but now to replicate the **Second** Restored Mankind), and to "have dominion … over everything that lives on earth" – other than humans.

At several points I'll repeat John G. Lake's words: "If a man is in Christ, he is God's son, man's servant, and the devil's master". I've never seen such a concise statement of the "mind of Christ" (1 Cor 2:16). I will present much more on that as we go.

The Second Mankind

You will see, cover-to-cover – that we are called to be recreated to the **Second Mankind**, "converted" upon our surrender to the Love of God, to *do the will of God on Earth*. This is not an improvement program, but a death and resurrection followed by an active yet restful walk.

As we will see, there is a salvation event followed by a salvation process, despite the best attempts of man to deny the process part. Sometimes it is indeed battle – but it is winning battle nevertheless, and you can know this and *see this* even when it hurts.

Raised in Power and Glory

Bible Quotes are Word English Bible (WEB) except where noted.

Do You Desire "Rest"?
God offers *Restoration*

(Acts 3:18-21; 5:20 NKJV) But those things which God foretold by the mouth of <u>all</u> His prophets, that the Christ would suffer, He has thus <u>fulfilled</u>...

*<u>**Repent**</u> therefore and <u>**be converted**</u>, that your <u>sins may be blotted out</u>, so that times of <u>refreshing</u> may come from the presence of the Lord, and <u>that He may send Jesus Christ</u>, who was preached to you before, whom heaven must receive until the times of <u>**restoration of all things**</u>, which God has spoken by the mouth of <u>all</u> His holy prophets since the world began...*

"Go, stand in the temple and speak to the people all the words of this <u>life.</u>"

Of "That Which Was Lost"
But ... *What Was Lost?*

Peter explains that the **"Restoration of *All Things*"** is coming. He provided a small demonstration of God's goodness by the simple, immediate, and easy restoration of the body of a single man. This restoration *starts* with *individuals* but does not end there (Ps 8:6; Ps 115:16; Gen 15; Ps 110). It builds to the *Nations* (Rom 1; Rom 16) and builds to the *Earth* itself (Rom 8; Rev 21).

"Repent" and "Be Converted"

Popular Christianity has degenerated into a repentance that now merely means "sorry" and seeking the "free ticket"; Usually out if ignorance, the Baptism candidate expects relief from fear of Hell and to maybe get some improvement of the Old Mankind instead of "conversion" to become the Second Mankind. Nobody has even mentioned to these people, for example, 2 Peter 1:3-4 or Romans 6:7.

But these passages restore the essential truths that *actually make us free*. I know about true freedom, because I experienced it in a moment in 1999 and I enjoy it to this day. My greatest fulfillment comes now as I partner with Christ in me to witness of it and lead others to discover it.

As stated earlier – I present most passages in "two-page spreads" with the passages displayed on the left page and with my comments on the right page. Within the commentary I make connections (references) to other vison passages and other supporting passages. Please notice the consistency and coherency that emerges; The thing that materializes is "The Gospel of the Kingdom".

"Kindling" the Hope in Which we are Saved

I selected these passages because they speak plainly of the transforming truths that make us free; Not just free to be like "us", but free to be like the Lord Jesus Christ (1 John 4:17) which was the entire full objective of God in the redemption of man. There are numerous passages in the scriptures that speak of these things, but I am sure that this selection is adequate to start the fire in anybody that hungers and thirsts not only for forgiveness, but for righteousness, bringing a glorious awakening to dignity while demolishing fear. The passages shine the glory that we are to "see". Somehow, over the centuries, the body of Christ in America has deteriorated into the religious "organization" that lives in powerlessness and fear. The very truths that would make them free are hidden in plain sight; but with the reduced-gospel talking points always kept front and center, *they cannot even see* the breakthrough truths.

Bible Quotes are Word English Bible (WEB) except where noted.

Bear Again
The Image of God; No Shame!

As my testimony elaborates, over the decades I have noticed many of these passages that speak of the actual power of God; and at points I experienced the sudden reality of that power. I came to see that Christ did not come merely that we could "get our heaven tickets punched" by believing the fact of the Atonement. I experienced the power of God at work in me when and as I surrendered my will to do His will. Not that I never strayed into "going my own way". I did and I returned under the chastening of God.

As I touched on earlier, the middle panel of the Poster shows there is always a *way*; a *hope*, a *call*; and a required *response* of sowing that leads to reaping *life*.

We <u>See</u>; Then we <u>Divest</u> & <u>Re-Invest</u>

In general, as we read the Word of God – or hear it,

1. The "Word of Truth" meets our eyes or ears and gets to our brains.
2. It touches our hearts (the heart is the seat of the "will").
3. Our hearts (our wills) make sound and joyful investment decisions.

An investment is an "entrusting"; As mentioned earlier, in Greek this is the same verb as "believing". It is a *committing of something* to one that can magnify its value.

But this entrusting is not "passive". One who has entrusted Himself "to" Christ has entrusted himself "into" Christ (legitimate translation of John 3:16) to **do His will** (righteousness) **by His power** ("Grace) rather than *go our own way* (God's definition of sin provided in Isaiah 53) by our own self-righteousness.

In the most repeated words of Christ ("Follow Me" in Mt 16:24 a few pages ahead), He "invites" us into an investment that produces an infinite and eternal return. He doesn't command it; He doesn't seize our assets; He announces it "on the exchange" as an FPO (final public offering). The investments we must make – the things we must commit – are **<u>"counterfeit" and "contraband"</u>**. This is how Grace is <u>Costly</u> but really <u>free</u>. Peer into the truth of God; Let it move you to make the trade in your spirits, and then move out – in freedom – to make the exchanges needed in our souls.

In Matthew 17 Jesus gave us the analogy of planting a seed – even a mustard seed, the tiniest of all seeds – to get in return a huge tree that is a refuge and a joy "to many". In John 12, He repeated the analogy and hinted that what is multiplied is the number of New Mankind people on the Earth.

Embrace His Promise
And Partake of His Nature!

Let's gaze into the promises of God and see His Glory! He has died and risen not just "FOR us", but "AS us" to be our righteousness and our Life. We are to partaking in the Life of God. As we shall see, Christ came to restore man to fellowship with God to break the penalty and power of sin; He commands us to then practice obeying His command to love as He loved, under mercy. It's a "do-over" under wonderful conditions of His very presence in us and with us.

For Millions of Christians, Bible-Reading ... Hurts!

For millions of Christians – or ex-Christians – reading their Bible makes them sleepy or gives them a headache. This is the direct natural result of reading material that contradicts what they have been taught in church, with the added extra of knowing deep down that we might still be in our sins.

In my decades of experience in *major* denominations and non-denominations, I have come to identify the most significant "disconnects. In some cases, what is said that is *unscriptural*; in other cases, the truth is systematically *omitted*.

I estimate that in 90% of churches today, narratives have evolved to where:

- The most pervasive *theme – Dominion of Man on Earth* – is buried.
- The most-repeated saying of Christ – "lose life to find it" – is buried.
- The means of escaping the power of sin – See Romans 6 – is buried.
- Many of the most incredible and wonderful passages are buried.

The purposes of the enemy in promoting these are:

1. *Keeping Holiness "Optional"* – this prevents true conversions, while it mass-produces false assurance; and
2. *Keeping even true Christians defeated* – the enemy wants to control and torment man and to mock the power of God.

The Centerline Theme is Dominion – But <u>Not</u> over Man

Dominion – In Christ - Is the Centerline Theme of the Bible. It is in view in *more chapters than any other concept in the entire Bible*

- It is the Original Assignment to Us by God
- It is What Christ Demonstrated, Taught, & Commissioned
- Equipping us to Overcome the Enemy is the Ultimate Expression of His Kindness toward Us through the Ages.

Raised in Power and Glory

Bible Quotes are Word English Bible (WEB) except where noted.

Let's Be Honest
About the Need to Persevere

Hebrews 6:4-6 For concerning those who were once enlightened and tasted of the heavenly gift, and were made partakers of the Holy Spirit, and tasted the good word of God, and the powers of the age to come, and then fell away, it is impossible to renew them again to repentance; seeing they crucify the Son of God for themselves again, and put him to open shame.

2 Peter 2:20 For if, after they have escaped the defilement of the world through the knowledge of the Lord and Savior Jesus Christ, they are again entangled in it and overcome, the last state has become worse for them than the first.

Matthew 24:10-14 Then many will stumble, and will deliver up one another, and will hate one another. Many false prophets will arise, and will lead many astray. Because iniquity will be multiplied, the love of many will grow cold. But he who endures to the end, the same will be saved. This Good News of the Kingdom will be preached in the whole world for a testimony to all the nations, and then the end will come.

1 Corinthians 9:27 but I beat my body and bring it into submission, lest by any means, after I have preached to others, I myself should be rejected.

Galatians 5:19-21 Now the deeds of the flesh are obvious, which are: adultery, sexual immorality, uncleanness, lustfulness, idolatry, sorcery, hatred, strife, jealousies, outbursts of anger, rivalries, divisions, heresies, envy, murders, drunkenness, orgies, and things like these; of which I forewarn you, even as I also forewarned you, that those who practice such things will not inherit God's Kingdom.

Rev 3:5 He who overcomes will be arrayed in white garments, and I will in no way blot his name out of the book of life, and I will confess his name before my Father, and before his angels.

Scriptures are Plain
And Stakes Could Not be Higher

I cannot in good conscience "dance around" this issue. If we read carefully, without the Reformation lenses, we see that *every one of these exhortations – warnings – is written to Christians*, not unbelievers. It is up to each and every one of us to decide who is to be feared – God or Man. This should be *sobering*, but not "scary". When we submit to the Word of God, we find He provides the Hope (Col 1:27; the power (Rom 6 entire); and manifest presence inside us (John 14:19;23) that it takes for us to persevere as He requires. He has given us all we need for life and godliness (2 Pet 1:3).

If you have been taught otherwise God will be merciful to you; But now that you know, it is extremely important that you obey the Word of God rather than try to protect your good standing in a community of false teaching.

> *2 Timothy 2:12-13 If we endure, we will also reign with him. If we deny him, he also will deny us. If we are faithless, he remains faithful. For he can't deny himself."*

> *John 15:6-10 If a man doesn't remain in me, he is thrown out as a branch, and is withered; and they gather them, throw them into the fire, and they are burned. If you keep my commandments, you will remain in my love; even as I have kept my Father's commandments, and remain in his love.*

> *Luke 8:13 Those on the rock are they who, when they hear, receive the word with joy; but these have no root, who believe for a while, then fall away in time of temptation.*

> *Rev 2:10 Be faithful to death, and I will give you the crown of life.*

> *1 John 2:24 let that remain in you which you heard from the beginning. If that which you heard from the beginning remains in you, you also will remain in the Son, and in the Father.*

> *Colossians 1:22-23 yet now he has reconciled in the body of his flesh through death, to present you holy and without defect and blameless before him, if it is so that you continue in the faith, grounded and steadfast, and not moved away from the hope of the Good News which you heard, ...*

Bible Quotes are Word English Bible (WEB) except where noted.

Some Valid Definitions
That Resolve Contradictions

As you read, please "carefully-and-prayerfully" consider the following definitions of the a few of the most important words in the Bible. Compare the popular definition in column two with the definition I propose in column three. As you work through the two hundred passages I bring out in this book, you will find that column two definitions are absolutely inconsistent with the scriptures, while the column three definitions are fully consistent – not just "among themselves", but with the scriptures.

Term (Greek, Hebrew)	Popular Definition and Usage, denying Power	Other Fully Valid and Biblical Definitions Consistent with Bible Context
Grace (Charis)	Forgiveness now, Heaven eventually	**Everything we need** for the Life of God and godliness; It is the right and the way to become one of the Second Mankind. All the rest is religion at best.
Baptism (Baptidzo)	Sins washed away	Entry Into **death and rebirth**, the end of going my own way; the start of doing the will of God; Pledge of a good conscience toward God
Believe in (Pisteuo Eis)	Accept fact of payment for sins	Commit to; **Entrust into**; Adhere to; Obey
Faith (Pistis, Ehmoonah)	Believing in Christ for forgiveness	Belief, faithfulness, **fidelity**, allegiance (Centurion!) Hebrew: Trusting **loyalty;** as that of the **Centurion**
Conversion (Epistrepho)	Joining a church, or receiving baptism signifying forgiveness of sins	Born into the **Lineage** of Christ; **Innermost nature recreated** in righteousness and true holiness.
Salvation (Sodzo)	Avoiding Hell	**Rescue & restoration** from the consequences of the fall of man and the works of the enemy
Repentance (Metanoia)	Regret	**Forsaking sin**; Decision to serve God, not self

Good works (Agathos ergon)	Passive automatic activity from gratitude for forgiveness	**Actively obeying Christ's commands by His power; by His Life in you, having been freed**
Righteousness (Dikaiosune)	Legal Acquittal; The state of being forgiven	**Actual** rightness of character and action; specifically, the **righteousness from God**
Eternal Life (Zoe aonion)	Living forever	The Life **of God** (Greek Zeo) through the ages
Sin (hamartia)	Sins	Sins, **sinfulness**; sin principle, sin **nature**; Context is extremely important for Hamartia
Meekness (Prahooce)	Poor sinner saved by grace	**Strength**, under **control**; as that of the **Centurion**
Glory	No, no! – only God gets glory	**Freed** from corruption, **partaking in God's nature** having been born of Him; **Overcoming** the true enemy by Christ living in you & you in Him
In Christ	Forgiven	Having forsaken sin; born with His nature. Filled with His Spirit; Abiding in Him, obeying His commands

I wish to note right here – that the definitions of "faith (pistis) and "meekness" (prahooce) reflect the mind of Christ, and they are also the mind of a Christian (1 Cor 2:16).

If you peer deeply and honestly into the Word of God – setting aside all bias long enough to see what the Bible actually teaches on these things, then the most wonderful thing occurs! You will hunger and thirst for righteousness and you will be filled (Matt 5:6); You will want to be "like Him" (1 Jn 4:17), and indeed you will get your transformation underway.

Bottom line: Popular definitions of "Christianity Words" have been morphed to support a fact-faith, once-and-done way of getting to Heaven and still get to go our own way. But the Bible plainly teaches that we must persevere doing God's will rather than our own until the end of our life in this age. But this entire Book is devoted to showing tht God has indeed given us everything we need – if we will only make use of it! And we have a merciful High Priest that has compassion – not to rebellion, but to humble cooperation.

Bible Quotes are Word English Bible (WEB) except where noted.

Pistis: Allegiance, Loyalty, Fidelity, Faithfulness

The Greek word *pistis* is almost universally translated "faith" in English bibles. But that very word also means the things we see in the title of this page. All these things are wrapped up together in pistis.

Our flesh will not like this, but we must not isolate and camp on just the one single aspect that absolves us of all responsibility.

We obtain our initial rescue when we embrace the kindness of the crucifixion act of Christ on our behalf; But our ultimate salvation – once we are truly free – depends on our faithfulness.

This is a lifelong practice of love, obedience, and perseverance; and we have a merciful High Priest for when we do fail (1 John 2:1).

A Simple Biblical Model of "Justification"

Millions demand that grace means "we are just forgiven", once and for all. But this violates hundreds of Old Testament and New Testament passages.

As we shall see, nearly all the hardest passages (hardest to understand or hardest to swallow!) fall into place if we see Justification as follows:

1. "Being justified" is a "state". It is the *state of being right with God*.
2. There is an "event" of justification, which is simply our surrender to do the will of God, and our confession of Christ as King. It is simply the event at which we have *gotten right with God*. The Greek word "sodzo" that is usually translated "saved" simply means "rescued".
3. To be remain saved, we *keep ourselves right with God*. We do this by our practice of obeying His commands and putting sin to death. We do this *by His power*, and therefore it is still "by faith through grace". The Greek word *pistis* that is usually translated "faith" also means "faithfulness".

The most important truth in the Gospel really is this simple.

Faith in Action
is Faithfulness and Fidelity

Dear reader, I suggest that when you encounter the word faith" in an English bible, you consider *the context* and notice how clear it becomes if you substitute "Faithfulness" or "Fidelity", or "Allegiance".

"Allegiance" in particular resonates when the Kingship – the Lordship – of Jesus Christ is in view. Allegiance is the right translation wherever we are called to action.

The Most Massive "Puzzle Piece Drop"

For most American Christians, nothing will produce a more massive burst of clarity in your Bible than this realization that the enemy has gotten pistis translated as "faith" everywhere.

On the topic of systematic false translation, please notice a few more. Bible Scholar David Bercot points these out in his excellent *Historic Fatih Commentary Series*. His writings are amazingly effective in removing our distorted FOG (Forgiveness-Only Gospel) lenses; These are Bible-reading lenses that we have been subconsciously wearing since the Reformation.

I suspect that every pastor or teacher that loves truth and has not made these discoveries will joyfully devour these revelations. This is because clarity always produces confidence and peace; and these in turn produce boldness in preaching and in personal evangelism.

"Law" in Romans and Galatians

An insidious distortion is present in some translations in connection with the word "law" or "Law". Everywhere we see this word in Paul's letters to the Romans (which was actually to the Jews in Rome) and to the Galatians, Paul is referring to the **_Law of Moses_**. He is referring to this *particular* "law" and therefore the "L" should be capitalized.

But by leaving the "L" in lowercase, some translations systematically lead us to believe that *grace is opposed to law in general*, and that grace promotes "do whatever you want and still go to Heaven". Romans Chapter 6 is dedicated to refuting that teaching, but it never sees the light of day in popular preaching.

The truth is that the grace of God – the forgiveness of past sins combined with the power and ery going forward, enable us to fulful the commands of Christ to love as He loved (Romans 8:1, 4).

Bible Quotes are Word English Bible (WEB) except where noted.

PART 1:
THE MISSING PIECES

The Epistles Explain
The Restored Species of Mankind

I find it beautiful to see that the passages from the Epistles **explain** the Life that is behind the Dominion that *Christ lived, taught, and commissioned* in the Gospels. Actually, He *commissioned* Dominion first in Genesis 1:26-27 and repeated it at the start of subsequent ages. 1 Cor 2:8 explains exactly why Christ didn't explain it in His direct teachings until after His resurrection.

Nearly everyone has been told – that is, it has been communicated directly or by technology – that the Blood of Christ has *paid for sins*. The tragedy of the day is that we stop there, as if that is the entirety of The Gospel.

The truth of the matter is that the very same Blood *ratified the New Covenant*; and by that Covenant **Christ restores in us what was lost**:

1. Union with God, with direct personal fellowship – companionship
2. Breaking of the compulsive power of sin
3. Rebirth as a Son of God
4. The indwelling Spirit of God, whom He gives to those that obey Him
5. A teachable heart – and both the desire and the power to do His will on this earth and in this age
6. Dominion. It is not universal in this age, but it manifests and puts the enemy on notice wherever God's people go. Specifically, it is Superiority over all the work of the enemy – *inwardly* in our spirits, our souls, and our bodies – and *outwardly* as we go forth to continue the liberating work of Christ until He appears.

When you see these wonderful benefits of the New Covenant – which are in the Gospel itself – your entire Bible to make sense. As a simple example – the Old Testament is a long sequence of obediences and rebellions – and the corresponding defeats (enslavements, captivities) or exploits (dominion, glory) that follow.

Now, of course, "knowing" these things that the New Covenant restores doesn't put you into that Covenant. So let me make this personal. Speaking the truth in love, I will alternate between "we" and "I" in the statements that follow.

In your heart – the portion of your will that is looking at the promises of God – will you surrender into Christ? He is what God in Christ calls us to do:

See the glory of Christ – His love **and His power** – and the FACT that He calls you to ***become that kind of being***.

> A person ripe for conversion is thinking the following:
>
> "I am now walking around, but condemned and dead and decaying; I am sold into the Corruption of the world. But I want to be *alive*, at any cost."
>
> "I want to be like Him".

Trust His promise that He is absolutely willing and fully able to restore the image of God into you;

> "He became like me so that I could become like Him".
>
> "If I will surrender my rebellion; plant myself like a seed – as He did – then yes, I do believe that He will raise me as that kind of being".

Entrust your life to Him; Obey His command to deny yourself and love as He loved; Planting yourself as a seed, losing your life to find it (Matthew, Mark, Luke, and John).

> "I am yours (and you are mine)". My will is now subsumed into yours (and your will is becoming mine); My life is yours (and yours is mine) I am buried in you (and I have your life living inside me); I live and move in your name – (and you live in me as a member of your very own body).
>
> I have renounced the so-called glory of man (and you have given me your glory)."

Persevere in Him:

> "You have restored in me that which was lost. Hallelujah!!!
>
> "You alone have the Words of Life. You have made the Way of Life! I will remain in you; I will not deny you; I will continue in faithfulness and allegiance; When I fail in weakness, I have an advocate; Therefore, I remain surrendered."
>
> "Through perseverance in doing good, I seek after glory, honor, and immortality; and you shall reward me with eternal life" (Rom 2:7).

Bible Quotes are Word English Bible (WEB) except where noted.

Taking the first letters of the verbs of the above "steps", we see "STEP". It is easy to remember.

Now See the Blood Covenant

The pure and innocent Blood of Christ ratified the New Covenant with all its terms, the foremost of which is reunion of God with man – "My Union with God" – "Christ in me, my hope of glory" (Col 1:27). Be very careful here! Do NOT translate this simply as "My hope of **going to heaven**!!!". If you make it mean that – as millions have been *trained in church* to do – then you and your children will remain alone and defeated. I say this in all compassion! But if we can embrace the plain truth of the Word of God – embrace it enough to *obey* **the Gospel** (Millions of pseudo-Christians recoil at that phrase, but Paul does not, John does not; James does not; Peter does not). Let's restart that statement now…

Each of us must enter into the Covenant,

> "I must enter into Blood Covenant with the King of Kings."

Then we see the thing that has been missing for millions. We see that holiness is righteousness forming in the soul – The fruit of the right tree. We enter under the service – and the banner and the Name – of Christ. God must see His own righteousness in us; He gives His Spirit to those who obey Him; they overcome the profound lies of the ages and they manifest as Sons of God.

Based on these passages we can now form a series of very natural connections. Because we have surrendered into Christ, to embrace the whole New Covenant – **not just amnesty** – there are no more contradictions for us. We *can now easily connect hundreds of passages* that were just fragments under a forgiveness-only gospel.

Rebellion is what destroyed the first mankind. The Second Man, the Last Adam (Christ) became us and surrendered unto death as us. Now, to be "In Christ" we must **surrender** as He did and then **persevere** to the end as He did.

This is the full Word of God and it will not change to fit our traditions.

For most of us this means we must at some point renouncing the sinful species of our parents and siblings and of ourselves; We, like every human – MUST **renounce the fallen, self-absorbed species that we are**. Will we remain under condemnation? Will we follow a man-invented narrative to destruction? Or will we transfer into the Second Mankind and live the Life of God forever?

In all kindness yet urgency, I hope you will choose the New Lineage and Live. I hope you will escape the corruption and partake in His nature!

Being in Christ

Those that are in Christ have not only seen that by Christ's death we <u>*can*</u> crucify our flesh (overcome it); They <u>*have done so*</u> and they continue to suppress it by the power of God in them, as a way of life (Gal 5:24; Matt 16:24; Romans 8:13). Ignore that at your peril! But if you have surrendered yourself into Christ and are remaining in Him then you know that you have passed from death to Life.

Hungering for Righteousness – or Just for Amnesty?

You do not have to "struggle intellectually" to figure out if you are "in Christ". You will not need a theologian to explain it to you. Rather you will of course know whether you are hungering for righteousness or just for amnesty.

If you hunger for *mere amnesty* – and if you come to *see that Christ paid for that*, then of course you will embrace it, and you will indeed be forgiven. If you furthermore see that Christ died "as you" (and He did as we shall see), then you will feel the chains drop as well. You "got saved" and are free indeed

The catch is, of course, once we are "free indeed", we are responsible for what we do with that freedom – to practice obeying God in love and faith for the rest of our days, actively cooperating with His overcoming power.

If we obey Him, this simply manifests who it is that loves Him and the One that sent Him. It is exactly why we will be judged not merely by what we believe; but by what we "do" with what we believe.

And all the apparent contradictions of the scriptures evaporate; and all the theological gymnastics and sophistry of the theologians gets exposed for what it is. The truth becomes simple and clear and beautiful!

In some Christian "organizations" the entire objective is to win your loyalty and your finances and leave you enslaved. The schemes were not invented by theologians but by the enemy himself.

Anybody is free to escape, but escaping takes courage and is not for cowards. But the discomforts of this escape are not worth comparing to the freedom and joy that will result from it.

Bible Quotes are Word English Bible (WEB) except where noted.

Clearing the FOG
The Forgiveness-Only Gospel

If we will read and hear and heed the scriptures *without our "forgiveness-only" glasses on*, we will see the glory of God in them once again. We will see that God, in Christ, has indeed given us everything we need for life (not just natural life as we know it, but the Zoe Life of God) and godliness itself (2 Pet 1:3-4).

There are hundreds of passages of scripture that speak of each of the following elements – and each of them is a dimension of the New Covenant beyond forgiveness. To be sure, The Blood of Christ bought forgiveness, but it ratified a Blood Covenant that is *far, far bigger than forgiveness alone.*

The most profound element that is missing from our Gospel is the **Second Mankind**, which is the restart of the Human race and the enabler of the holiness that God requires of us fruit of the right tree. Notice that in the lineage listed in Luke 3 – only the *First* man and the *Last* man listed are "Sons of God".

The first mankind had lost its connection with God and every man in that lineage is born in the enemy camp and under judgement; But the Second Mankind is born of God and partakes of His nature so that the righteousness requirement of the Law can be fulfilled in us who walk by His Spirit in us. This is easy to state – it is simply how salvation works; yet we almost never hear it stated.

To See God's Call
To Holiness, Glory, and Dominion

Holiness, glory, and dominion are highly interrelated elements of incredible dignity; John chapters 13 forward describe them in detail, but the church has all but left them behind in favor of just "getting saved".

Holiness is the detachment of the Second Man from the stain of the Corruption due to evil desire; That evil flows in from the World and the default constitution of man is void of the presence or the power of God to resist that deadly infection.

Holiness is being set apart from the power of darkness, to do the will of God. Holiness is the bearing once again the fruits of the Spirit in the soul. Holiness is the gardening into our souls the righteousness of God that has been born in our spirits. We must renew our minds and our actions by His power and by the sustained act of our wills. The Old Man *cannot* do it; The New Man *can*. This is how the burden becomes light (Mt 11:28); This is why Revelation states plainly – eight times that salvation is to those that "overcome" (Most are in Rev. 3).

Glory is "the image of God" seen without having to be spoken. In the Old Testament Hebrew language, it appears as "glowing"; or as "winning overwhelmingly" in a class all its own. In the New Testament Greek, it appears as "the unspoken yet manifest presence of God". Romans 3:23 states the problem: "all have sinned and fall short of the glory of God", but not a single Bible tract I have seen in my forty-five years as a Christian has stated the answer to the root problem plainly stated – "fallen short of the glory of God". The church seems to want to proclaim only two things: (a) get saved; and (b) go your own way as a poor sinner going to Heaven someday.

"Glory" is precisely "that which was lost" by the First Adam. The Second Man, the Last Adam, came to restore it.

Dominion – is dominating, and a Kingdom is the Domain of a particular King. Corrupted mankind wants to control other people; But Christ demonstrated that those that would inherit all things must be (as John G. Lake has summarized it):

> "God's son, man's servant, and the devil's master."

False Christianity calls itself the bride of Christ, *but will always deny one or more of the above three elements*. Only those who will serve man can be born out of the lineage of the fallen Adam, and only God's sons are the devil's master.

Bible Quotes are Word English Bible (WEB) except where noted.

The scriptures show that dominion of this sort is what Christ proclaimed, demonstrated, taught, trained, equipped, and commissioned. It is the "Gospel of the Kingdom" (Matthew 24:14).

Popular Christianity still proclaims merely a Gospel of forgiveness; and then wonders why a missionary reports ten converts for the whole year; or a Pastor is overwhelmed and burnt out, seeing himself, his family, and his whole congregation worn out by the enemy – and living in defeat.

Demonstrating weakness (no authority over the power of the enemy) does more harm than good to the glory of God! Therefore, no missionary should leave home without it. *If there is no strength, there is no witness.*

Come tell me to my face that I am wrong about this.

But There Is a Way

But there is a "Way"; though indeed it is a stumbling block to the proud. The way to strength, freedom, joy, glory, honor, and immortality ... passes through humbling and surrender. Not just a surrender into passivity, but a humble-yet-bold exchange of the Old Man in us for the New Man that Christ promises. We must lose our life to find it (the most repeated saying of Christ, never once shown in any Bible tract I have seen). It is the planting of a seed known as "my life", knowing that something unexplainable will happen while it is buried and hidden; that the thing we seek will emerge.

There are hundreds – I dare say a *thousand* if we are attuned to them – of passages that show God's intention for mankind to have dominion restored on the earth. The catch is, that we – by the power of God – are to overcome the enemy within before we get to overcome the enemy without. Please look for these themes even if you have never heard of them in church or even never been in a church. You will see them everywhere.

All this is to restore not just "*those* who were lost" (The Bible doesn't say that at all!), but rather "that which was lost". God wants us to bear His image, and to no longer fall short of the glory of God; and He has made the way for it.

This is the Gospel of the Kingdom.

There is a remnant that is emerging as we approach the end of this age. It consists of those that will surrender the going of their own way; will forsake sin by the power of God; will then obey all that Christ actually taught and commanded – by His indwelling power and righteousness.

Are you in?

Bible Quotes are Word English Bible (WEB) except where noted.

The Way of Holiness
The Redeemed Shall Walk There

(Isaiah 35:8-10 KJV)
And a highway will be there, and a way, and it shall be called <u>The way of holiness</u>; the unclean shall not pass over it; but it shall be for those: the wayfaring men, though fools, shall not err therein. No lion shall be there, nor any ravenous beast shall go up thereon, it shall not be found there; but the redeemed shall walk there:

And the ransomed of the LORD shall return, and come to Zion with songs and everlasting joy upon their heads: they shall obtain joy and gladness, and sorrow and sighing shall flee away.

A "Highway"
No Ravenous Beast Shall Be There

Even though there has always been a remnant of people humbly surrendered to do the will of God, many traditions have degenerated into unscriptural teachings that preserve a "form" of religion – or maybe a grand "culture", but on a day-to-day practical level, families are routinely defeated by the enemy.

Marriages are routinely destroyed as husbands and wives lack the power to live in unity. The divorce rate among professing Christian exceeds that of non-Christians. Furthermore, at the time I write this, American society is now deeply infiltrated by spiritism, occult, and outright devil-worship; and *just about everybody knows it*.

The thing is, Christians seem to have no suggestions as to what can be done, despite the fact that there is a very clear "Way" that Christ presents. He walked it and said, "Follow Me". The fact of the matter is, the road to "glory" – and glory is "winning" – leads through self-denial; and sadly, this for many people is a deal-breaker. They reject Christ out-of-hand, Who is "the Way, the Truth, and the Life" (John 14). They "move on" like sheep – and "go their own way" (Isaiah 53).

God *knows in advance* who will respond to Him in humility, but this doesn't negate our true free will. He chooses ("elect" means choose") to give grace to the humble, and He predestines them "to be conformed into the image of His Son, *__the firstborn among many brothers__*" (Rom 8:29).

So, we see that, rightly understood of foreknowledge, "predestination" is true! … and **yet it leaves us fully responsible to choose to obey God**. And God is good – not unjust as is implied by the *arbitrary* predestination teachings. As we shall see from the Word of God, the Way that Christ calls us to follow is a way of peace and rest, because those that give themselves to His care have the benefit of "no condemnation"; no "consciousness of sin".

Above all, it is a way of peace, because those in Christ enjoy the awareness of the presence of God living in them and speaking with them and through them!

Hope, as in *Joyful Expectation*

Those surrendered into Christ (yes, the word is "into"!) "See His glory" – and they are filled with the joyful knowledge that God is able to do what He has promised; He will confirm them to the image of Christ – provided they will use the power of God (NOT mere human will-power!) to resist sin to the day of their natural death.

Bible Quotes are Word English Bible (WEB) except where noted.

Spirit vs. Soul vs. Body: What *Am* I?

(1 Thessalonians 5:23) May the God of peace himself sanctify you completely. May your whole spirit, soul, and body be preserved blameless at the coming of our Lord Jesus Christ.

> We are "in" a body, of course, but we "are" a spirit

(Romans 8:16) The Spirit himself testifies with our spirit that we are children of God;

> And We "have" a soul

(Hebrews 4:12) For the word of God is living and active, and sharper than any two-edged sword, piercing even to the dividing of soul and spirit ...

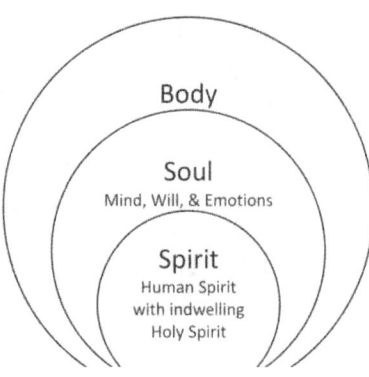

Body

Soul
Mind, Will, & Emotions

Spirit
Human Spirit
with indwelling
Holy Spirit

Sown in Weakness and Shame

Your Spirit is "You" and You're No Longer a Sinner

This truth from the Word of God can save you a lifetime of self-condemnation. If – and only – if – you are surrendered to forsake sin and do the will of God, then you are converted - Acts 3, *"repent* and be converted", not just "get saved"). You have been born of God, created in righteousness and true holiness (Eph 4:21). A conversion is a *conversion*, by burial and resurrection. We will see this in passages throughout this book.

But then the process of the cleansing of our souls is *our* job (Eph 4:21-23). By the power of His Spirit in us, "we" purify <u>ourselves</u> (1 John 3:3; Rom 8:13).

The vast majority of American preaching omits at least one of the above truths, leaving even true Christians suffering self-condemnation and defeat.

After we are truly converted – born again, we MUST NOT look at our souls and say – "that sin is just part of me". If we do so then we will not be able to pray the prayer of faith, without doubting or wavering (James).

The solution is to know what you are recreated as (Eph 4:24)– and it is not your "soul". So, when we sin, we just need our feet washed from contact with the earth (the World-system) – we don't have to "get saved" again (1 Jn 2:1). This is how we escape sin-consciousness (Heb 9, Heb 10).

In the simple diagram at left, the soul is the middle ring (which is purified over time because the sin is not "you" (Rom 7). The mind, which is in the soul, is responsible to direct itself to obey spirit rather than obey the flesh. If you are taught that this is automatic, then you will live in the same passivity and defeat that we see all over the church. The spirit is the innermost man; for every true follower of Christ, the spirit is a Son or daughter of God. NOT a "sinner".

The Soul is the "Man in the Middle"

The will is in the *soul*, however; it is right in the middle between spirit and body. It is the instrument by which we make decisions to nurture and live either "from the spirit" or "from the flesh". At any point in our lives – or at any point in a day for that matter – we in our souls decide whether we are sowing to the one or the other.

The kindness of God was demonstrated by the Blood of Christ. If, in response, we love Him enough to practice obeying Him, we find the power to do so; and we then "see" Him (Jn 14:19,23) and then the burden becomes a joy.

But the soul must make a choice - and persevere in it under mercy.

Bible Quotes are Word English Bible (WEB) except where noted.

PART 2: HIDDEN IN PLAIN SIGHT

The "Backbone" themes of the Bible have, of course always been there but Eclipsed by Forgiveness-Only Teaching. Forgiveness is indeed essential in that there is no salvation without it. But popular Christianity says it is "the only thing you need to know". Please know for sure that the *Blood of Christ **ratified a covenant**; a covenant which is **far bigger than forgiveness alone.***

In these passages we will see the New Covenant emerge with clarity. We will see that as our guilt is wiped away and we have been converted, Christ Himself comes to literally ***live within us***… and we are welcome to enter the throne room of the Father.

"In Christ"

For brevity, in this book I will sometimes refer to these passages as "Vision Passages". I believe that the Word of God presents to us two unspeakably powerful facts – big puzzle pieces if you will – that the church has lost sight of:

1. To be "In Christ" is to be no longer going our own way, but to be entrusting ourselves into Christ and doing the will of God (see Gal 5:24) rather than living according to the flesh – by His own power (2 Pet 1:3-4, Rom 6:7); and
2. We who are *In Christ* are <u>with Him where He is seated</u> and also <u>where He is walking</u>. There is both rest (in peace, refreshing, strength) and constant movement – in serving man, and in doing battle.

The basis of our being there is our Covenant <u>union</u> with Christ (the Isa 54), as Jesus states in His High Priestly Prayer (John 17). To be in Christ, we surrender the doing of our will; we have died by His power; so, we forsake sin by His power and are raised by His power (summarized in Romans 6-8 as we shall see). Now, let us identify with Him in <u>all the aspects</u> of His work and identity. Let's *partake in His Life*!

I know I just dropped a bomb of mystical phrases. Relax! The entire book – as its central purpose – will unpack each one and connect them into a simple backbone. The backbone is constructed of some of the most outrageous passages that many "churchgoing" readers were either never taught; or were blinded at the time they were taught.

"Mind-Blowing" is Good

We are commanded to renew our minds and be transformed by it (Rom 12:1-3). *Explosive demolition of unbelief and human traditions* was the norm in the early church. These passages are "cosmic and mystical". In our natural minds we cannot do anything with them; But God by His Spirit stands ready to reveal them to those that wish to partake in the divine nature – the nature of the *First*born Son of God – the One that walked the earth, and we beheld His glory.

Let the Word of God stir a hunger in you, and God will then satisfy it (Rev 22).

> *(Matthew 5:6) Blessed are those who hunger and thirst for righteousness, for they shall be filled.*

The Willingness and the Ability to Love as He Loved

One item is particularly noteworthy because the church in America has by and large lost sight of it: The New Covenant, as its central element invites us to the *means* of joyfully fulfilling His requirements by His very righteousness in us (Romans 8:4).

If we keep our vision centered on this beauty, then we will not drift off the road or "break down". (2 Peter 1 even promises this very thing). Confident hope keeps us on the "straight and narrow", the way that leads to life.

The promises in these passages are better than any promises man could ever conceive of, but they are set out before like a table (Ps 23, 1 Cor 2:9). The Truth of God emerges with a picture; and that picture is beautiful; and we embrace the Hope of it; and we do what it takes to obtain it; Not to *earn* it! But absolutely to obtain it.

Perhaps most reading this book are already converted to Sons of God, but not all.

The Spirit of God is *with you* as you read, even if He is not yet *in you*. Let the Word of God make you hungry – for the dignity of overcoming, of righteousness, of Sonship – and then Christ will satisfy your hunger!

The Backbone Appears

Many believers read their Bibles, and in their minds see a few clusters, but overall, it is a scattering of fragments; fragments of things heard, things read, things experienced. We all want to *make coherent, simple sense of it all*. But if we have been taught that the whole purpose of salvation is "forgiveness", then our Bible can never fully come together for us. This is because the blood of Christ not only forgives what we have done, but opened a way for a conversion out of what we *are* (were!). The death of Christ was the sacrifice that ratified –

Raised in Power and Glory

Bible Quotes are Word English Bible (WEB) except where noted.

legally enacted – a "New Covenant". This Covenant – most concisely stated in Ezekiel 36:25-27, confers to humans that are in that Covenant, a "newness of life" in our spirits and the dynamics of freedom into our souls. If we then utilize that power in the service of Christ, we experience a "restoration of dominion", a reversal of the work of the enemy.

If it is drummed into us that forgiveness is all there is until we get to Heaven, then the "puzzle" that is the Bible … is scattered fragments that simply will not come together. There seems to be no connection from the Old Testament to the

New, and there seems to be no connection of the New Testament to real life. So, the puzzle is as shown below; There is a small spot of brightness at the far left; a breakup, the crucifixion (purchasing reconciliation) in the center, and Heaven over on the right:

But if we take – as hypothesis – that the Bible is really about Covenant, rebirth, erasure of the consciousness of sin, of reversal of the work of the enemy in our souls, and *Dominion*, then an entirely different thing appears.

These vision passages bring out those typically buried themes from the Bible, to form the true "backbone" of the scripture "puzzle"! That is, if you can see these passages for what they are saying, then you will see numerous passages drop into place. You will see "forgiveness" fit in as the "foyer" to the palace of salvation.

As you go, this effect will *accelerate*! Many apparent contradictions will evaporate as the Mystery hidden through the Ages comes into focus. It is "Christ in you, the hope of glory" (Col 1:27). That phrase and others will be converted in your perception from poetry to promise, and the Truth will come alive in you as fact. Your experience of reading the Word of God should quickly

start to be like this:

Your own backbone – a new kind of strength – appears as Christ becomes your strength, your integrity, your peace; and your joyful hope. There were only two of the First Mankind before the fall, and they bore the image of God, and all other creatures were subject to them. But the Second Mankind is a royal priesthood, a holy nation (1 Pet 1). The Firstborn of the Second Mankind (in the middle of the puzzle centerline) is bringing many Sons to Glory (Heb 2) even through dark ages. That's why the end of the puzzle backbone shines as it does.

Bible Quotes are Word English Bible (WEB) except where noted.

Foundation & Pillars
Upon God's Love & Forbearance

Notice the "Pillars" on the Front Cover of the Book. They can represent these:

The First Fruits

His Image-Bearers are On the Earth Again
Carrying His Compassion, His Power, His Authority, His Joy
As God's sons, man's servants, and devil's masters (John G. Lake)

Dominion & Inheritance

Yet walking toward glory, honor, and immortality
Seated with Him in the Unseen
to Reign *with* Him *and Under Him*

The New Covenant in His Blood & The Second Mankind

Partaking in His Nature, Having Escaped the Corruption
His Freedom, His Righteousness, His Dignity
All Ultimately Based on the shedding of His Innocent Blood

God's Steadfast Love & Forbearance

Always Inviting to Reconciliation, Peace, and Rest
His Love, His Justice, and His Mercy are Ours –
"In Christ". To be "In Christ" is:
to be surrendered to Him and following Him.

He Who Loves Christ
Follows Him into *Strength*

The Way of Holiness is where Christ went – *before* He said *"Follow Me"*; He invites us to both follow Him there in the seen world, as we are seated with Him in the unseen world.

Please note that this "way" is not to be called the "Way of *Amnesty*" but "The Way of Holiness". We will see exactly why it is called that; The purpose of God in it is that we may be with Him where He is and at the same time, be like Him where we are.

But what do we most often hear to be the "Gospel"?

>Is it Forgiveness and Heaven? By a *gentle* Jesus?

No, we don't see that in the Bible. Let's embrace the whole truth of the matter. There is a surrender that turns a poor sinner into one who bears the armor of the righteousness that is of God. The true Gospel, to the one *who will walk in it*, brings Forgiveness, Sonship, actual righteousness, Dignity, Access, and Dominion, by a Lion of the Tribe of Judah. There is a forerunner that shows this way of Holiness and where it leads. He leads a lineage, a different Kind of generation. *Meekness* is "strength under control". That's different than mere "gentleness".

The conquerors are those that are no longer what they were, but have been buried, exchanged, and hid in Him by the full surrender of the going of their own way. The Heavens, the very courts of the Throne of God are open, for the Court of the Most High is now also their Home, and that God is now also their Father.

The gates are now wide open, for the Lord Jesus Christ is also their brother that has gone before. He is the High Priest that brought His own innocent Blood to obtain Mercy; This same Priest, by His Life-Giving Spirit, in His own words, has given us His glory (Jn 17).

This Lamb of God *is the Way of Holiness (John 14 "I am the Way ... ");* If and as we set our hearts on Him who is the Way, we enter that narrow gate; and in confident Hope we walk the road that we are on in the material world, which is far more than material. Let us operate by the *truth* that *overcomes present facts* and changes them.

Raised in Power and Glory

Bible Quotes are Word English Bible (WEB) except where noted.

Let us never apologize to the "religious establishment" for believing in the power of the true God. Let us taste it and learn to use it.

We are indeed to <u>*enter into his death and burial*</u>, but it is followed by resurrection, ascension, and seating. This is why we "proclaim His death until He comes" (1 Cor 11). But after His "seating", Christ and the Father did a "sending". We who wish to walk the road must first receive what He sends. He gives His Spirit to those who obey Him (John 14; Acts 5:32), and then he sends them to continue His work for the remainder of this age (Jn 20:21).

This "Way" was created by the Firstborn, He made that way to "bring *many Sons* to Glory" (Heb 2); to share with them true liberty and His very nature (2 Pet 1:4). Is that "born again" (John 3), "converted (Acts 3:19) nature *still* a sinner? ... NO! It has become a Son and an Overcomer as regards power and authority (Eph 1:17; 2:7; 4:13-24; 1 Jn 4:4; numerous others!). If you have been trained in "religion" then you might experience the FOG right now. Please embrace this precious truth, and you can experience the crumbling of that stronghold now.

Christ – as the Second Adam, is obeying God; He is doing this not just as the Son of God, but as the Son of Man. *He is being fruitful and multiplying…* in us! Isn't that simple? The enemy knows it is the beginning of the end; Now doing everything in his power to **keep the false church <u>false</u>** and **keep even most of the true church <u>powerless</u>**. On both fronts, the enemy must deceive with all his energy, using the same line: "we're just poor sinners saved by grace".

Now I say this in love: If you sought only ac*quittal,* and you did not *surrender your will and call on Jesus for life-exchange*, then you are indeed still a sinner; the liar has you where he wants you.

But even if you genuinely surrendered to God in response to the love He showed in Christ, having forsaken sin; been converted; and received deliverance; unless you take responsibility for your ***mind***, you are a nuclear warhead thinking you are … "just a sinner saved by grace".

Binding and blinding as many as possible, the enemy keeps even true Sons of God sidelined by sin-consciousness and defeat; It is the inevitably result of hyper-grace theology. As the Word of God shows, the Grace of Christianity first brings forgiveness of past sins by simply trusting on the ransom paid by Christ (Rom 3:27); but then the Grace of God also brings the actual power to overcome sin (2 Pet 1:3-4). The question then of course becomes – shall we now go on sinning? (Rom 6:1).

The Spirit of God whispers to our consciences "there is a problem not just with what we've done, but what we are", ... and *offers the trade*.

So, which is it? Are we the sons of the *First Adam?* or the *Second* Adam – the one *after the Lord's own heart*; who said "put a *new and right spirit within me?*". That was the exact promise (Ezekiel 36, Jeremiah 31, Isaiah 42). That promise is for you and for me and for anyone that will travel this particular road that Christ paved:

> "***If any man*** would come after me..." (all gospels).

Mercy opens the way and anyone may enter, even though it is God who knows our response in advance, and calls accordingly; It is not for us to presume that "we are the champions"; it is for us *to follow in the way of Holiness*.

For our part, we are called to open the gates of our hearts that He may come in, with "Clean hands and a pure heart" (Ps 24). The "clean hands" mean "no blood on them"; the "pure heart" is a converted – exchanged – heart.

> *(Psalms 24 NRSV) ...*
> *Who shall ascend the hill of the LORD? And who shall stand in his holy place? Those who have clean hands and pure hearts, who do not lift up their souls to what is false, and do not swear deceitfully.*
>
> *They will receive blessing from the LORD, and vindication from the God of their salvation. Such are those who seek him, who seek the face of the God of Jacob.*
>
> *Lift up your heads, O gates! and be lifted up, O ancient doors! that the King of glory may come in. Who is the King of glory? The LORD, strong and mighty, the LORD, mighty in battle. Lift up your heads, O gates! and be lifted up, O ancient doors! that the King of glory may come in.*
>
> *Who is this King of glory? The LORD of hosts, he is the King of glory. [Selah]*

This requires *not improvement*, but rather *a surrender*, an exchange:

> "Lose your life to find it ..." (all gospels)

Only His Life, His Righteousness, will be acceptable; So, He offers it to us on a trade-in basis only. Let us all lay down our selfish independence, receive the Life of God, yes – His Spirit is the main course; the heavenly gift, bringing the powers of the age to come (Heb 10).

Raised in Power and Glory

Bible Quotes are Word English Bible (WEB) except where noted.

By the Love of God:
All We Need is Provided

(1 Corinthians 1:30) Because of him, you are <u>in</u> Christ Jesus, who was made to us wisdom from God, and righteousness and sanctification, and redemption:

(1 Corinthians 3:11 NRSV) For no one can lay any foundation other than the one that has been laid; that foundation is Jesus Christ.

Yes, It's Mystical!
As the Word of God Explains

Many if not most people would prefer a Gospel that merely requires that we be intellectually persuaded of some philosophical arguments associated with Christianity. But God is not in the least interested in "intellectual" colleagues.

As we shall see over and over from the scriptures, God the Father is interested in more sons, and Christ the firstborn is looking for more brothers. As Watchman Nee has somewhere written, "The highest objectives of God towards man is to honor the name of His Son Jesus Christ, and to form us into His Image."

In Reading, Please Remember This

Throughout history, the religious traditions of man have always attempted to downplay – or *entirely remove* if possible – the hard sayings of Christ. I am speaking of the dreaded "O" word – "obey".

As much as our pride wants to just "get saved" and still go our own way, the only way to enter into Christ is to *surrender our self-will* (as an event) and *do the will of God by the power of God* (as a process).

Apart from Christ – living "in our own name", we are under wrath. But the greatest irony in the Gospel lies in the fact that only in this obedience – and active sustained surrender – do we find real freedom and joy.

We will see that, surrendered into Christ, we obtain everything we need not ony for life, but also for the godliness that God expects from us; and that's why it is quire reasonable for Him to expect it!

And yes, if we are practicing this righteousness, then there is mercy for when we fail in weakness.

Bible Quotes are Word English Bible (WEB) except where noted.

Cover Photo "Pillars" Form a "Backbone" of the Bible

Built upon the foundation, the "Pillars" constitute "The Abundance of Grace and the Gift of Righteousness" that invite us to "Reign in Life as Kings" (Rom 5:17). In the Cover photo for the book, you can see one of these massive pillars.

The Foundation and pillars *together* are the "Backbone" that runs through the Bible, making the 5000 puzzle pieces steadily drop into place. No more FOG (forgiveness-only gospel). Rather, God's work is For-Our-Glory! (1 Cor 2:7) … If we will humble ourselves to let Christ Himself be our righteousness.

I list them again below. I submit that "First Fruits", "Dominion", and the "New Man" (Second Mankind) deserve far more notice than they generally receive.

The First Fruits
His Image-Bearers are On the Earth Again
Carrying His Compassion, His Power, His Authority, His Joy

Dominion & Inheritance
Yet walking toward glory, honor, and immortality
Seated with Him in the Unseen - to Reign *with Him and Under*

The Covenant in His Blood & The New Man
Partaking in His Nature, Having Escaped the Corruption
His Freedom, His Righteousness, His Dignity
All Ultimately Based on the shedding of His Innocent Blood

God's Steadfast Love & Forbearance
Always Inviting to Reconciliation, Peace, and Rest
His Love, His Justice, and His Mercy are Ours – "In Christ"

The First Adam Corrupted;
The Second Adam Purifies

The Second Adam is ready and willing to purify us just as surely as the rebellion of the First Adam contaminated us.

Unfortunately, the mystery has been very effectively hidden by much of the church itself, as a result of the *subtle oversimplification* of terms and the systematic *omission* of any chapter that mentions human responsibility to obey God as a salvation matter.

Moreover, what is often passed off as the gospel is so extensively trimmed to remove the supernatural that *it is simply not the Gospel at all*. In popular thinking, "witnessing" goes something like the following:

1. It is difficult to get people into a church building, but it can be done if people are pressured enough. They have nothing to witness to, but they can at least be persuaded to invite people to church.
2. If a poor soul arrives on a Sunday, "Pastor" can tell them that Christ came to forgive sins – if they will bow their heads and repeat a prayer (Only pastor can do this part, of course), they are congratulated.
3. Some people actually surrender their lives to God and are truly saved despite the defective teaching; but most of those that have walked the aisle are unaffected (we know this by the divorce rate in the church decade after decade).
4. Even if they come back "to church on Sunday", they go about their lives, feeling forgiven for a while until they notice they are still enslaved.

Bottom Line: If you cannot honestly say you are "free indeed", then Christ is a liar or you are camping in the elementary school of salvation; sitting in the foyer of the palace, most likely because *you were never told there was more*. In some circles you are even actively told not only to accept *less*, but that you must settle for the sin bondage of the miserable wretch.[2]

There is more!

> Albert Einstein said: "Make it as simple as possible, but no simpler".

---

[22] This interpretation is only possible if we surgically omit Romans 6:13,7,21-22 and Romans 8:1-4, and 13.

Bible Quotes are Word English Bible (WEB) except where noted.

What about God's Reputation?

A forgiveness-only Gospel says: "If you were not chosen, then tough luck. But if you are chosen, you can be forgiven now! By the way, *don't expect freedom from your oppression in this life*". If we are **honest** about it, a God that shows partiality and offers no freedom in this life is very "bad" news. It makes God out to be crueler than the worst tyrant. There is no "unsearchable wisdom" in it.

But God desires that none should be lost, and calls humanity everywhere to repent and be saved (2 Pet 3:9, Acts 17:13, every "if any man", and dozens of "now choose" commands). Christ alone is the Ark that shall survive the flood, and seeing His truth and faithfulness we choose to get in or not. God of course sees in advance who will get in and stay in, and calls us.

But God gets no glory from Robots, so He did not just "program it all". Rather, He makes the "way to freedom"; That "way" includes forsaking sin; There is no getting around it – but He has broken the chains in the unseen, and He supplies the Life, the actual power to overcome the enemy.

With all due respect to teachers and preachers: If your Gospel is not focused on the multiplication of "manifest Sons and daughters of God", then your gospel is not Christianity; But if it does, then it is.

If your gospel does not make people *free indeed*, then it is not Christianity. But if it does, then it is.

The glory of God is in His kindness to us!!! The will of God is that we be conformed into the Image of His Son, the firstborn from among the dead; that in this World we become like Him. This is why we have no fear of the day of judgement (1 Jn 4:17).

The Mystical Truths are Important

Identifying with both the death and the life of Christ is not merely an interesting topic for the deeper seminary students or the "mystics". On the contrary, they were central, essential, common knowledge in the early church:

Romans 6:3 NRSV

Do you not know that all of us who have been baptized into Christ Jesus were baptized into his death?

To be sure, some "mystics" have been – as someone rightly said – "so heavenly minded they are no earthly good!". But at this time, nearly the entire church has become so earthly minded that their faith is reduced to "fact-faith" and there is no power to even speak of.

But God has, in fact, as part of the new Covenant itself, *mystically* provided the means by which we can understand the mystical things, and we are to tell of them! I am not speaking of a "secret society"; Rather, the Spirit of God is *given to all who will obey the gospel*; and that same Spirit gives the eyes to see and ears to hear the deep things of God (Acts 5:32).

> *(1 Corinthians 2:12-16) Now we have received not the spirit of the world, but the Spirit that is from God,*
>
> **so that we may understand the gifts bestowed on us by God.**
>
> *And **we speak of these things** in words not taught by human wisdom but taught by the Spirit, **interpreting spiritual things to those who are spiritual**.*
>
> *Those who are unspiritual do not receive the gifts of God's Spirit, for they are foolishness to them, and they are unable to understand them because they are spiritually discerned.*
>
> ***Those who are spiritual discern all things**, and they are themselves subject to no one else's scrutiny. "For who has known the mind of the Lord so as to instruct him?"*
>
> **But we have the mind of Christ.**

Now let's look at the pillar components in more detail. When we come to a mind-blowing statement, let's let it blow our minds – because what emerges in its place as we do so is the mind of Christ. God is that big, and this truth makes us free.

Bible Quotes are Word English Bible (WEB) except where noted.

Foundation: God's
Steadfast Love & Forbearance

He is Just

(Ezekiel 18:20 NRSV) The person who sins shall die.

A child shall not suffer for the iniquity of a parent, nor a parent suffer for the iniquity of a child;

the righteousness of the righteous shall be his own, and the wickedness of the wicked shall be his own.

Don't Despair!!! By His Grace - Christ Died AS us

Yet Merciful

(Exodus 34:6-7) The LORD passed before him, and proclaimed, "The LORD, the LORD, a God merciful and gracious, slow to anger, and abounding in steadfast love and faithfulness,

keeping steadfast love for the thousandth generation, forgiving iniquity and transgression and sin,

yet by no means clearing the guilty, but visiting the iniquity of the parents upon the children and the children's children, to the third and the fourth generation."

The Humble Receive This Mercy

(1 Cor 1:30-31 NRSV) "HE WHO GLORIES, LET HIM GLORY IN THE LORD."

He is Absolutely *Just*
... Yet He is Also *Merciful*

These two passages (Ezekiel and Exodus) look as if they are contradictory but are not. The first declares that both righteousness and wickedness are real, and that they each bring consequences.

The second shows that mercy and forgiveness are available – and always have been – to those that turn away from their rebellion and turn back to God. Each of us has the power and responsibility to do what is right and to train our children in that way. If we choose sin, then we can produce *generations* lost in sin, with its consequences coming upon them. If we choose righteousness then we can produce *generations blessed*. Nevertheless, each individual has enough conscience to see and to choose. The issue is, *will we justify our sin just because our parents justified their sin?*

Always Inviting to Reconciliation, Peace, and Rest

God, of course, is not glorified when preprogrammed humans turn to Him. Love could not exist without true *freedom to choose God or to reject Him*. It was not God's will that man would rebel; but it certainly was God's will that genuine love could exist in man, and that rebellion was possible. He himself provided the solution to both: *Perfect* "Justice" and *Perfect* "Mercy"! As a result, our redemption is as nearby as an instant *exchange* transaction.

His Love, Justice, and Mercy are Ours In Christ

Notice in the Exodus passage we see generations of people that love God and generations of those that hate Him. See the New Man passages, Romans 5:17, 2 Cor 5:17, and 1 Cor 15:40. They both speak of the *Two Mankinds* and how you get from one to the other. The Covenant Blood of Christ is the basis of all mercy – calling for conversion across this line; so that man might receive and live from the righteousness of God. Every man must choose his Lineage!

If you hunger *for the righteousness of God* and ask for it from the heart – then you shall have it. How can we say this? We know it because Christ became sin for us so that we might become His righteousness.

One Mankind *fulfills* the just requirement of the Law (Rom 8:4) and bears the image of God (1 Jn 4:17). The other *does not* because it *cannot*. *We choose the right lineage and live from His strength and Freedom*. It truly is that *simple*; for the humble it is not only *simple* but also *"easy"* (Matt 11:30).

Let us not settle for anything less than this!

Bible Quotes are Word English Bible (WEB) except where noted.

Pillar: The New Covenant
Promised, Ratified, Fulfilled

What was Promised Beforehand

*(Ezekiel 36:25-29) I will **sprinkle clean water on you**, and you shall be clean. **I will cleanse you** from all your filthiness and from all your idols. **I will also give you a new heart, and I will put a new spirit within you**; I will take away the stony heart out of your flesh, and I will give you a heart of flesh. I will **put my spirit within you**, and cause you to walk in my statutes. You will keep my ordinances and do them. You will dwell in the land that I gave to your fathers;*
you will be my people, and I will be your God.

Ratified in Christ's Blood; Now Fulfilled

(1 Cor 11:25) ... the <u>new</u> covenant in <u>My</u> blood...

*(Hebrews 10:2-17) Or else, wouldn't they [sacrifices] have ceased to be offered, since the worshipers, having been once cleansed, **would have had no more consciousness of sins**? ... For it is impossible for the blood of bulls and goats to take away sins... Then I said, 'Behold, I have come to do your will, O God' (in the scroll of the book it is written of me)." ... then he added, "See, I have come to do your will." **He <u>takes away the first</u> that He may <u>establish the second</u>**. By which will we have been sanctified through the offering of the body of Jesus Christ **<u>once for all</u>**. ... But He, when He had offered once sacrifice for sins forever, sat down at the right hand of God, from that time waiting "**<u>until his enemies are made the footstool of his feet.</u>**" For by one offering he has perfected forever those who are being sanctified. The Holy Spirit also testifies to us, for after saying, "This is the covenant that I will make with them: 'after those days', says the Lord, '<u>**will put my laws in their hearts, and I will also write them on their mind**</u>"; '"*
then He says,
"I will remember their sins and their iniquities no more."

Unites Us with God
In a Solemn *Blood Covenant*

Covenant High Priest

Christ our "High Priest" is not of the order of Aaron the Levite, but of the order of "Melchizedek" mentioned in Genesis 14. The name means "Priest of the Most High God". As our High Priest, He has no beginning and no end; He holds *the power of an indestructible life*; and He is Good!

The New Covenant that is the essence of Christianity is a "Blood Covenant" such as all primitive cultures understood as the most solemn bond there can be between two persons – and perhaps those that they represent. Some of its elements are as follows.

Representatives, Sacrifices, and Promises

Christ as *Son of God* Represents God (Righteousness of God) to Man; Christ as an Innocent *Son of Man* Represents Man to God. Abraham saw it and was glad (John 8:56; Gen 15)! He Himself is the dual Sacrifice – both of man to God and of God to man. Sprinkling from sins and freedom from sinfulness itself.

"The Gift": A New Spirit – the Spirit of Truth

His spirit in us is "The Heavenly Gift" (Heb 6); He is the gift of actual righteousness (2 Cor 5:17).

A New heart of flesh for a heart of stone

The heart (likely speaking of the will) He gives us is moldable and teachable. It is not the stubborn kind.

Sharing of Wine is Mingling of Blood – <u>Union!</u>

There is no such thing as thankfully receiving forgiveness without an intent to obey God by His power. If the element of *true surrender and life exchange* is missing, then no transaction has taken place. Lack of Union – or the mere unawareness of it – is the basis of all defeat that we see in Christianity today.

In these formatted (paperback and hardcover) versions of *Follow the Firstborn*, I am including two important graphics that do not "present well" in the eBook edition. I also add some commentary. These spreads are also publicly available electronically under *resources* at secondmannow.net.

These two selections in particular are helpful in communicating the more "mystical" central truths of the Gospel that are harder to describe in words alone.

Bible Quotes are Word English Bible (WEB) except where noted.

Not Just "Secure" But Secure *In Christ*

To Be "In Christ"
Is to Live to Do His Will

In *Follow the Firstborn*, I have described our union with Christ and with God the Father in various ways, but as publishing time approaches, I have become convinced that a graphic will help to solidify the concept.

As mentioned, the idea of "in" Christ or "through" Christ occurs about 165 times in the New Testament. Its importance literally cannot be overstated.

In John chapters 13 to 17 we see a steady development of the connections:

- between "obeying Christ's commands" and seeing Him
- between "obeying Christ's commands" and receiving whatever we ask

Also, as I have described, the Gospel is the announcement of the ratification fo the awaited "New Covenant" (Ezek 36); and the benefits we receive are literally the benefits of going where Christ has gone… if we follow Him".

This graphic shows a kind of "telescoping" in which (a) Christ is in God by a sustained surrender to do the will of God; and (b) we are in Christ by a sustained surrender to do the will of Christ. In the graphic we can see these "ins" wherever circled persons get "into" the other circles (persons) by aligning their wills to the will of the other.

Exactly like a class-action lawsuit judgment – the award to the oppressed - the promised benefits of the covenant belong to those that are in the class by virtue of practicing obedience to the command of Christ.

And we know the commands of Christ. He names His "new one" in John 13. The first verse states the command; The second one shows what marks those that are in Christ.

> *A new commandment I give to you, that you love one another. Just as I have loved you, you also love one another. By this everyone will know that you are my disciples, if you have love for one another."*
>
> *(John 13:34-35)*

If we continue to *practice* obeying Christ – by His power – then we are remaining in His love (John 15:10). It's not about perfection, but it is about perseverance. And He has given us everything we need!

Bible Quotes are Word English Bible (WEB) except where noted.

The New Covenant
Sacrifices & Exchange of Gifts

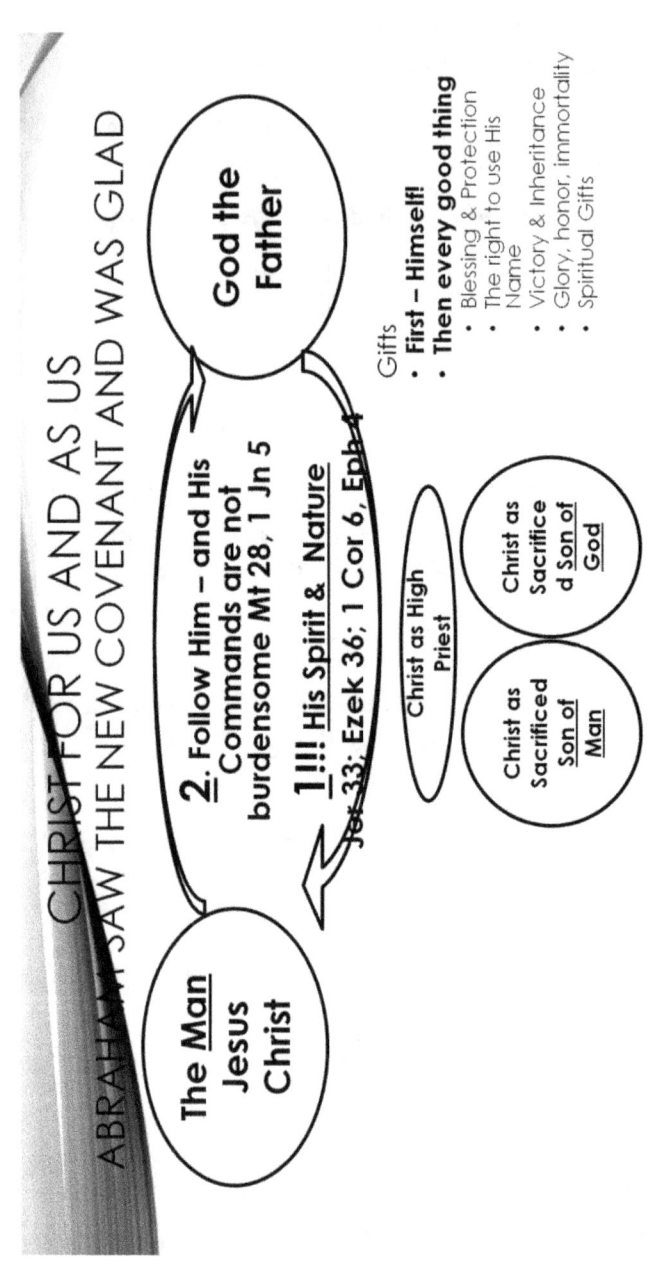

For Both Sides
God Provided the Sacrifice

In Follow the Firstborn, we looked at several of the announcements of the New Covenant in Isaiah, Ezekiel, Daniel, Jeremiah. A "Blood Covenant" was commonly understood in ancient cultures, as it is even to this day in many cultures. This graphic depicts a few of the important elements of the <u>*New Covenant*</u> specifically.

> *He took bread, and when he had given thanks, he broke, and gave it to them, saying, "This is my body which is given for you. Do this in memory of me." Likewise, he took the cup after supper, saying, "This cup is the new covenant in my blood, which is poured out for you." (Luke 22:19-20)*

Sacrifices

Christ, when becoming man, never ceased being God as well; However, He did lay aside His inherent powers (Phil 2:6). In this way He succeeded in obeying God where the first Adam failed.

As man, God in Christ made the sacrifice *as man* that brought us peace. God the Father gave His only Son, as the sacrifice from His side (see 1 Tim 2:5).

Exchange of Gifts

The immediate and central gifts from God are His Nature and His Spirit. For our part, we trade our life for His life – that is, we stop doing our own will and start doing His will.

Unselfish Desires Restored

Life becomes wonderful as God changes our desires and then fulfills them. This is the "Following Him" that causes every blessing He won to become ours as an inheritance upon His death; and each of them has "first fruits" in this mortal life.

> *Whoever confesses that Jesus is the Son of God, God remains in him, and he in God. 16 We know and have believed the love which God has for us. God is love, and he who remains in love remains in God, and God remains in him. 17 In this love has been made perfect among us, that we may have boldness in the day of judgment, because as he is, even so are we in this world. (1 John 4:15-17)*

Bible Quotes are Word English Bible (WEB) except where noted.

The Shedding of Christ's Innocent Blood

Without the shedding of blood there is no forgiveness of sins (Lev 17:11); but the Shedding of the Blood of Christ "ratified" the New Covenant, putting it into effect (Luke 22:19-21). The Old creation is *not merely forgiven but destroyed*. Christ became Sin (2 Cor 5:17), and the Father destroyed it (Isa 53:4). We were crucified with Him and in Him (Gal 2:20; 1 Cor 1:30). He died *AS you* (Rom 5:17).

When persons enter into this Covenant, they are making *the most solemn of all commitments*, because in His love Christ offers not only absolute forgiveness of sins and absolute reconciliation, but also *the joining of Himself to us by the sharing of His Spirit* – which is His Nature (1 Cor 6:17).

Notice the Pattern

Natural intimacy is patterned after this joining of Christ to His Bride (Isa 54:5; Eph 5:25; Rev 19:7; 2 Cor 11:2; Rev 21:2; Jn 3:29); but every element of Christ's joining to us is *unselfish*; it is from love that comes from *His being*; not from his admiration of us; It is the bond of perfect faithfulness to provide everything we need for healing and wholeness of spirit, soul, and body.

> *(Isa 54:5-8 NRSV) For your Maker is your husband, the LORD of hosts is his name; the Holy One of Israel is your Redeemer, the God of the whole earth he is called ...*
>
> *For a brief moment I abandoned you, but with great compassion I will gather you. In overflowing wrath for a moment, I hid my face from you, but with everlasting love I will have compassion on you, says the LORD, your Redeemer.*

We who surrender to receive Christ are the "Bride of Christ"; and we will bear fruit that abides. This is *the fruit of actual holiness that brings eternal life* (Rom 2:7; Rom 6:22; from 8:1-4). It is *His righteousness* in us. The question to each of us is:

How badly do I want it?

Spiritual Children and Grandchildren

Union with God carries the power to restore anything that is broken.

If a husband and wife both surrender into Christ, they obtain the ability to love unconditionally. In both parties, bitterness breaks; dignity arises, and every aspect of each personality *heals*. Health appears and eyes once again reflect peace and gladness. The couple then smiles each morning because they know what God has done for them; together they possess the secret and life itself has become a different thing; a wonderful thing. They have become innocent and free.

Then He Rewards Us for Living from His Own Goodness

He will observe the righteousness that we receive from Him and that we have nurtured – Yes, it is *His*! and He will reward us with everything we need for life and godliness – but most notably His very presence and nature mingled with our own. All we must do is make the life-trade and walk according to the Spirit rather than according to the flesh – because we finally, literally, in truth, have the power to do so (Rom 8:13).

Arising out of our union with Christ, there is another component of fruitfulness – spiritual descendants! We see it in the words of Christ and also back in Isaiah:

> *(John 12:24-25) Mosty certainly I tell you, unless a grain of wheat falls into the earth and dies, it remains by itself alone;*
> ***but if it dies, it bears much fruit.***

> *He who loves his life will lose it. He who hates his life in this world will keep it for eternal life. If anyone serves me, let him follow me. Where I am, there will my servant also be.* ***If anyone serves me, the Father will honor him.***

> *(Isa 49:20-22) The children of your bereavement will say in your ears: "The place is too small for me; give me a place to live in." Then you will say in your heart,* ***"Who has conceived these for me, since I have been bereaved of my children, and am solitary, an exile, and wandering, an exile, wandering back and forth? Who has brought these up? Behold, I was alone. Where were these?"***

> *Thus says the Lord Yahweh: Behold, I will lift up my hand to the nations, ... and they shall bring your sons in their bosom, and your daughters shall be carried on their shoulders.*

Notice: "losing your life to find it" (surrendering of self will) is directly connected with *planting a seed in hope*; the hope of being *no longer alone*. Not only that, but those who surrender their self-life for the sake of union will gain not only one companion, but will see "much grain". In this way Christ is bringing many Sons to glory – and He is not ashamed to call them His brothers – *because they are born of the same Father*.

Bible Quotes are Word English Bible (WEB) except where noted.

Pillar: The Second Man
The "Mankind *Do-Over*"!

If you see all that these passages are saying, then you know the Gospel.

*(Romans 5:17) ... by the trespass of the one, **death reigned through the one**; so much more will those who receive the abundance of grace and the <u>free gift of righteousness reign in life</u> through the one, Jesus Christ.*

*(2 Cor 5:17-21) Therefore if anyone is **in Christ**, he is a **new creation**. The old things have passed away; Behold, all things have become new! But all things are of God, ... For Him who knew no sin **became sin on our behalf**, so that **in him** <u>we might become</u> the righteousness of God.*

A Biblical Definition of Grace, Almost Never Heard

*(2 Peter 1:34) Seeing that His divine power has granted to us all things that pertain to life and godliness, through the knowledge of him who called us <u>to his own glory and virtue</u>, ... that through these **you may become partakers of the divine nature, <u>having escaped</u> the corruption that is in the world by lust**.*

*(Eph 4:22-24) That **<u>you put away</u>**, ..., the old man that grows corrupt after the lusts of deceit; and that **<u>you be renewed</u>** in the spirit of your mind, and **<u>put on the new man, who in the likeness of God has been created in righteousness and holiness of truth</u>**.*

*(Acts 5:16-20) The multitude also came ... bringing the sick people, and those who were tormented by unclean spirits, and <u>they were **all** healed</u>. But the high priest ... filled with jealousy, and arrested the apostles and put them in public custody. But an angel of the Lord opened the prison doors by night, brought them out, and said, "Go, stand and speak in the temple to the people <u>all the words of this life.</u>"*

Are We Still Sinners?
Not if We are Born Again

Yes – *we have sin* (John 1), but if we have been *reborn – converted* – born again – we are no longer sinners as a matter of innermost nature. The scriptures are clear on this!

When we are definitively surrendered, we have had our bath! (John 13:1-17). "I will sprinkle clean water on you, and you shall be clean" (Ezekiel 36:25 – believe it!). Then when we sin in weakness, we need only our feet washed (1 John 1:9).

The New Mankind isn't God[3], but the New Mankind **_partakes in the Nature of God_**! This is – literally – the "heart" of the Gospel. When you have truly escaped the corruption that is in the world through lust, and are truly partaking of the divine nature, you know freedom. It's for all.

The person *that I was is dead and buried*. The world-system, the "cosmos" that had power over me *is now powerless over me*. I am unresponsive to its lures (see Gal 6:14-15). The curse of sin and death is broken for me; I am no longer a sinner in the lineage of sinners, but am now in the Lineage of Christ, as a point of fact.

I have received the abundance of grace and the gift of *righteousness*, and shall now reign in life through the one (Romans 5:17). I have been translated out of the power of darkness and into the Kingdom of the beloved Son (Col 2).

His Freedom, His Righteousness, and His Dignity

The Apostles and the early church demonstrated the "life of God" (Zoe).

To *partake* in the Nature of God – including his righteousness – is to enjoy unspeakable *dignity*. This is far more satisfying than forgiveness alone. If you haven't tasted of the heavenly gift and the powers of the age to come (Eph 2:7; Heb 6:4-6), then (a) if you are not yet converted by surrender then please do so; or (b) if you already are surrendered, then please know that you have His Spirit in you and you are invited to go deeper.

As the New Mankind, we become the righteousness of *Christ*; Christ died for us *while we were yet sinners* (Eph 2:5), but we were at this point **no longer *"sinners"*** (1 Pet 4:16-17). They had become like Christ, in innermost constitution, *in this life* (1 Jn 4:17; Titus 2:11).

---

[3] though Christ Himself has the right to name "mighty ones" (John 10:54)

Bible Quotes are Word English Bible (WEB) except where noted.

The term "Christian" means "Little Christ". The Lord Jesus is not ashamed to call them **His brothers** (Heb 2) **because they are like Him**, and He is **bringing many Sons to glory** (Heb 2:10-11).

If your tradition has never mentioned these amazing, profound truths; wonderful beyond words, then that is precisely why you have remained in defeat. You absolutely come out from them (Mark 7:13). Who will you please? God or man? God only calls you to *do what's best for you* by His power.

What Does the "Establishment" think About It?

Leaders in the religious establishment are always the most threatened by Version 2.0 mankind, because these leaders are only mere mortals (1 Cor 3:3).

They are coming to nothing now because the Jesus whom they crucified, has – by His death! – begun *replicating himself* (John 12:24). Have you ever stepped on a spider egg to smush it – only to see a hundred of them scurrying about? That's likely how they felt, but times 1000.

Had they anticipated it, they would not have crucified Him (1 Cor 2:6). Despite persecution, being of the New Mankind is still the most wonderful thing a human can experience; Even in persecution we will take great joy in the privilege of suffering for His name (Mt 5:10-12; 10:22-25). How's that?! He manifests himself to those that obey Him (John 14:19,23).

The Second Mankind is a re-do of the human race. God, in Christ, offers to re-create you into His own Lineage, as brother or sister of His firstborn; to make His home in you; to cleanse you and to form you; to live in union with you.

Bible Quotes are Word English Bible (WEB) except where noted.

Pillar: Dominion & Inheritance

(Psalms 8:3-6) When I consider the heavens, the work of your fingers, the moon and the stars that you have ordained; what is man that you are think of him, what is the son of man that you care for him?

*Yet you have made him a little lower than the angels, and **crowned him with glory and honor You make him ruler** over the works of your hands; you have **put all things under his feet** ...*

*(Psalms 115:16) The heavens are the heavens of Yahweh, but the earth has He given to **the children of men**.*

(Eph 1:18-23) ... that... you may know what is the hope of his calling, and what are the riches of the glory of his inheritance in the saints,
and what is the <u>exceeding greatness of his power</u> toward us who believe, according to that working of the strength of His might which He worked in Christ when he raised him from the dead and made him to sit at his right hand in the heavenly places, <u>far above all rule and authority and power and dominion, and every name that is named, not only in this age but also in that which is to come.</u>

He <u>put all things in subjection under his feet</u> and gave Him to be head over all things in the assembly,

<u>which is his body, the fullness of him who fills all in all.</u>

If you are surrendered to God ...
In the Unseen, *you are seated with Him there* (Eph 2:6)!

Sown in Weakness and Shame

Life as a Son of God
Is Hope, Peace, and Joy

I Live Free from Sin -Consciousness

I am Bearing His Image as I was meant to (Gen 1:26); Not only is guilt gone, but both guilt *and shame* are ancient history (literally – they were *buried* with Christ when He *became* our sin).

I have power over sin, and of course I do not practice it; By the work of Christ, I no longer even **carry a consciousness of sins** (Heb 10:2). I stay the course in putting sin to death by the power of the spirit (Rom 8:13); and if I do sin in weakness, I have Jesus Christ the righteous as my *advocate* (1 John 2:1).

Seated with Him - to Reign with Him and Under Him

I am more than content to be seated with Christ – to Reign with Him and under Him. I have no need of independence; rather I delight in *inter*dependence. I need and utilize His power in me; and He needs and utilizes my physical body on the earth. I am His eyes, His feet, and His mouthpiece on earth.

I Receive what I Ask

With thankfulness, I indeed can *take for granted* what I ask of God – because I am a Son and it has been granted (Rom 8:32; Jn 14:12-14). This means I can pray the prayer of faith without condemnation; without doubting; and without wavering (James 1), and I then receive what I ask for (Mark 11:22-24).

Doing the Business of Liberation

I am the Body of Christ now, continuing His work on the Earth until He returns. Like the Centurion I am under authority and in authority. I say go and "it" goes. I am dominating the enemy and I am liberating the oppressed. There is joy in battle when it's not even fair.

Knowing the Joy that Lies Ahead

In all of it, I am always aware that I am receiving a Kingdom of glory, honor, and immortality. I'm walking in freedom and joy to that Kingdom.

Bible Quotes are Word English Bible (WEB) except where noted.

In this Age: First Fruits
In Spirit, Soul, and Body

(Rom 8:23 NRSV) ... and not only the creation, but we ourselves, who have the first fruits of the Spirit, groan inwardly while we wait for adoption, the redemption of our bodies. For in hope we were saved...

(Matthew 8:16-17) When evening came, they brought to him many possessed with demons. He cast out the spirits with a word, and healed all who were sick; that it might be fulfilled which was spoken through Isaiah the prophet, saying, "He took our infirmities, and bore our diseases."

JON FARMER FOLLOW THE FIRSTBORN

Not the Ultimate But the Earnest

Healing In My Own Body

Healing is the *first fruits* of *immortality*, until mortality is swallowed up by immortality (1 Cor 15).

Surely, he has *borne* our *sicknesses* and carried our *pains*, exactly as He has *borne* our *sins* and our *sin* (Isa 53:4, 11). Matthew tells us that Christ *healed all*, at that to fulfill what was said by the prophet Isaiah (Mt 8:17). No passage anywhere tells us this has "ceased". Indeed, in many quarters it is re-emerging today.

Sadly, many cannot see it because they are immersed in cultures of false teachings. Many do obtain salvation in these environments, but it is "despite" the teachings, not because of it. Meanwhile they and their loved ones suffer lives of defeat. From Him to who much is given, much will be expected (see Luke 12:48). I believe we can rightly infer that "less" is expected from them that are raised in such environments. But the scriptures are there for all to see; therefore, there will still be consequences.

The same spirit that raised Christ … **will give life to your mortal bodies** (Rom 8:11). This is the same Spirit of God and of course the same power. By this power Jesus walked in perfect health as man so as to serve God; By this same power the twelve and then then seventy and the early church – walked in health in order to minister.

Healing In My Own Soul – But Not Passive!

There will come a day when we see him face to face and become *perfectly* like Him; and He who has this hope *purifies himself* (1 Jn 3:3). We surrender the counterfeit- life fragments under the loving discipline of the Father (Heb 12).

I tis our own job to renew our minds to the Word of God, to tear down strongholds – which are lies – and replace them with truth.

We increasingly have confidence for the day of judgement, because *as He is, so are we in this World* (1 Jn 4:17). Salvation is not by "how much holiness", but rather "of the right tree".

Administering Healing and Deliverance; Loving as He Loved

We are called to love even the unlovely; bringing more than "sympathy" (Jn 20:21).

Bible Quotes are Word English Bible (WEB) except where noted.

The power of God at work through Christ first **_put the enemy on notice_** that there is another Kingdom on the scene (Earth). The resurrection of Christ was the death of the devil's hope. Pentecost was the devil's dread; and we now put him to flight (Luke 10; Matthew 8:17; Matthew 10; Mark 16). What is the Gospel that must be preached to all the earth – and then the end shall come? It is not "the gospel of amnesty", but **_the Gospel of the Kingdom_** (Matt 24;14). So, we see – the Love of God manifests as a *liberating* army. Love is War directed at the *real* enemy, which is *not man*. Right spiritual warfare is love rightly directed; it is violence against the captors.

Even our dominion can be suppressed through error perpetrated by the church itself. This happened through the dark ages, and it has happened in recent centuries as well; But now as the battle lines of the ultimate war are being drawn, the enemy is recruiting as hard as ever; but likewise, God's people – those that know the One that is them – are growing strong, learning to speak life and undo the work of that enemy.

> *(Mat 9:8) When the multitudes saw it, they marveled and glorified God,* **_who had given such authority to men_**.

Christ was the appearance of the grace of God that brings salvation (Titus 2). At the same time, He was the inaugural appearance of the *Kingdom* of God ("He has now become both Lord and Christ", Acts).

The Kingdom of God manifested in power in the early church for three centuries at the start of the age, putting all rulers on notice – until the church allowed itself to be allied with *political power* of enforcement with an unregenerate emperor, and blended with paganism.[4]

Nevertheless, the true Kingdom of God – the one that shall never end – is now increasingly manifesting as we approach the end of this age.

In the unseen, the King is now already seated in authority (the one intercessor between God and man, the man Jesus Christ, 2 Tim.). Likewise, those that worship Him and serve Him in truth are also already seated with Him and in Him (Eph 1:17ff, Eph 2:6ff). Progressively that truth is manifesting and will manifest apocalyptically (Rev. 19, Rom 8:28; 1 Jn 3:3).

Will you be found in Christ when He appears?

---

[4] David Bercot's *Historic Faith Commentary* Series quotes church writers 100 A.D. forward

Bible Quotes are Word English Bible (WEB) except where noted.

PART 3: DOMINION GIVEN ... *FORFEITED; STILL AWAITING*

In the poster, we see the Dominion theme stretching "End to End" from the creation of man all the way to the "Restoration of All Things" and the "World that is to Come".

This panel is shaped like a smile, because *nothing less than real progress toward restored dominion will put a true and lasting smile on a human's face*. A person that is forgiven yet still oppressed and defeated, cannot produce an honest smile of joy. Furthermore, if there is no strength, there is no witness.

I have positioned this theme in its "end to end" place in hope that you will keep it in mind as you study all the vision passages. Christ's intention was – and is – to restore His *image* and this *dominion* to man, but first He had to reconcile man to God. In other words, *forgiveness* is "*legal groundwork*", but **union with God, image-bearing, and dominion are the "purposes"**.

Indeed – for many, many readers in the "Bible Belt" – these are the themes that paint the full Glory and Grace of God they have never seen or heard of; If that's you, then you can get these truths into your DNA, you will have your breakthrough and your life will never again be the same.

"Under Our Feet"

The phrases "under his feet", "under our feet", "under your feet", etc. are among the most-quoted passages in the Bible! It simply speaks of "dominating" the enemy. In both Old Testament and New Testament, dominion is the "dominant" theme if we will see it for ourselves and admit it.

The Gospels and Epistles present this "under our feet" promise as being finally *fulfilled!!* Yet oddly, it is <u>never, ever quoted in the vast majority of American churches</u>. Who is behind such a systematic omission?

The Truth is, that the innocent Blood of Christ indeed paid for the sins of the whole World (1 John 2:2); but as we shall see, that Blood of Christ also bought restored union with God, dominion, freedom, strength, and dignity.

That Blood *ratified a Covenant* – and all benefits of the New Covenant are reserved for those that truly enter that Covenant by Life-Exchange.

As we will see from the scriptures, this doesn't mean these benefits are automatically all ours to receive passively if we "just believe it". Most Christians, if they are honest, know from experience that such an approach leaves them in defeat.

Again, the scriptures tell us that "man" is not our true enemy – though the true enemy uses humans to try to get to us. Inside the single chapter Luke 10, we see that God's intention is for us to be: "God's son, man's servant, and the devil's master" (John G. Lake condensed it that way). When popular Christianity says, "accept forgiveness and you are saved", is it any wonder the world equates Christianity with *weakness*? When popular Christianity manifests no power over sin, much less devils, is it any wonder that so many turn to the devil himself seeking dominion? They reasonably conclude that the devil won at calvary.

On the other hand, a human that sees the glory of Christ – in a true Christian – will hunger for what they see, and they will find it. This is how evangelism worked in the early centuries. Jesus had "restored that which was lost" (the dominion aspect), but the church has lost it again.

Fortunately, the way back is still there, and many thousands are discovering that The New Covenant still stands with its door open wide. The way of dominion – *inward* conquering of sin and *outward* conquering of the enemy – is still there. Having given us everything we need for life (the life of God), and godliness (2 Pet 1:3-4), God now invites us all to escape the power of sin, partake in His nature, enter fellowship with Him, and "overcome".

In the following pages we will bring out a sampling of "under our feet" passages from throughout the bible.

Bible Quotes are Word English Bible (WEB) except where noted.

The Beginning:
All Things Under Our Feet

There is more to say of these dominion passages, so I repeat them here:

> *(Genesis 21:26-28) ... "Let us make man <u>in our image</u>, after our likeness; ... and God said to them, "Be fruitful, multiply, fill the earth, and subdue it; and <u>have dominion</u> over the fish of the sea, over the birds of the sky, and <u>over every living thing that moves upon the earth</u>."*

> *(Psalms 8:36) When I consider Your heavens, the work of Your fingers, The moon and the stars, which You have ordained, What is <u>man that</u> You think of him, and the son of man that you care for him?*

> *For You have made him a little lower than the angels,*
> *and crowned him with glory and honor.*
> *You have made him to have dominion over the works of Your hands; You have put all things under his feet,*

> *(Psalms 115:16) The **heaven**, even the heavens, are the **LORD's**; But the **earth** He has given **to the children of men**.*

A Profound Expression of God's Love

Millions and millions of churchgoers – that would readily identify as "Christian" – have not encountered the fundamental truth that God "crowned us with glory and honor" and "assigned the Earth to us". Passages like these speak of the real and true "Great Commission" – and indeed the *only* commission. Passages in Matthew 10, Matthew 28, Mark 16, and Luke 10 are really "reintroductions" of the original great commission as Jesus worked to "restore *that which was lost*".

Psalm 8 above shows that God's love toward us is not just to forgiven our sins, but to "crown us with glory and honor". Does that word "glory" make you a little uncomfortable? If you were raised in a religious church, then you will squirm, thinking "only God gets the glory – I'm just a sinner".

But if you are reading this without any brainwashing to undo, then it is pure beauty. God's intention to "crown us with glory" – to enjoy the dignity of His nature; His freedom; His strength, and His dominion – is all over the true Gospel!

Bible Quotes are Word English Bible (WEB) except where noted.

We Gave It Away
Seeking Personal Dominion

(Luke 4:5-6) The devil, leading Him up on a high mountain, showed Him all the kingdoms of the world in a moment of time. And the devil said to Him,

"I will give you all this <u>authority</u>, and their <u>glory</u>,

for <u>it has been delivered to me</u>, and I give it to whomever I want

And So, the Battle Begins

(Genesis 3:15) I will put hostility between you [serpent] and the woman [Eve], and between your offspring and her offspring;

He [the woman's offspring, mankind"] **will bruise your head***,*

and you [devil] will **<u>bruise his heel</u>***.*

Notice the focus here is not "forgiveness". Rather, there is an insubordination; a stripping of authority; a loss of power; and the introduction of shame instead of glory.

Going forward, we see that there is "battle". The loss of dominion and the struggle to regain it are together the context for nearly every subsequent book of the entire Bible. The Old Testament shows cycle after cycle of rebellions toward God in our wills into defeat, and also surrenders into obedience to God (by inward surrender) bringing victory. The curious ceremonial Law of Moses provided advance pictures (See Hebrews 1) of the Grace which was to come. Even Old Testament humans could obtain the grace of God looking forward (Ps. 103).

And that grace included "dominion" (e.g. redemption out of destruction; restoration of justice to the oppressed), not just *forgiveness.*

But you might ask: "But ... Who gets saved? After all – that's what counts, right?" That seems important ... so let's look into it!

Who Will Be Satisfied
To Rule With & *Under* Christ?

In the introduction to the Book of Revelation, Jesus explains who shall be saved. Curiously, there is no direct mention of forgiveness, but **_"overcoming" is everywhere_**:

> *(Revelation 2:7) He who has an ear, let him hear what the Spirit says to the assemblies. To him who **overcomes** I will give to eat from the tree of life, which is in the Paradise of my God.*

> *(Revelation 2:11) He who has an ear, let him hear what the Spirit says to the assemblies. He who **overcomes** won't be harmed by the second death.*

> *(Revelation 2:17) He who has an ear, let him hear what the Spirit says to the assemblies. To him who **overcomes**, to him I will give of the hidden manna, and I will give him a white stone, and on the stone a new name written, which no one knows but he who receives it.*

> *(Revelation 2:26) He who **overcomes**, and he who **keeps my works to the end**, to him I will give authority over the nations.*

> *(Revelation 2:28) Even as I also received authority from my Father. To the one who **overcomes** I will give him the morning star.*

> *(Revelation 3:21) He who **overcomes**, I will give to him to sit down with me on my throne, as I also overcame, and sat down with my Father on his throne.*

He Who Has Ears to Hear

Notice "He who has an ear, let him hear". The enemy has succeeded in pushing Forgiveness-only Gospel (FOG) to the point that they cannot even see these verses much less understand, much less heed them. My prayer is that every reader will see these clearly, see Romans 6:7 clearly; Romans 8:1-4 clearly and then see the above verses as wonderful invitations – not only unacceptable warnings.

Bible Quotes are Word English Bible (WEB) except where noted.

If we have heard only popular Christianity or "religion", then this doesn't even seem like it belongs in the bible!! But it is the Lord Jesus Christ speaking. How does it square with the standard notion of "grace"? **It doesn't fit at all**.

Overcoming?! But Pastor Says I'm Just a Sinner!

But even more seriously – this "overcoming" sounds *terribly infeasible* to anyone that is trapped in sin – and this includes selfishness and pride in all its forms. But the Good News is that Christ has made the way for us to overcome sin, and this way is by *our being surrendered into Christ*, and *Christ literally making His home in us*. Then, and only then, do we find that we finally have the power to obey God (Romans 6:7, 14, 21-22). Furthermore, if we fail in weakness, we have a compassionate and faithful High Priest (1 John 2:1).

Overcoming Sin

So – to "Overcome" is to *Overcome Sin*. Popular Christianity says that on account of "grace", there is "no longer any requirement to overcome sin" – we simply need to accept the forgiveness of Christ. It proclaims that "the wage of sin is no longer death". This is even more serious than an enlightened society telling us that "crime is no longer illegal" (I heard this phrase from Bill Ackman). Yet tens of millions have taken that bait.

The truth is that the road to Eternal Life merely "begins" with the forgiveness of sins. "Eternal Life" itself may be defined as "glory, honor, and immortality" (see Rom 2:7 – a good companion to Rev 2:7!) and a *mature* Christian *crushes Satan under his feet*. That is glory. It is the glory of the reversal of a battle, with a definitive finish. Human "glory" is "winning contests among humans". The Glory Christ came to bring us to (Heb 2) is to overcome the spiritual enemy that has enslaved us all; and then to join the liberation army to release others. And that's just in *this* life; The age to come then takes it to a "whole 'nother level" (1 Cor 15:40; Rev 19).

Let's now take a tour of some "under our feet" passages, noting that they are sprinkled through the Bible from cover to cover. If you have been trained to read your Bible trying to see "forgiveness" as "the main point", the you might just not see any coherency at all on any given day.

One might wonder why the Old Testament is just a story of battles and heroes, always fighting – **never kicking back to just trust that their sins are forgiven**. Even David and Joshua – among the most celebrated and honored mere humans in the Old Testament – were most famous for their *skill in battle*. Those heroes did their exploits *by faith*. Their faith was not "their **reason to not have to obey God**"; Rather, their faith (trusting) was *the means by which they were faithful to obey* God and able to "overcome" the enemy.

By definitive and sustained surrender to forsake sin and do the will of God, we are reborn. We ask and are filled with His Spirit; We then have the very power to ***obey God by <u>His own righteousness</u>*** – not our own power and our own righteousness.

The God of the Old Testament is the God of the New Testament; but the New Covenant is far superior to the Old! The Good News is that we can have Christ in us, and this is to be our expectation of … glory (Col 1:27).

Bible Quotes are Word English Bible (WEB) except where noted.

The Dominion Intent
Stands Through the Ages

In this section we take a short drive-by through the Old Testament to see God speaking through the prophets to remind the Israelites that *Dominion* is still on the table. I included a few New Testament quotes of the same – to show you in advance that the New Testament promise is aimed at fulfilling the *original* great commission, which is a commission to *have dominion over ...* and *every creeping thing*.

If you see this, you see the backbone of your Bible; When you see that God in Christ invites you to experience new birth as a Son or daughter of God – following Christ the firstborn from the dead – you will feel your very own backbone appear and begin to grow.

If you have read this far, then you are already hungry for righteousness – and you will be filled (Matt 5:6). This happened to me in 2019. It will certainly happen to you if you are hungry enough to renew your mind to the truth by the Word of God.

(Psalms 110:1) Yahweh says to my Lord,
"Sit at my right hand,
*until I **make your enemies your footstool for your feet.**" Yahweh will send out the rod of your strength out of Zion.*

Rule among your enemies.

Your people offer themselves willingly in the day of your power, in holy array. Out of the womb of the morning, you have the dew of your youth.
Yahweh has sworn, and will not change his mind: "You are a priest forever in the order of Melchizedek."
The Lord is at your right hand. He will crush kings in the day of his wrath.
He will judge among the nations. He will heap up dead bodies. He will crush the ruler of the whole earth.

He will drink of the brook on the way; therefore he will lift up his head.

Gospel of the Kingdom:
Invitation to Dominion

David was (and is) a man "after God's own heart"; and here we see that David appears to be a major champion of dominion.

The next age is the Millennial Reign of Christ on this Earth (Rev. 19 and 20). I say only half-jokingly that I do not get into detail on these chapters here because I am trying to get this book out and circulated well before the end of this age.

The "Gospel of the *Kingdom* shall be preached". It is the Gospel of Dominion in the Millennial Age.

Suffice to say that:

(a) Christians – those that belong to Christ; those that received the abundance of grace and gift of righteousness – are to be overcomers;
(b) For each of us – our station in the coming age is a function of what we do with the full grace of God – not just forgiveness! – in this age that is coming to a close.

The Dominion theme holds strong through the Bible literally into eternity!

Who has tasted the heavenly gift and the powers of the age to come (Heb 6), and will actually exercise those powers as the body of Christ, in His liberating Army, in this present age?

That man will be place over a city (Matt 25:23).

> *(Matthew 24:12-14) Because iniquity will be multiplied, the love of many will grow cold. But he who endures to the end, the same will be saved.*
>
> *This Good News of the Kingdom will be preached in the whole world for a testimony to all the nations, and then the end will come.*
>
> *(Rev 2:7) ... He who overcomes, I will give to eat from the tree of life, which is in the Paradise of my God.*

> *(Revelation 2:11) ... He who overcomes won't be harmed by the second death.*
>
> *(Joshua 1:3-4) I have given you every place that the sole of your foot will tread on, ... No man will be able to stand before you all the days of your life...*
>
> *(Joshua 10:21-25) Joshua said ... "Come near.* ***Put your feet on the necks of these kings." They came near, and put their feet on their necks****. ... for Yahweh will do this to all your enemies against whom you fight."*

Bible Quotes are Word English Bible (WEB) except where noted.

I can't help it. I have to show you Luke 10! When we are like Christ in this age, we no longer fear judgement, because as He is, so are we.

> *(Luke 10:17-20) The seventy returned with joy, saying, "Lord, even the demons are subject to us in your name!" He said to them, "I saw Satan having fallen like lightning from heaven.*
>
> *Behold,* ***I give you authority to tread on serpents and scorpions, and over all the power of the enemy****. Nothing will in any way hurt you. 20 Nevertheless, don't rejoice in this, that the spirits are subject to you, but rejoice that your names are written in heaven."*

We shall see in the *central* sections of the Poster:

- The Work of Christ, not just "***for*** us", but "***as*** us", so that we may follow
- What it means to be "in Christ" and the way we come to enter into Him, hidden with Him, in Covenant with Him, United with the Father
- The nature of "following Him".

But first, I want to show that "union with God" and "Dominion" are the things that "were lost"; and that God has every intention to deliver the first fruits of these in this age.

Bible Quotes are Word English Bible (WEB) except where noted.

A Cloud of Witnesses
Sons Being Brought to Glory

From beginning to end, the plan of dominion for man has never changed.

The problem is, contrary to nearly almost all Gospel tracts in the Western World at this time, Eternal Life is the reward of Holiness, not just of "believing" (Rom 2:7; Rom 6:21-22 – not just Romans 6:23).

1. Initial Salvation is by believing; and at that time, we receive everything we need for life and godliness – including companionship with God.
2. Final Salvation is by persevering in love and allegiance, obeying His command to love.

Some Important Details

Our flesh may recoil at this, but it is the plain truth of the full and true Gospel. It has been God's promise all along and has been there in black and white. For someone that has been a "churchgoer" for years, the problem is simply that they only see the Bible through the lenses that have been put on them. If this is you, please – please – take off the tinted glasses and read the Word of God for what it says. Believe the words of Jesus over the words of any pastor and over the sophistry of the theologians.

What is new to the New Covenant, is the *means of the righteousness God requires*; both the desire (the new heart) and the ability (the power of His Spirit in us) to do what He commands. Don't worry "Old Testament people were all lost"; they were not. Christ preached to them when He descended (1 Peter) and many were seen on the surface of the Earth again. I think this was to give them the opportunity to witness that Christ is Lord and that He raises the dead (Romans 10:9-10).

In all this, when we who are in Christ fail in weakness, we have an advocate (1 John 2:1). But here is the point: God in Christ has provided the means of the righteousness He requires (Rom 8:4). Will we walk in it? That is the question we face each morning.

> *(Matthew 11:12) From the days of John the Baptizer until now, the Kingdom of Heaven suffers violence,*
> ***and the violent take it by force.***

Glory is "Winning"
But the Opponent is Not Man

The remainder of the Book will elaborate on this, but suffice for now to show that the Gospel, The New Covenant, the New Testament – are entirely about fulfilling the innermost desire for the restoration of dominion on Earth.

(Luke 20:42-43) David himself said ...
'THE LORD SAID TO MY LORD,
"SIT AT MY RIGHT HAND,
*UNTIL I **MAKE YOUR ENEMIES THE FOOTSTOOL**
OF YOUR FEET"

(Acts 2:34-35) ... The Lord said to my Lord,
"Sit by my right hand,
until I make your enemies your footstool..."

(2 Corinthians 3:18) ***But we all**, with unveiled face seeing the glory of the Lord as in a mirror, **are transformed into the same image from glory to glory**, even as from the Lord, the Spirit.*

(Hebrews 10:12-13) but He, when He had offered one sacrifice for sins forever,
sat down at the right hand of God;
*from that time waiting until His enemies **are made the footstool of His feet**.*

(Romans 16:20) And the God of peace
will quickly crush Satan under <u>your</u> feet.
The grace of our Lord Jesus Christ
be with you.

This "glory" is for those that will deny themselves, forsake sin, and turn to serve God. The glory lies in two victories – the overcoming of the sin that is in our souls, banishing "shame" (not just guilt), and also the overcoming of the spiritual enemy that would otherwise wreak havoc of the lives of those around us.

As we approach the end of this age, the Sons of God will become manifest, and it will be seen to all that the Lord is indeed a man of war, and He brings warrior-glory to His people.

Raised in Power and Glory

Bible Quotes are Word English Bible (WEB) except where noted.

Dominion: For Him Who ... "*Overcomes*"?

Here we see the people of God, the followers of Christ, being added to the great cloud of witnesses. In their lives of the present age, they invested in various degrees the grace they are given. They manifested various degrees of the glory of Christ, but they all bore at least some fruit of the right tree – even if they lived only long enough to confess their allegiance to Him.

You should now be noticing the trend – Heaven is not promised to "to those who have believed in Christ for the Forgiveness of Sins". It is promised to those who "overcome". And we overcome by the means He has given us – not rituals, but life-surrender, mind-renewal, and perseverance in obeying His command to love.

Please consider the simple phrase:

I'm Free Indeed. Now What?

1. Christ forgives past sins; Everybody will claim that part. It is precious beyond words, but that is not the full gospel.
2. Those that are humble before God will forsake sin, making the life-exchange transaction. God breaks the compulsive power of sin; Comes to live inside us by His Spirit; Even gives us the power to minister and to command the enemy spirits in His name. (Rom 3:27; Rom 6:7; Jn 14:17; Mark 16:17)
3. Now that He has given us *everything we need for life and godliness,* He says: "***What will you now do with this freedom***? Will you still go your own way and serve your own selfish desires? Or will you, by the power of My Spirit within you, put to death the deeds of selfishness and pride, and obey my commands?" (Rom 8:1; 8:13; Jn 15:10; Jn 15:22).
4. Those that *love Him* will *obey Him*; those that do not, will not (Jn 14:19,23).
5. He who does the will of God endures forever (Rom 2:7; 1 Jn 2:17).

This is how salvation works. Again, you will see hundreds of passages find their places in full consistency. It's plain and simple, and you understand it without a Master's in Divinity.

The "Do-Over"
Under Wonderful Conditions

If we step back from "pop-Christianity" to read the New Testament – Gospels and Epistles and Revelation – to register in our minds *for what is actually saying without omitting what we might have been taught to omit* – then we will see exactly how salvation works.

This truth is so simple that it takes armies of theologians to cover over it and give you an excuse to **go your own way** and still feel **assured of Heaven**.

Christ makes us "free indeed", and then *what we do with that freedom* declares to all who it is that loves Him and who does not. Our obedience or continued disobedience, then, is Christ's absolutely just basis for our outcome on the day of judgement. The Apostle John even states point-blank how this works.

> *(John 15:22) If I had not come and spoken to them, they would not have had sin; but now they have no excuse for their sin.*

It is stated plainly in many other scriptures as well, as we shall see, but these are scriptures that are systematically hidden from today's "Churchianity". As we move forward int the heart of *Follow the Firstborn*, you will see massive alignment of scriptures all making sense together. If you have endured decades of the most popular traditional teachings then you will see the walls of confusion coming down.

Now – if your response before God is pride, as in "I don't need a savior and I will not have a 'Lord'" – then this will certainly make you angry! But of course, I know that if you have made it this far into the book, you do seek the Kingdom of God, not the Kingdom of man. So – if your response before God is humility (and keep in mind that He foreknew it would be, before the World was created) then you will see the light of His goodness and His promises and **you will joyfully run into that light and embrace those promises**. You will simply see from the scriptures how it works, and my aim is that you will walk in ever more freedom and joy in the Way that the Lord Jesus Christ has made for you.

If you persevere you will indeed overcome; and you will qualify for the eight blessings named in Revelation Chapter two that are "for Him who overcomes". There is nothing automatic about it, but it is the dynamic of Hope and Freedom.

Let's look at a few of these promises.

Bible Quotes are Word English Bible (WEB) except where noted.

Christ Shall Reign
And in Him, We Shall Reign

(Daniel 7:27) The kingdom and the dominion ... Will be given <u>to ... the saints of the Most High</u>...

(Revelation 2:7,11) ... To him who overcomes, I will give to eat from the tree of life which is in the paradise of my God.

... He who overcomes Won't be harmed by the second death.

(Revelation 22:5) And <u>they shall reign</u> forever and ever.

To Him Who Conquers
Glory, Honor, Immortality

There are 11 instances – mostly in Rev 2 - showing that "overcoming" (also translated conquering) is a prerequisite to a *salvation* result; therefore, no serious Bible student can infer that this conquering is *optional*. There is a school of theology that says it is "automatic", but the true present state of the church tells us plainly that it is not, and there are dozens of imperatives and warnings to be diligent; even "diligent to make our calling and election sure" (2 Peter 1:10).

The key is that we must conquer by the *means God has provided*. Throughout the Epistles – if we will read them with clear lenses, we see that overcoming the work of the enemy in our own souls is by *His* power, but by *our* action and perseverance (Rom 2:7; 6:21-22; 8:13). We are motivated by hope (Rom 5:1-5; Col 1:3) and empowered by God's provision (2 Pet 1:3-10).

The central "act" of Christ was His ratifying of the New Covenant in His innocent blood. This opens the way for those that actually enter that covenant by life-exchange; It is the restoration of the fellowship and life of God within us (Col 1:27).

Bible Quotes are Word English Bible (WEB) except where noted.

Restoration of All Things
Peace, Joy, Glory, and Honor

(Revelation 21:1-8) I saw a new heaven and a new earth, for the first heaven and the first earth have passed away and the sea is no more. I saw the holy city, New Jerusalem, coming down out of heaven from God, prepared like a bride adorned for her husband.

I heard a loud voice out of heaven saying, "Behold, God's dwelling is with people, and He will dwell with them, and they will be His people, and God Himself will be with them as their God. He will wipe away every tear from their eyes; Death will be no more; Neither will there be mourning, nor crying, nor pain, any more. The first things have passed away."

He who sits on the throne said, "Behold, I am making all things new." ...

6 ... I will give freely to him who is thirsty from the spring of the water of life. He who overcomes, I will give him these things.

I will be his God and he shall be My son.

But for the cowardly, unbelieving, sinners, abominable, murderers, sexually immoral, sorcerers, idolaters, and all liars, their part is in the lake that burns with fire ... which is the second death."

(Revelation 22:1-3,5 NKJV) And he showed me a pure river of water of life, clear as crystal, proceeding from the throne of God and of the Lamb. In the middle of its street, and on either side of the river, was the tree of life, which bore twelve fruits, each tree yielding its fruit every month. The leaves of the tree were for the healing of the nations. And there shall be no more curse, but the throne of God and of the Lamb shall be in it, and His servants shall serve Him... 5 There shall be no night there: They need no lamp nor light of the sun, for the Lord God gives them light. And they shall reign forever and ever.

I dare not comment on these two passages. Let us meditate on them until the hope wells up and we see the call of the love of God toward us.

Everything that Creeps...
Would You Crush Them?

> *(Luke 10:19) Now after these things, <u>the Lord also appointed seventy others</u>, and sent them two by two ahead of him into every city and place, where He was about to come. Then He said to them, "... And <u>heal the sick who are therein</u>, and tell them, '<u>God's Kingdom</u> has come near to you.' ..."*
>
> *The seventy returned with joy, saying, "Lord, <u>even the **demons** are subject to us in Your name.</u>" And He said to them, "I saw **<u>Satan</u>** having fallen like lightning from heaven. Behold, I give you the authority to **<u>tread</u>** on **<u>serpents</u>** and **<u>scorpions</u>**, and over all the power of the **<u>enemy</u>**. Nothing will in any way hurt you."*

Bible Quotes are Word English Bible (WEB) except where noted.

The Kingdom of God
Allows *Violence*?

(Matthew 11:12) From the days of John the Baptizer until now, the Kingdom of Heaven suffers violence, and the violent take it by force.

(Psalms 110:1) Yahweh says to my Lord, "Sit at my right hand until I make your enemies your footstool…"

(Acts 2:33-34) The Lord said to my Lord, "Sit by my right hand till I make your enemies a footstool for your feet."

To Be Again Crowned
With Glory & Honor

The creation speaks of the unfathomable glory of God (Rom 1). Among other things, "glory" is about winning – especially in a massive reversal or ambush.

God's purpose toward man was, and is, and shall be, exactly as it says here. We were originally created a little lower in authority than the angels, yet He crowned us with glory and placed us in authority over the Earth and things in it.

He *crowns* us with glory and honor. This speaks of Kingship, of Dominion. There is no shame in this picture. No "worm of the dust", no "poor sinner" as many have so often been told by Gnostics. He wants to relate to us by *the sharing of His nature*. He seeks this friendship – ***and we should treasure it***!

Who are we to deny Him that? Why would we to deny *ourselves* that?! He does not take back the words that come from His mouth (Isa 55:11); It's His purpose.

Given His eternal power, why would He care to even "visit" us, much less *come to dwell and abide in us*? But "Christ in you" is the Gospel itself (Colossians 1:27). How could we possibly refuse so great a salvation (Heb 2:3-4)?

God speaks here of "man" as in "mankind", and also speaks of the "Son of Man" - as if there is a ***special man that represents mankind***. Indeed, this is the mystery hidden from before the ages but is now revealed (1 Cor 2).

1. The First Mankind – under the First Adam – was given dominion, as God placed all things under his feet.
2. That first mankind gave it away, not content to reign with God, demanding instead to be higher; to be independent, to go His own way, and to decide for himself what was good and what was evil.
3. Christ – the Last Adam and the Second Mankind (1 Cor 15), won back the dominion on the Earth by winning us the right to become once again the Sons of God; to become once again the Image-Bearers, crowned with glory and honor.

How does that happen for our individual lives? The way *Christ walked* as He said "Follow Me" is the way He calls us to walk. I believe it is precisely what was foreshadowed by the "King's Highway" or "Way of Holiness" described in Isaiah 35. We will now begin a tour through the "precious promises" (2 Peter 1:3-4). These should awaken our hunger and become our experience!

Bible Quotes are Word English Bible (WEB) except where noted.

PART 4: NEW COVENANT PROMISE & ARRIVAL

The Good News is literally the bringing of the Long-awaited "New Covenant". Protestants commonly purport to exalt the Word of God; but in my personal experience of evangelical churches, 99 out of 100 cannot name a third of the provisions of that covenant named in the prophets, or even tell you where any of them appears. The 99 will name only "forgiveness" and "Heaven".

We must ask, then – if mainstream Christianity is not familiar with the New Covenant, why is this? It is because the New Covenant is designed not just to forgive sins, but produce the fruit of holiness; and because seekers generally don't want to hear about holiness unless it is made out to be either optional or automatic?

It is not the purpose of this book to explore the many facets of the New Covenant in detail, but to soundly bring the central benefits of it – including "the powers of the age to come" – back into the consciousness of the church.

The "Old" Covenant was a temporary measure, "covering over" sins, but not taking away the core problem, which was, of course, the _**sin nature**_.

I find it helpful to think of the following simple "Title and subtitle" as the heart of the New Covenant:

A New Spirit and a New Heart

The Desire and the Ability to Do what is Right

Omit These Two – and You No Longer Have Christianity! But focus on them as you peer into the whole Word of God, and you will see a thousand puzzle pieces drop into place.

The New Covenant was described in different aspects by _all_ the prophets (Acts 3); but these few passages taken together describe its provisions. The most important such promise by God is His promise to "put His Spirit into man. This is paramount because without a _conversion_ of our spirits, and a filling with His own Spirit, _we simply cannot obey God_ (Rom 7); This is what makes the New

Covenant *better than the Old Covenant that it replaces*. It's why we needed a New Covenant (Rom 8:4).

A Highway

He Came to Bring Many Sons to Glory; Let's Follow

Christ presented the Love and the Glory of the Father for all to see, living a life of submission to the Father, and said: "Follow Me". It is the invitation to partake in the divine nature (2 Pet 1). So, we see that Christ called us both *by* and *to* His own glory (Heb 2, to bring many Sons to glory); He ascended carrying His own innocent Blood that was to ratify the New Covenant; He brought that blood into the Holy of Holies *as our High Priest* – and He did this *with us in Him, as we shall see*. Finally, He sends His Spirit to those that are ready to obey Him by His power (Acts 5:32, Rom 8:13), and we are made complete. Any that will serve Him are in Him and live from that Union.

This Highway of Holiness has been laid out and elaborated clearly in the New Covenant (New Testament). In the Early church, the Gospel itself was called "The Way". It is still the way we are to follow. In the poster layout, this is the first tier of the center panel.

Invited to Make the Trade

Many teach that we need "only believe", … but without being clear on ***what it is*** that we must believe and its implications. We are to believe what the early church believed – that this is the King and his people that shall reign forever (Daniel 7:27; Psalms 110). We are commanded to "follow Him" in denying "the going of our own way" and in resisting sin as a process. This is "faith" (fidelity, faithfulness is the same Greek word *pistis!*). This second tier of the center poster panel focuses on this *event* of repentance and conversion; and on important things that happen in us that we might not be aware of.

And Follow Him

Actively following is a salvation matter, but we do this restfully (Mt 1:28) in confident hope of appearing with Him (Col 1:3-5; Col 3:3). We walk as the converted species of Mankind – made free and strong by his death and His Life (1 Cor 1:31).

In the poster this "walk" is shown on the third tier of the center panel.

Bible Quotes are Word English Bible (WEB) except where noted.

PART 4A:
A NEW SPIRIT
AND A NEW HEART

A New Spirit? A New Heart? Psalm 51 shows us that David was "after them"!. The self-righteous leaders of Israel lived in misery because they, like all of us, could not do *by their own fallen constitution* what the righteous requirement of God had demanded, because the sin that was in them was actually "them" (Rom 7:17)!! We need to be born into Mankind 2.0.

> *(Romans 7:8) But sin, finding occasion through the commandment, produced in me all kinds of coveting. For apart from the Law, sin is dead.*

David's desire was to do the will of God (Acts 13:22). But he learned that he needed a new heart and a new spirit in order to do it. And he wanted more than forgiveness. The Holy Spirit was with him, but he knew he needed the Spirit of God "in Him".

> *(Psalms 51:9-11 NRSV) Hide your face from my sins, and blot out all my iniquities. Create in me a clean heart, O God, and put a new and right spirit within me. Do not cast me away from your presence, and do not take your holy spirit from me.*

Israel knew of their own failure only too well; the entire Old Testament is the account of lost battles *inward* – the battle striving and failing to do what is right; and also of lost dominion *outward*; the battle striving and failing to bear the image of God; the despair of dominion lost. But it also foreshadows things to come, and a King to come. God, at points when they were baptized into Moses (following Him out of Egypt, doing His will), **_gave His glory to Israel_**. They had supernatural dominion at times. They had tasted of the heavenly gift – not even *in* them, just **with** them! So – when God by His prophets tells Israel He will *put His Spirit into them*, then:

That is what they (the humble) were looking for, and *that* is the living water.

They believed that God was both able and faithful to do what he had promised – so they *followed*; They "stopped going their own way" (Isa 53).

Sown in Weakness and Shame

Forgiveness + ...
Desire + Power = Free Indeed

Forgiveness is Just the Foyer

Will we settle for a "Forgiveness-only Gospel?" even though Jesus Himself said the following?

> *(John 8:35-36) And a slave does not abide in the house forever, but a son abides forever. Therefore, if the Son makes you free, you shall be free indeed.*

I believe that, if we are honest, not a single one of us can experience confidence for the day of judgment if we are living enslaved and defeated, trying to just stay grateful for forgiveness.

Old Covenant vs. New Covenant

The Old Covenant – centered in the Law of Moses, sought to restrain evil through penalties. Yet genetic Israel, political Israel; military Israel – simply wanted personal power and personal reputation.

The irony is that if we will humble ourselves to serve God *by His power*, then we will "overcome" and this leads to life. "True Israel" is not based on physical bloodline; It is based on surrender to obey God by His life inside us.

Everything We Need; But Not Automatic

As we shall see in detail, God has – by His power – given us everything we need "for life and for godliness" (see 2 Peter 1:3-4) – and this includes freedom from enslavement to sin.

Initial salvation is by belief in the atoning work of Christ and in the event of our surrender that results in being recreated and filled with the Spirit of God. However, that event simply gets us "back to the garden", with residue in the soul, yet now with both the desire and the power to obey God in our spirits.

Therefore "Judging by Our Deeds" is Just

This is precisely why it is totally just – in our *final* salvation - for Christ to judge us by our deeds, and not by our beliefs. If you reread your entire New Testament with this model in mind, you will not only see that it is true; you will see that the New Testament makes perfect, natural sense.

The question is, as Jesus would say, "do we have ears to hear"? Should we please man? Or God?

Bible Quotes are Word English Bible (WEB) except where noted.

The Days are Coming
I Will Make a *New* Covenant

Forgiveness of Sins
Power to Do what is Right
Restored Companionship with God Himself

(Jeremiah 31:31-34) "Behold the days come," says Yahweh, "that I will make a <u>new covenant</u> with the house of Israel and the house of Judah. ..."

But <u>this is the covenant that I will make</u> with the house of Israel after those days, says Yahweh:

<u>*I will put my Law within them, and I will write it on their hearts;*</u> *and* <u>*I will be their God, and they shall be my people.*</u>
They will no longer each teach his neighbor ... "Know Yahweh;' for **they will all know me**, *from their least to their greatest," says Yahweh:*

"for I will forgive their iniquity, and I will remember their sin no more."

Sown in Weakness and Shame

Forgiveness of Sins:
Merely the *Foyer* of the *Palace*

The cup of communion is the cup of the *New Covenant* in in His blood; That covenant has many profound benefits, *only the first of which is forgiveness*. Many passages describe the rest, but Ezekiel 36 lays out the key provisions in a few verses.

Sadly, today's popular Christianity takes the single verse Jer. 31:34 and runs with it, as if the New Covenant brings *forgiveness <u>alone</u>*. The shedding of the Blood of Christ is the Blood Covenant sacrifice that enacted a class-action lawsuit judgement, even transferring us out of the power of the enemy and into the Kingdom of God (Col 2).

If so, what are the awards of the lawsuit? As regards holiness – and the ability to meet the righteous requirements of the Law – His death "as us" breaks the power of sin; and His Spirit in us adds the positive power to both will and to do that which is right. In short, His power has given us everything we need for Life and godliness (2 Pet 1:3-4). Then, the question is:

If God gives us the power to obey Him – and plainly He says He will – then, will we? *Will we forsake our sin*? Will we put it to death by His power in us?

This is not a "rewards" issue – but a "salvation" issue:

> ***Romans 6:1-2*** *What shall we say then? Shall we continue in sin that grace may abound? May it never be! <u>We who died to sin</u>, how could we live in it any longer?...*
>
> ***John 15:22*** *If I had not come and spoken to them, they would not have had sin, but now they have <u>no excuse for their sin</u>.*
>
> ***Romans 8:13-14*** *For if you live after the flesh, you must die; but <u>if by the Spirit you put to death the deeds of the body, you will live</u>. For as many as are led by the Spirit of God, these are children of God.*

To him who will insist on *going his own way*, this is <u>bad news</u>. The "obedience thing" is an eternal life matter! … But the humble hear it and are glad – it is the <u>best possible news</u> (See Rom 6:7; 8:2). They are ready to trade a life for … a LIFE! It is the start of a "do-over" but with the Spirit of God in us and with us, making the burden light (Mt 28:11).

Bible Quotes are Word English Bible (WEB) except where noted.

New <u>Heart</u>, New <u>Spirit;</u>
Freedom, Provision, <u>Belonging</u>

(Ezekiel 36:25-29) I will sprinkle clean water upon you, and you will be clean. I will cleanse you from all your filthiness, and from all your idols.

A <u>new heart</u> I will give you, and a <u>new spirit</u> I will put within you;

and I will remove from your body the heart of stone and <u>give you a heart of flesh</u>.
I will <u>put my spirit within you</u>, and cause you to walk in my statutes. You will keep my ordinances and do them.

Then *you will dwell in the land that I gave to your fathers; and you shall be my people, and I will be your God.*
I will save you from all your uncleanness, and I will call for the grain, and will multiply it...

An Inner Constitution
Possessing the Mind of Christ

It is difficult to emphasize anything in this passage – because every phrase is profound. It resonates at every level: Covenant Union, The Second Man, and Dominion. The strong and steadfast Lovingkindness of God is all over it; and He showers us with kindness.

The first two verses correspond perfectly with 2 Peter 1:3-4 ("Partaking in the divine nature, having escaped the corruption in the World through lust"). Notice:

- The New Spirit – "The heavenly gift; the divine nature itself; Christ in You, the hope of glory (Col 1:27).
- New Heart – the seat of the *will* – the breaking of stubbornness; replacing it with a desire to do what is right.
- Deliverance of both the inner<u>most</u> man (spirit), and inner man (soul).
- Deliverance from the action of that sin upon our flesh – healing.
- Rest and prosperity – dwelling in a land that produces its fruit without toil.
- Union with God; We are distinct but no longer separated from God.

This is Grace" – that God piled our sin onto Christ – actually *made Him Sin* and destroyed Him, with us in Him (1 Cor 1:30-31; 2 Cor 5:21). Forgiveness is not the totality of Grace, but **that nuclear act of forgiveness is the <u>legal foundation</u> <u>for the fullness of Grace</u>** which is "everything we need" for life and godliness.

The faithful High Priest that mediates this covenant is not only in us and interceding for us, and He is also our advocate because He knows our frame. In a blessed hope we now purify ourselves (Rom 8:13; 1 John 3:3) because the burden of it is finally light. I hope that all readers can see clearly that the Grace of God is bigger than forgiveness. Evangelism must be restored to what it was in the first centuries.

> The New Covenant – the Good News Itself – is that we can serve God without fear because He gives us both the desire and the power to do what He requires; that we can once again bear His image, enjoy dominion, and live in fellowship with Him

Bible Quotes are Word English Bible (WEB) except where noted.

Christ will not "take you over". He stands at the door and knocks (Rev 3:20), offering to become our righteousness (1 Cor 1:31), and this changes everything (2 Cor 5:17) ... If we will make the trade or deny the First Adam and step into the Second Mankind. He is the Last Adam we will see – so let us *live by His own Righteousness*.

> *(Isaiah 43:25) I, even I, am He who blots out your transgressions for my own sake; and <u>I will not remember your sins</u>.*

> *(Isaiah 53:10-11) Yet it pleased Yahweh to bruise him. He has caused him to suffer. When you make his soul an offering for sin, <u>he will see his offspring. He will prolong his days, and Yahweh's pleasure will prosper in his hand</u>. After the suffering of his soul he shall see light and be satisfied.*

> *My righteous servant shall justify many by the knowledge of himself, and he will bear their iniquities.*

> *If you take away one single thing from this book, the following is a good one to grasp. I will repeat it at a few points in the book. You will see it echoed directly or indirectly in all of the vision passages.*

The New Covenant Presents the Precious Promises

If we are actively affirming, embracing, and pursuing what the New Covenant promises; if we hold to that hope enough to trade in our lives for it, then we are Christians; and our destiny is to reign with Him forever and ever.

The Purpose: Restored Union, Freedom, and Restored Dominion
The Terms: Believe in Christ's payment; Forsake Sin and Practice Obeying His commands until the end
The *Legal* Basis: The Innocent Blood of God Incarnate

The Shedding
Of <u>Innocent</u> Blood was Required

The restoration of all things begins with reconciliation *through* the one *through whom* all things were created (Col 1:16-17).

Man stood guilty, and no man possessed the "rightness" that would constitute an acceptable payment. But without the shedding of innocent blood there is no forgiveness of sins! Therefore, God in His love provided that payment through His Son. As we shall see in the next section, Christ, by carrying His own innocent blood to the throne of the Father, has *united us with the Father*.

We receive this amnesty – and its unspeakable benefits – only if we surrender our rebellion and serve Him by His own nature that has been implanted in us.

In the society of fallen mankind, "Fathers" are doing nothing but reproducing fallen mankind.

But Christ - the Firstborn from among the dead – is now "bringing many Sons to glory" (Heb 2:15). The Father of the Second Mankind is *God Himself* (Jn 1:13)

Unlike a "Father" under the First mankind,

The Father of the Second Mankind is Good
---

*(1 John 2.2 NRSV) and he is the atoning sacrifice for our sins, and not for ours only but also **for the sins of the whole world**.*

But of course – ultimately not everybody is saved; Even though all are freely justified, not all love Christ enough to obey Him and remain in His love (John 15:10) – with our advocate always there as we confess our sins (1 Jn 1:9).

Bible Quotes are Word English Bible (WEB) except where noted.

He Bore Our Sickness
and Carried Our Pains

~700 BC:

(Isaiah 52:14-53:12) Just as many were astonished at you (**his appearance was so marred more than any man**, *and his form more than the sons of men) — so he will cleanse many nations ...*

<u>Who has believed</u> *what we have heard? And to whom has the arm of the LORD been revealed? ...*

*Surely **he** has borne **our** sickness and carried **our** suffering; yet we considered him plagued, struck by God, and afflicted.*
*But **he** was pierced for **our** transgressions, crushed for **our** iniquities; the punishment that brought **us** peace was on **him**, and by **his** wounds **we** are healed.*
All we like sheep have gone astray; <u>**Everyone** has turned to his own way</u>, *and Yahweh has laid on **him** the* <u>iniquity of **us** all</u> ...

*<u>**He**</u> will see his **offspring**. He will prolong his days ...*

*After the suffering of his soul, he will see the light and be satisfied. My righteous **[tsadiq]** servant will justify **[tsadaq - make righteous – see 2 Cor 5:21]** many by the knowledge of Himself; and **he** will bear **their** iniquities.*

*Therefore I will give him a portion with the great, and <u>**he** will divide the plunder with the strong; because he poured out his soul to death</u>, ... yet **he** bore the sin of **many**, and made intercession for the <u>transgressors</u>.*

Sown in Weakness and Shame

He Will See the Fruit
of His Travail and Be Satisfied

This passage – spanning Isaiah 52 to 53 – is like no other passage in the Bible, depicting Christ crucified about 700 years before the event. From the time of Christ forward, it has no longer been permitted to be read aloud in synagogues. I think this chapter is the clearest picture of the love of God – as a single chapter – that we have. Take your physical Bible and part it exactly halfway – and you might just land on it.

Please note the underlined words; they point out the most important ***exchange*** that ever occurred. It is the physical act of ratifying the New Covenant that brings peace and wholeness to all who will receive Him. Holiness is righteousness in the soul, expressed through word and deed. Will we *see His glory* and surrender our rebellion?

It is no mere coincidence that this chapter connects with most or all of these vision passages! It is very helpful to see the connection to 2 Cor 5:21 (next passage) and to John 3:14-15 – He "became sin" for us that we might *become the righteousness of God*; This is the ultimate dignity! We can be changed instantly by seeing this exchange offered to us and surrendering to the Love of God. It is for you and for me!

Verse 4 shows that He bore our sicknesses and carried away our pains. In the Hebrew, they are the same verbs used to describe what He did with our sins and our iniquities; He bore them away, just as on the Day of Atonement in the Old Testament, the second Lamb carried the sins of the people to the wilderness to be devoured by beasts (exodus).

The Jews wanted Dominion over their oppressors, they did not want a *suffering* King, much less a *crucified* one. But take heart – Christ shall "divide the spoil with the *great*" (the last verse shown in bold; other translations render that *the strong*).

Hmmm ... The "Great"? the Strong"? Who would that be? If we have to think about it, then that means we are under a spirit of "religion" that keeps us deceived and oppressed under a "poor sinner" mindset, and also under self-condemnation and consciousness of sins. "The Strong" are those at peace by His sacrifice; born of God, that have escaped the corruption and are partaking in His nature; It is those that know Him. It is these that shall grow strong and do exploits. This entire book focuses on the passages that go to this theme of dominion (John 1:12; 2 Pet 1:3-4; Daniel 11:32).

Bible Quotes are Word English Bible (WEB) except where noted.

The Spirit of God
Poured Out for All Mankind

(Joel 2:28-29) "It will happen afterward that I will <u>pour out My Spirit</u> on all flesh; and your sons and your daughters will prophesy.
Your old men will dream dreams, your young men will see visions.
And also on the servants and handmaids in those days, <u>I will pour out my Spirit.</u>"

We Should Hunger for It
It is Intended for Us All

The highest gift of God toward man is His very presence on us and in us.

It is the power to live a life that is pleasing to Him, and "he who does the will of the Lord endures forever" (1 John 3:22).

This is why we see in Ezekiel, Jeremiah, Joel, and Isaiah looking so intently upon "the Spirit of God" and speaking of it as the centerpiece of the New Covenant itself. So, we find in the New Testament that indwelling presence of God, by His Spirit in us, is the essence of the Gospel itself. It is *Christ in you, the hope of glory*" (Col 1:27).

The Spirit of God in us, of course, is not just for "special experiences" as a human would define that. But rather the Spirit of God reveals all the God freely gives to those that being to Him (1 Cor 2, the whole chapter); to those that have given themselves back to Him in response to the proof of His goodness.

The Spirit of God in us brings us the mind of Christ; the perfect fellowship with God; the ability to love as He loved – truly unselfish and unconditional; He brings us the power to know and to do just as Christ did – and even greater works (John 14).

He brings us authority over all the power of the enemy.

I become Like Him (1 Jn 4:17; Matt. 10).

At the pinnacle of "grace" is that I am born of Him (John 1:12); He becomes my God and Father (John 17), and I belong to Him and He belongs to me (Song of Solomon; Ezekiel 36; Jer 31; Rev 22) …

Again – this is so, so much more than "forgiveness now and Heaven someday".

Bible Quotes are Word English Bible (WEB) except where noted.

PART 4B: THE ARRIVAL OF WHAT WAS PROMISED

All of Ancient Israel would have certainly known of the outrageously wonderful New-Covenant promise of *God dwelling in them*. *Some* would welcome the fellowship of God, partaking in His nature, and enjoying His provision, and living free of oppression. *Others*, amazingly, would be blind to the mercy and justice and joy, and simply seek to obtain power to oppress others.

In John 14 we see Jesus speaking plainly of the institution of the New Covenant. We see all three persons of the godhead coming to dwell in man. We also see that in order to obtain this indwelling, we must <u>*obey God as*</u> a matter of practice. He says it over and over, yet most of the church does not even bring up chapter 14, much less mention the prerequisite of practicing obedience as a salvation matter.

If we want to enjoy "power", then we must understand that the only arrangement that God supports is (as John G. Lake phrased it):

> If a man is in Christ, he is God's son, man's servant, and the devil's master.

We will probe more deeply into the implications of those three components, but for now I urge you to notice that the supernatural power Grants His people is for undoing the work of the enemy in themselves and others – continuing Christ's work of setting captives free.

Bible Quotes are Word English Bible (WEB) except where noted.

We will Love Him,
Make Our Home with Him

(John 14:6-31) Jesus said to him, "<u>I am the way, the truth, and the life</u>. No one comes to the Father except through me. ... from now on you know Him and have seen Him." ... He who has seen me has seen the Father; ...

Believe me that I am in the Father and the Father in me,

or else believe me for the sake of the works themselves. "Most assuredly, I say to you, he who believes in me, the works that I do he will do also; and he will do greater works than these, because I am going to my Father. And whatever you ask in My name, that I will do, that the Father may be glorified in the Son...
If you ask anything in My name, I will do it.

<u>If you love Me, keep My commandments</u>. And I will pray to the Father, and he <u>will give you another Counselor, that he may abide with you forever— the Spirit of truth</u>, whom the world cannot receive, because it doesn't see him; neither knows him; You know him, for He lives with you and <u>will be in you</u> ...

"<u>Yet a little while,</u> and the world will see me no more, but you will see me. Because I live, you will live also. At that day you

will know that I am in my Father, and you in me, and I in you.

If a man loves me he will keep my word. My Father will love him, and

We will come to him and make Our home with him. ...

"I have said these things to you while still living with you. But the Counselor, the Holy Spirit, whom the Father will send in my name, he will teach you all things, and will remind you of all that I said to you."

Sown in Weakness and Shame

Surrender into Union with God Through Christ

I included nearly the whole chapter here; Please notice – Jesus describes His union with the Father and the Spirit, and invites us into it; and describes its benefits (greater works, seeing God, and joy).

In Absolute Union yet Distinct

Underline = God is one being, with three persons in eternal Union and unity.

The Trinity are "in" each other – in perfect unity, yet are distinct and equal. The Father is *superordinate* to Son and Spirit, but not *superior*. As Sons of the same Father after the Firstborn (John 1:12), *we are subordinate to be sure, but we are Sons of the same Father nonetheless* and partaking in the Divine nature (2 Pet 1; Col 2:9).

Even we are called to Union with God, while yet being distinct (He even has new names for us since we were born of God). Christ came to bring many Sons to glory and is not ashamed to call us His brothers (Heb 2), so why are we ashamed? "Mind renewal" is learning to accept this truth that makes us free; but the first element of that truth is the realization that we have died (Gal 2;20; Rom 6:7, 21-22; 7:17) Chains must break or no amount of struggling will succeed.

Indeed, Jesus Christ is King of Kings and Lord of Lords! Nevertheless, we are to be unashamed to call Him "brother". Can you handle it? Christ certainly hopes you can, because that's what He paid for!

Obedience is the Cost – Religiously Incorrect, but True

Bold = **Obedience** is the cost of Entering into Covenant – also known as **repentance**. As a Christian Culture we have gradually, stealthily, made "Repentance" murky so we can get people to walk the aisle with an acknowledgement of guilt feelings and desire to get forgiven. We are at the point where repentance no longer carries even the thought of *actually forsaking sin by the power of the death of Christ* (Rom 6; Gal 6; 2 Cor 5:12, 21). This leaves us feeling ***sorry*** for sin(s) yet ***lacking the ability to overcome*** that sin. I have been in that "misery-of-the-Pharisee". It is not fun; What's so sad is that it is not even necessary.

The Truth is we are forgiven the moment we **truly turn to God to forsake sin** (As with Abraham's faith, noted in Rom 4). But if we are demanding to be "saved by faith" ***rather than** have actual righteousness*", then we have been misled with a doctrine of devils. There is a crucial distinction here! The church must get this right!

The Gospel proclaims the *means* of the righteousness God requires, not the excuse for lives of sin.

Our repentance by the conviction and convincing of the Holy Spirit, brings us into "conversion" and into union and fellowship with the Father, the Son, and the Spirit. This is a change of *lineage* and a change in *allegiance*.

If – and only if – our repentance was a change of allegiance, then it was real. But how deep is that allegiance? In our society, "Allegiance" might seem murky or abstract, just like "Kingdom".

It goes as deep as deep can be! In a true conversion there must be a reckoning that what we are deserves its condemnation to death; a recognition that God, out of His love proven by Christ, offers the very life of Christ – and the genuine righteousness of Christ – to us in exchange. The most-repeated command of Christ is that we would "lose our life to find it". Baptism speaks directly of this death and resurrection. Romans 6 tells exactly how humans get free from the power of sin, but most modern preaching simply skips the whole chapter except for verse 23 out of context… But anybody that is "of the truth" will step into that light when they see it. So, so many would crave the dignity and joy of carrying and manifesting the light of Christ, in both love and power … if they were only told of it – or would read it for themselves.

When we see the glory of Christ and the sinfulness of the constitution that we are born under, we will gladly make the trade.

Now let's look at some details of both the costs and benefits.

In John 14, Jesus states – and immediately repeats – the covenant entry requirement, which is actually "obeying His commands" (verses 21 and 23). If we have Christ in us – *with His righteousness in each of us and with power of sin broken* – then this is not a hard saying at all. Rather, it is the open door to unspeakable dignity and joy. We are going to cast out fear of the day of judgement (1 Jn 4:17).

But if we are seeking a self-righteousness by the power of the first mankind, we will be offended and frustrated as we strive in futility and shame. But He whom the Son sets free is free indeed.

Overcoming and Joy are by Union

Sin is "going our own way"; it is selfish-independence, and self-righteousness, apart from the righteousness of God.

Righteousness is by *Union with Christ*; That Union is through the blood of Christ and it becomes ours when we *forsake* "the going of our own way" (AKA sin). We can never forsake sin *just by accepting forgiveness!* Church – Haven't we proven this to ourselves for years? Decades? Centuries? Millennia?

We forsake sin by the power of God – by *identifying with* His death and resurrection (Rom 6) and ascension to the Father (Eph 1:19; 2:6; John 20:17). Christ is the Second Adam, the Second Mankind; and He died not just "for us", but "as us". We must see our sin crucified (John 3:*14-15*). It is the defining context of "John 3:16"; Yet sadly, the vast majority of believers – if you read verse 14 to them – could not tell you where it is.

But it starts with Obedience – *Entrusting* belief which brings us into Covenant. It is not "entrusting that he paid for your sins"!!! Rather, it is *entrusting yourself to follow Him* because you trust Him for what will appear, given some patience. It is to transfer your allegiance from *yourself* to the King whose Kingdom shall stand.

At this very last supper Christ and the twelve all drank from the cup. Christ ratified the New Covenant in His Blood which not only brings mankind (all that are in Him) – into "peace" with God as "fire insurance" – but also brings them into *Union with God* and gets the Spirit of God ***into them*** upon request (more detail is to come).

The Centurion simply "Re-presented" His Sender

Matthew 8:9-13 For I also am a man *under authority*, having soldiers under me. And I say to this one, "*'Go,' and he goes*; and to another, *'Come,' and he comes*; and to my servant, *'Do this,' and he does it.*" 10 When Jesus heard it, He marveled, and said to those who followed, "Assuredly, I say to you, *I have not found such great faith, not even in Israel*! …" Then Jesus said to the centurion, "Go your way; and *as you have believed, so let it be done for you.*" And his servant was healed that same hour.

Curry R. Blake is the World's foremost trainer in Divine Healing. He tells us "If we understand faith, we understand authority. If we understand authority, we understand faith". Blake infers this directly from Christ's honoring of the Centurion's faith.

Who has sent *us*? Who do we "re-present"? Knowing this at the core of our being frees us to be bold as a lion. The issue is the "*quality*" of faith – not the "*quantity*". It is faith as allegiance and fidelity, not just believing the fact of the atonement.

Bible Quotes are Word English Bible (WEB) except where noted.

The New Covenant *Fulfilled* as the Father is Glorified in Us

Consider John 14:12, an amazing promise. Power and joy (greater works; anything!) that come from *Being Sent by All Three*. We who entrust ourselves into Christ (truly repent) are *indwelt by all three*. Each of us now, as a man in whom the fulness of God is pleased to dwell – may do the works Christ did, and even greater. Not my idea. Read the Word of God on the matter (John 14).

Exactly like the Centurion – if we understand the authority of the one that has sent us (Mt 28:18ff); and know the power of the fullness of God that dwells in us, then everything changes… We shall operate in exactly the conditions by which Christ operated. The degree of our experience is paced by the shedding of our unbelief.

Our Joy is made complete when we are pleasing to the One we were created to please; as we carry the dignity of a Son of God; *the honor of bearing His image*.

Parents – you know you long to see the good and honorable values that are in you, **appearing in your children**. If you see it, you have "glorified" them; Moreover, their virtues are your glory, and they glorify you. They "honor" you. Compare to Psalms 8:6). It all works together!

This is why we are baptized in the name of all three. In the gospels, the disciples were merely sent by the Son, not all three. Furthermore, they had the Spirit of God *with them* but not *in them*. So of course, we will do greater works – if we will renew our minds and reject all traditions that deny the power of God.

Connect this with John 14 and 17

Our bearing *the image of the Firstborn* brings Joy to the Father, Joy to the Firstborn, and Joy to the Spirit. They are glorified in us; and we are glorified in them. The Life of overcoming becomes possible through not only our Union with Christ but with the Father as well. And as we have seen previously, we are INDWELT AND SENT by ALL THREE – AND THEY AGREE. This is why we will do *even greater works* (John 14:12). It is glorious grace, and is *vastly, VASTLY* beyond forgiveness alone. Think of the glory that will come to the reputation of God when his people start "winning" over the work of the enemy in sickness and oppression.

Taking glory to the next level, we must get our eyes off of ourselves and see the *Body of Christ* sent – not just us as *individuals* sent.

The twelve followed Christ and did His works; the seventy followed Christ and did His works; The great commission is actually clear and consistent with all scripture if we will merely combine the original great commission (Gen 1:26-28); Matthew 28:18; Mark 17-20). If we are baptized into the fellowship (John 20) of all three persons of the single *being* which is God – and know it - then we will do even greater works.

That is communion; dominion restored, and an unspeakably precious promise (2 Peter 1:3-4). Christ the King is inaugurated; His Kingdom has begun to manifest, and it does so in the lives of the people that carry His indwelling presence and do His will.

Bible Quotes are Word English Bible (WEB) except where noted.

This High Priest
Did what "The Law" Could Not

The Old Covenant could only point out our sins and "cover them". It could never fix the root cause of sins, which is our damaged innermost constitution that leaves us vulnerable to temptation to sin.

But if a New Adam, with the innocent Blood of God could come onto the scene … would be born into the realm of Earth, would live without sin, and then give Himself as ransom, … then we would have the legal right to _transfer our allegiance_ to _that one_; That transference is repentance and faith.

Not only would He ransom us out of the bondage and its trajectory of fear and death; He would also give His own _loving, but also_ **_conquering_** – "nature" to each of us who will trade what we have (which is nothing) for what He is (a Son of God).

He came to bring many sons to Glory (Heb 2:15). We surrender that we might become … Still Poor Sinners – saved by grace? No!!! Worms in the Dust, groveling and begging that God would come down? That He would "show up" in our church service? No!!! This is diametrically opposite to Christianity. Be "converted"!

Grace is "everything we need for life – _the very Life of God, "Zoe"_ – Christ in Us, being born as His "Kind".

> To all who believe – in His "_Name_" – that is, in His "_Lineage_" …
>
> He gives the right to become that Second Mankind. That's the Gospel!

(John 1:12 NRSV) But to all who received him, who believed in his name, he gave power to become children of God …

Sown in Weakness and Shame

Restoring Desire & Power
To Do What is Right

Knowing the full purposes of Christ is immensely important. If we are only aware of a small portion of His purpose, then by faith we can obtain only that small portion.

Now, Christ told us that He came "to restore that which was lost" (Luke 19:10). So, it would be very appropriate to ask: "What was lost?" It was the *original state of Mankind before the rebellion.*

The prime things lost were mutual belonging with God; the bearing of the Image of God; and dominion over every living thing on the Earth – except mankind of course. The First Adam had naturally subdued even the creeping things on the earth. He had done so by bearing the image of God, by the indwelling nature of God that had been breathed into him.

Note that the Father glorifies the Firstborn Son that does His will; In turn, the *Firstborn* Son *glorifies* (brings to glory and strength) those of us that will follow Him, to do the will of God. That is what it means to be "baptized into" Him: Believe this and you will have a breakthrough!

When Christ speaks of us "dying", He is speaking of *laying down our right to go our own way and do our own pleasure.*

Notice how Jesus fulfills the original great commission to be fruitful and multiply:

> *(John 12:24 NRSV) Very truly, I tell you, unless a grain of wheat falls into the earth and dies, it remains just a single grain; but if it dies, it bears much fruit.*

We are called to put sin to death by His power – not fun – but we will be more than satisfied as we observe the nature of Christ arise in us (Rom 5:5) and even the presence of God in us (Jn 14:19, 23).

In this section we have seen the prophets telling of the coming New Covenant; Under this Covenant God Himself would be coming to dwell in us and profoundly change us, *giving us the joy of His **manifest presence**; and giving us both the **desire and the power** to do what He commands*. How would this appear?

Bible Quotes are Word English Bible (WEB) except where noted.

PART 5: CHRIST THE SECOND MAN MADE THE WAY

Even Christ Himself, was called by the Father and was motivated by a very specific "hope" that relates to the original great commission – "be fruitful and multiply" and "have dominion" – in fact all the elements that we see in Psalms 8 and Genesis 1.

Our default state, that which each of us in this age is born into, is *the contaminated selfish mankind that has no connection to the only true God*; and no supply of life. So, we inexorably descend into death. The First Adam chose to go his own way, and we are born into the enemy camp of selfish independence. Even under the first Adam we are able to do *some* good. The vast majority of mothers and fathers are at least occasionally able to have compassion on a child and make some sacrifice to care for it. There are others that can lead campaigns of compassion for others. At the other extreme, there are people that have fully seared their consciences are pursue nothing but selfish gain at any and all cost to others.

So, we have what we might call people of light and people of darkness; but only on a *relative* scale. Not one bears the image of God and projects His glory on the scale that is needed to overcome the work of the enemy in their spirits and souls, much less in the world around them.

A "progenitor" is the "original" of something that will be – or has been – replicated. Every man is born into the wrong *lineage*, descended from the selfish progenitor. The infected Adam succeeded in "being fruitful and multiplying" (Gen 1:28).

Each of us eventually realizes that something wonderful was lost and is now out of reach. It is the glory and joy of unity with our maker; and the joy of dignity and dominion. The situation is worse than merely "something good out of reach"; At this time, nearly everyone knows there is a powerful spiritual enemy that drives people to ultimate measures to dominating others for personal gain and power.

On the other hand, nearly every man or woman remembers the innocence and simplicity of their childhood. We all want freedom – the lightness – of perfect provision and love. We see it slip away. This is because every human is born disconnected from Life. Anchored and trapped in the tragic lineage of the First Adam.

But God, in His amazing love, has given the World nothing less than a *Second* Adam, and ***He will even live in us***. This is the ultimate Do-Over of mankind. This second man was born into the realm of human authority on Earth – that is, born of woman; yet He was conceived by the Spirit of God.

Christ became the original, the firstborn from the dead, that walked in sound and full possession of all that was lost; This is what the Bible calls "glory". Christ is the ***progenitor of the Second Mankind***. He is the heirloom seed of the Sons of God.

Do you want to be like Him? Not just in power, but in Love?

He calls us to "follow Him", "come after him"; to "lose our life to find it". It is not merely to change our lifestyle, but to exchange our life itself. The Gospel is not a simply a command to change what we "do"; but a call to *ex*-change what we "*Are*".

To be saved, we *see* in this "Christ" the "rightness" of God demonstrated in the realm of earth (John 1:1-14). We are to ***Trust*** that He is able to crucify the Old Adam in us; to recreate us after His own nature (Eph 4:24) and dwell in us (Col 1:27). We see that ***He restores what was lost***. In short, we see that He is most definitely what we need. *He* is what we must *become*.

We see the love of God toward us in the innocence and suffering of this Christ, and we love Him (john 14:23); We ***Entrust ourselves into Him***, that is, we "repent" we resolve to obey His command to love as He loved; But this time, we get to live and love *by His nature in us*, which is pure and innocent and entirely unfallen. In our souls there is still residue that we are responsible for, but it is not "us", and we have the have the power to dismantle it.

Any man's attempt to "get saved" without the life-exchange and the *conscious desire of the New Mankind* is the prime strategy of the deceiver. The dying and rising must happen; the seed must be planted before it can germinate. As I mentioned earlier, this is *Baptism*, and Jesus had to *go through it all* before we can – so that we can. He overcomes the World, the flesh, and the devil – not so that we *don't have to*, but ***so that we can***. He is the Way, and His command is "follow me".

I urge you to study the frame headings; say them in sequence so that they form a complete sentence; Then as you increasingly understand it, practice saying it in your own words as clearly and boldly as you can. Once you do this you will find not only that your own hunger for righteousness will rise dramatically.

If you will take this approach to learning all three of the central tiers; letting them awaken hope in you, then you will find your breakthroughs; You will also be able to share the Gospel accurately and effectively; The promises of that Gospel will once again be big enough that the World will begin to take them seriously again.

Bible Quotes are Word English Bible (WEB) except where noted.

The Last Adam,
The Second Mankind

*(1 Cor 15:42-49) The body is sown perishable, it is raised in <u>imperishable</u>.
It is sown in dishonor, it is raised in <u>glory</u>.
It is sown in weakness; it is raised in <u>power</u>.
It is sown a natural body, it is raised a <u>spiritual body</u>...*

*And so it is written, "The first man, Adam, became a living being".
The <u>last Adam</u> became a <u>life-giving spirit</u>...*

The <u>first man</u> is of the earth, made of dust; the <u>second Man</u> is the Lord from heaven.

...

As we have borne the image of those made of dust, let's also <u>bear the image of the heavenly</u>.

Sown in Weakness and Shame

Sown in Weakness, Shame
Raised in Power & Glory

The spatial arrangement of the central panel of the poster is very, very important at this point. It shows that on each of three different levels (the three "tiers"), there are the following elements:

1. A **call** given
2. A **hope** provided
3. A **response** required
4. **Results** that will accrue if the response is made

Before we focus on this central panel, I wish to briefly refresh our minds to the essential promise of reaping the Second Mankind if we sow – ***bury*** – the First Mankind. That is "baptism".

So let us first get the "Central ***Heading*** Panel" firmly into our minds. It is the title of this very book page. If you put it into the center of your consciousness, you will have a glimpse of the center of "mind of Christ" (1 Cor 2:16; Phil 2:5-11).

Most of popular Christianity has been conditioned to believe that the road to Glory does not go through self-denial and calls it "grace". The scary contrary passages are avoided where possible. Theologians that "know the Bible languages" are well paid to deal with it.

But if we will see the Word of God without lenses colored by tradition; and see the "hope" – we will find the wonderful provisions God has made though the work of His Firstborn Son.

If you grasp the above, and surrender your rebellion; and seek the righteousness of God – not just forgiveness – Then you will be reborn in spirit after the pattern of God (Eph 4:24); you will ask for His indwelling spirit and He will not withhold it; and you will overcome in your soul (Rom 8:1-4; 13).

Before long, you will see fruit of the right tree (Rom 5:5 and elsewhere).

Then going forward, as you study the Word of God, it will rapidly make perfect and beautiful sense, cover to cover.

May we all accept – and chose to walk in – the bigger Grace; the Grace that fully and truly honors God. The grace of God that provides everything we need to follow the Firstborn from among the dead.

Bible Quotes are Word English Bible (WEB) except where noted.

I Give You as a Covenant
To Restore What was Lost

From His Mouth Issues a Sword

Isaiah 49:1-7 "Listen, islands, to me. ... <u>Yahweh has called Me from the womb</u>; From the inside of my mother, he has mentioned my name.

Isaiah 49:2 He has <u>made my mouth like a sharp sword</u>. He has hidden me in the shadow of his hand. He has made me a polished shaft. He has kept me close in his quiver".

Isaiah 49: 6 Indeed he says, "It is too light a thing that you should be my servant to raise up the tribes of Jacob, and to <u>restore</u> the preserved ones of Israel?
<u>*I will also give you as a light to the nations,*</u>
<u>*That you may be my salvation to the end of the earth.*</u>*'" ...*

Bringing Restoration, Freedom, and Dignity

Isaiah 49:8-9 ... I will ... give You for <u>a covenant of the people,</u>
<u>*...*</u> *saying to those who are bound, "Come out!" ... you may say to the prisoners, "Go forth!". To those who are in darkness, <u>"Show yourselves!"</u> ...*

Isaiah 49:11 I will make all of my mountains a road, And my highways shall be exalted.

Overcoming the True Enemy

Isaiah 49:25 But Yahweh says: "Even the captives of the mighty shall be taken away, ... For I will contend with him who contends with you, And I will save your children.

Even Christ Embraced
... *Hope of What is Promised*

I had a season of serious despair a few years back. In a dream, a man (an angel) simply turned toward me and said "Isaiah 49 is for Jon"; then he turned away and the dream was done, and I woke up. I fumbled for a pen and wrote "Isa 49" on whatever felt like paper; then I went back to sleep.

In the morning, I looked it up. A few phrases in this passage "rang a bell", but prior to this event I never could have told you what was in Isaiah 49 if asked. Now it is among the most precious chapters in the Bible for me! Why has it almost never been presented "in church"? Who is behind its omission?

The answer is that the enemy makes sure that "poor sinners" are too humble to seek anything like "dominion". But if this chapter speaks of Christ and we are to have the mind of Christ (1 Cor 2:16), then there are things for us to see in here!

Now, let me be clear. These words are from God the Father to Christ the incarnate Son. I, of course, am not Christ, and I am not being given as a Covenant. It is the assignment of Christ alone. But I found in this chapter the heart of the Father towards Jesus, and I saw that the Father has the same heart for me; because I am now a son (small "s") of God as well. This is why the Angel said it was for me.

Please notice the following from the headings I have placed at left:

From His Mouth Issues a Sword

This speaks directly of Revelation 19, where we see Christ coming not as the suffering servant, but as the leader of the army of Heaven bringing the final and complete defeat of the enemy.

The Father Gives the Son for a Covenant

The Lord Jesus Himself is the sacrifice and guarantor (1 John 2:1) of the New Covenant.

The glory that Christ manifested is the nature God offered to man (2 Peter 1:3-4) as the chief objective of the mission. Reconciliation and Restoration are the highest objectives of redemption; and forgiveness of sins is merely the precious legal groundwork for them. We will discuss "glory" in more detail soon.

There is a kind of "telescoping" relationship from the Father to Christ to Us. Jesus was sent by the Father and obeyed the will of the Father – and was

Bible Quotes are Word English Bible (WEB) except where noted.

thereby "In" the Father. Likewise, we are sent by Jesus Christ (John 21:22) and obey His command to love as He loved; and this is how we remain in His love (John 15:11). In this way, we are to live "In Christ". Christ is perfectly secure! And we are secure if we are "In Christ".

Restoring Freedom and Dignity

As we will see very clearly when we get to the second tier, Christ bought – and brought us true freedom from the compulsive power of sin. That sin was compulsive simply because we <u>were</u> sinners (can a zebra change his stripes?). But one born of God is of course, no longer a sinner.

As we then use our true freedom to progressively overcome the residual sin that is in our souls, we are *changed*.

Wait a minute – who is doing this work? Is it "God? Or is it "us"? The answer is "yes". It is our active use of His power and with His active guidance (Phil 2:12-13).

And so, we begin to bear the acceptable fruit of true righteousness. It is the "fruit of the good tree". If we are "of the light", then we gladly run into the light and we are delighted that we are being confirmed to the image of the firstborn Son. That is *dignity like no other dignity*.

Overcoming the True Enemy

Nobody gets outward victory until inward victory is underway". Not that it must be "complete", but it must be underway. This is why American Popular Christianity remains, by and large, defeated. More specifically, if we believe the lie that holiness – separation from the corruption of the world – is either *not required for salvation*" or that it is, but is "*automatic*", then we *remain in defeat*. That is not "having life and having it more abundantly" (John 10:10).

But the Covenant that Christ ratified made the way for the restoration of peace, strength, freedom, dignity, and overcoming. As we shall see, He had to pioneer through the whole trail.

Bible Quotes are Word English Bible (WEB) except where noted.

To Crown **Mankind** with ... *Glory* and *Honor*?

(Psalms 8:4-5) what is man, that you think of him? What is the son of man, that you care for him? For you have made him a little lower than the angels, and crowned him with glory and honor.

(2 Corinthians 3:15-18) But to this day, when Moses is read, a veil lies on their heart. But whenever one turns to the Lord, the veil is taken away. Now the Lord is the Spirit and where the Spirit of the Lord is, there is liberty. But we all, with unveiled face seeing the glory of the Lord as in a mirror, are transformed into the same image from glory to glory, even as from the Lord, the Spirit.

(Colossians 1:26-27) the mystery which has been hidden for ages and generations. But now it has been revealed to his saints, to whom God was pleased to make known what are the riches of the glory of this mystery among the Gentiles, which is Christ in you, the hope of glory.

(John 17:22) The glory which you have given me, I have given to them; that they may be one, even as we are one.

Glorify:
To Bring Glory to Another

We have to define "glory" very carefully, and we have to distinguish the aspects of "glory" that God does or does not share with man. Many in the church have heard "All have sinned *and fallen short of the glory of God*". The Gospel News is that Christ has come to "solve" even **the *second half* of that verse** (1 Jn 4:17).

Christ came to restore that which was lost – all of it. Let's bring out a few definitions here. These adjustments cause numerous difficult passages to fall into place (their place in the puzzle).

In the definitions I choose, I am not simply extracting the cheapest grace I can find. Rather, given that many words have radically different alternative meanings dependent on context – I am choosing the set of valid definitions that does not produce contradictions. As it turns out, it is the set of definitions that upholds not only "forgiveness" passages, but also the "holiness" demands.

As it turns out, the Word of God reveals itself to be very, very consistent if we can see that "grace" goes beyond forgiveness, to include both *the desire and the power to do what is right*.

Freedom may be scary to those have been trained to fear it. But freedom is glorious to the Sons of God (Romans 8:21).

Evil: Going our own way, making our own rules; Seeking glory by our own resources of the first mankind; Asserting personal righteousness of our own.

Righteousness: Buried and raised with Christ; and united with God; Living in right relationship with God, sourced with the actual Righteousness of Christ.

Good: Overcoming the true enemy, as servant of man, by the power of God.

Grace: All that we need for the Life of God and for Actual Righteousness (2 Pet 1).

Glory: Greek *Doxa* – Unspoken yet manifest presence of God.

Glorify: *Bring to Another the Image of God*.

Some of you have seen this in … Basketball: Chicago Bulls: Jackson and Jordan and Pippin and Rodman – the *"glory of the **assist**"*. The *send* and the *pass* and the *pick* and the *slam* all *glorify* each other when they work together;

they *leverage* each other; many people that are beaten down by life will watch this "glory" on a court or a field.

Consider the Olympic Games. Originally, the emperor would place "crowns" on the victors. In our modern Olympic Games, the victory of those sent "glorifies" the nation that has sent them.

Yet even all this is just the glory that appears when *mere humans* will set aside the need for *personal* glory and serve with one another in a bigger objective.

The analogy to the Kingdom of God is obvious. In Spiritual Life: The Father and Firstborn send The Spirit into us; and we share in the dance; We partake in the divine nature (2 Pet 1:4) and we honor Him back. God is glorified in His kindness toward us – *and in the fact that we use our real freedom to serve Him*.

Those in Christ are not mere humans (1 Cor 3:1-3) and there is "always" an *assist* in play (Mark 16:20). We are called to the complete joy by experiencing winning battle for the Kingdom of God, trouncing the enemy together – by His power and our action.

What Makes this Dance Special

Describing John 17, some of the early church "fathers" used the Greek word "perichoresis", literally "around-dancing". Those in Christ are to enjoy a dance of unity. In Him we live and move, and have our being (Acts 17:28).

Loving cooperation mimics the "dance" of John 17 in which every partner is working toward the objective of *"the restoration of all things"* (Acts 3); Peter actually calls the news of this restoration "the gospel"! Participating in it is the dance of <u>union, joy, and overcoming</u> – and we are all invited. In this dance, no partner glorifies Himself; Rather, each glories the others. It's a dance because we are taking turns stepping on the neck of the enemy. Christ alone could not "dance"; but now that He has us (His brothers) and we have Him, we *can*.

Mind-renewal is required! Not long ago I heard a worship leader pray on behalf of the congregation, saying "Lord, we're all poor sinners". By now you should be able to see who it was that promoted that mentality into the church. While we were **yet** sinners, yes, of course we **were**! But we are no longer sinners, and it is not even us who sin, but *it is merely the sin that dwells in us*. Once the zebra is no longer a zebra, he can do something about those stripes. We will see that by the real power of God, we truly can resist sin ... *by actively cooperating with the power and presence of God – his glory – within us. That's* grace!

Sown in Weakness and Shame

Bible Quotes are Word English Bible (WEB) except where noted.

To Bring Many Sons
To Companionship and Glory

(Hebrews 2:5-16) For he didn't subject the world to come ... to angels but one has somewhere testified, saying:

"What is man that you think of him, or the son of man, that you care for him?
You made him a little lower than the angels.
You crowned him with glory and honor

You have put all things in subjection under his feet.
... 10 For it became him, ... for whom are all things ...,

> in bringing many children to glory,

to make the author of their salvation perfect through sufferings.

> Heb 2:11 For <u>both he who sanctifies and those who are sanctified are all from one, ...</u>
> <u>He is not ashamed to call them brethren"</u>

(John 12:24) Most assuredly, I say to you, unless a grain of wheat falls into the earth and dies, it remains by itself alone;
but if it dies, it produces much fruit.

Sown in Weakness and Shame

Not Ashamed
To Call Us His Brothers and Sisters!

Calling us His brothers and sisters, Christ was not "being nice." He was referring to the many "Sons of God" that He was bringing to Glory – born of the same Father and by the same Spirit. We don't always feel it, **but it's true** – if we have surrendered to *do the will of God* rather than *go our own way*.

Dominion was assigned to mankind; even though the first Mankind abdicated that authority, the Second Mankind won it back. He is now replicating Himself and the Image Bearers are back. His people are manifesting His glory and bearing the first fruits of their inheritance!

In this chapter we see an important link – Jesus Christ has restored the very dominion of man that had been plainly promised in Psalms 8 (one of our first vision passages). The price was high – Jesus set aside His innate powers and privileges (Phil 2:6), took on human flesh; denied Himself and obeyed the Father to the end; Finally, He took all sin upon Himself, "becoming" Sin itself. His purpose in that suffering is plainly stated here – to bring many Sons to glory; and He is not ashamed to call us His brothers, because we are born of the same Father and constituted by the same spirit.

Dignity and Dominion

Are you "just a poor sinner saved by grace"? *Not if you are saved*. If you are "in Christ', you are not merely deeply thankful for forgiveness of sins, but you no longer carry sin consciousness (1 Jn 2:1; Hebrews 9, Hebrews 10). You are a Son of God and brother of the Lord Jesus Christ (Hebrews 2). We must renew our minds to this!

You are the possessor of an unspeakable Dignity, and growing from glory to glory as you put sin to death and put on righteousness by the power of His righteousness in your nature; Once you know it, it dissolves any and all shame. No exceptions. The person that carried the wounds, the shame, the regrets, the errors … is dead and buried (John 3:14-15; 2 Cor 5:21). The Lord Jesus has given you beauty for ashes (Is 61). You are a beautiful new creation, patterned after God Himself (Eph 4:24). You have the power to deny the flesh and overcome the enemy (Rom 8:1-4, 13). Furthermore, you are complete in Him who is head over all rule and authority (Col 2:9). In your Union with both the Father and the Son you will do even greater works than Christ did (John 14:12).

(Dan 11:32) … those who know their God will be strong, and take action.

Bible Quotes are Word English Bible (WEB) except where noted.

Christ *Became* Sin
Then was Raised in Glory

Please do not be offended by this image. It honestly depicts what the innocent Jesus Christ became for us, *so that we might become His righteousness*. The Word of God states this plainly (2 Cor 5:21) and it is the very thing that sets us free (Rom 6:7) but it has been buried by the church.

The first two verses below provide the context – the meaning - for the most well-known verse in the entire Bible – and 99% are completely unaware of it:

(John 3:14-16) ***As Moses lifted up the serpent in the wilderness****, even so must the Son of Man be lifted up, that whoever believes in him should not perish, but have eternal life. For God so loved the world that He gave His only begotten Son, that whosoever believes in Him should not perish, but have eternal life.*

(2 Cor 5:14) For the love of Christ constrains us; because we judge thus, that one died for all, therefore all died.

Sown in Weakness and Shame

What's There to "See"?
More than "Sins Forgiven"

What did the Apostles see when they saw Jesus crucified? To gain the free-indeed, you must see more than just "sins forgiven"!

You must see the *enemy disabled*. You must see *your sin packed into Christ* (Isa 53, 2 Cor 5:21) and *destroyed*. You must *yourself* crucified (Gal 2:20).

Ransom Payment for All Sins of All Time

(Isa 52:13) Behold, my servant will deal wisely. He will be exalted and lifted up, and will be very high. Just as many were astonished at you (his appearance was marred more than any man, and his form more than the sons of men), so he will cleanse many nations. Kings will shut their mouths at him: for they will see that which had not been told them; and they will understand that which they had not heard.

The Liar, The Poisoner, the Accuser Crucified

(Numbers 21:9) Moses made a serpent of brass, and set it on a pole. If a serpent had bitten any man, when he looked at the serpent of brass, he lived.

"Sin in the Flesh" Crucified ... FREEDOM

(Rom 8:3-4) For what the Law couldn't do, in that it was weak through the flesh, God did, sending his own Son in the likeness of sinful flesh and for sin, he condemned sin in the flesh; that the ordinance of the Law might be fulfilled in us, who walk not after the flesh, but after the Spirit.

A Life-Exchange Offer

(2 Cor 5:14,21) ... that one died for all, therefore all died. He died for all, that those who live should no longer live to themselves, but for Him who for their sakes died and rose again ...
For him who knew no sin **he made be sin on our behalf***, so that in him we might become the righteousness of God.*

Bible Quotes are Word English Bible (WEB) except where noted.

Our Own Death – and this is Cause for Joy!

(Rom 6:3,7) Or don't you know that all we who were baptized into Christ Jesus were baptized into his death? ... For he who has died has been freed from sin.

Conversion experiences vary widely! But there are some aspects of this event that millions of Christians are never informed of.

A Forgiveness-Only Gospel, with or without Repentance

Many have heard a "Romans Road" version of salvation that makes it simply about payment for sins, with absolutely nothing said about the core purpose of that Blood, which was to ratify the New Covenant, which meets all the needs of man, beginning with restoration of companionship and indwelling.

If someone seeks the forgiveness of sins without the full intention of forsaking sin, there is simply no salvation there.

But "with" repentance – which is surrender of selfishness, to do the will of God by His power – there is true rebirth and true salvation. There is a change of nature, of innermost constitution.

When I must state the gospel in 30 seconds or less, I always start with:

> "If we will surrender our rebellion and forsake sin, then God will ..."

Some will see the crucified Christ; and will see that He died "for" them; In a quick moment they know that they know that their sins are forgiven because they have been "paid for". It is deep and massive relief!! As Jesus has said, "he who has been forgiven much, loves much".

But Jesus also said "He whom the Son sets free is free indeed". That person is no longer a sinner by nature; Nevertheless, they might live the rest of their life in defeat – *without victory over the compulsive power of sin.* Even if they are genuinely born again (converted), they will find an ***extremely frustrating experience***. As Steve Backlund has said: "If we *believe* we are *still sinners*, we will sin by faith!!!

Yet others also "see" that Christ died not only for them", but "as them"! They see that "the soul that sins shall die" (Levitcus17:11) ... and ...

> ***I just died***! ... Thank you, Jesus, and thank you Father!!!

> Now I shall be raised! As a son, I can ask and receive the promise (Gal 4).

Sown in Weakness and Shame

What a world of difference this makes! I experienced it in 1999, twenty years after my conversion and after twenty years of unnecessary misery (Rom 7:25).

As the popular song rightly says "I'll never know how much it cost to see my *sin* upon that cross" (Hillsong Worship). Notice that, in that stanza, "sin" is singular!!! It is the sin nature that was destroyed from our inner constitution! Consider the above passages with this in mind, and you just might feel it "break" in an instant. You must know it. Please gaze into it until you know it.

You will never be the same, I promise this; But more importantly, God promised it. It is "sins remembered no more" that we saw in Jeremiah; but it is also the "Heart of flesh" and the "My own Spirit in you" from Ezekiel.

When we preach a forgiveness-only gospel, we sell God short and we introduce people into lives of self-condemnation because they need to know that God has died "as" them to make them free to obey Him – and to do so without fear.

Bible Quotes are Word English Bible (WEB) except where noted.

Christ: The Bread of Life
Let's Be *Nourished* by Him!

*John 6:28 They said therefore to him, "What must we do, that we may **work the works of God?"** ...*

(John 6:31-54) 31 Our fathers ate the manna in the wilderness. As it is written, 'He gave them bread out of heaven to eat.'" 32 Jesus therefore said to them, "Most certainly, I tell you, it wasn't Moses who gave you the bread out of heaven, but my Father gives you the true bread out of heaven. For the bread of God is that which comes down out of heaven and gives life to the world." 34 They said therefore to him, "Lord, always give us this bread." 35 Jesus said to them, "I am the bread of life. Whoever comes to me will not be hungry, and whoever believes in me will never be thirsty.

40 This is the will of the one who sent me, that everyone who sees the Son, and believes in him, should have eternal life; and I will raise him up at the last day." ...

44 No one can come to me unless the Father who sent me draws him, and I will raise him up in the last day... Most certainly, I tell you, he who believes in me has eternal life. I am the bread of life. Your fathers ate the manna in the wilderness, and they died. This is the bread which comes down out of heaven, that anyone may eat of it and not die.

51 I am the living bread which came down out of heaven. If anyone eats of this bread, he will live forever. Yes, the bread which I will give for the life of the world is my flesh." 52 The Jews therefore contended with one another, saying, "How can this man give us his flesh to eat?"

53 Jesus therefore said to them, "Most certainly I tell you, unless you eat the flesh of the Son of Man and drink his blood, you don't have life in yourselves. 54 He who eats my flesh and drinks my blood has eternal life, and I will raise him up at the last day.

Sown in Weakness and Shame

Be Nourished
The Sacrificial Lamb of God

They wanted Dominion immediately "added to them", but it would require a different kind of nourishment; a different kind of "Life".

We can multiply the reference "John 3:14-16" (from the preceding spread) times two to get "John 6:28-32". John 6 explains what the wandering Israelites saw that saved them, and it also explains what we are to see in the crucifixion.

In the Numbers 21 passage the Israelites were complaining about the food – the "manna from Heaven"; but then many found healing – in both souls and bodies – by seeing that sin itself had been destroyed and finding life by knowing it.

Let's say that you have worked your body into exhaustion, and then you are treated to a meal that recharges you, nourishes you, and you quickly recover your strength.

The bread-side of communion (representing the body of Christ) is our "eating of the flesh" of the Son of Man to find the life of His body, giving healing to our bodies (Rom 8:11). The wine-side of communion represents the Innocent Blood of Christ shed – for the nourishment and restoration of our souls.

But the very core of reunion with God is the New Covenant itself (Ezek 36; Jer 31; Isa 49; numerous others). Abraham saw that covenant ceremony in advance, and rejoiced that he might see the day of it (John 8:56).

Blood Covenants

A "Blood Covenant" is the most solemn and permanent *mutual* commitment two parties can make. It is understood in most cultures outside of America.

There is always the shedding of blood; sometimes the mingling of blood; there are promises for those who are faithful; there are penalties for those who are not; there are gifts exchanged; there are representatives (possibly sons of the kings or chiefs, signifying that it applies to generations).

Jesus plainly stated that He ratified that Covenant by His own blood:

> *"This is my blood of the New covenant" (Matt 26:38)*

We see the mingling of natures (Son of Man with Son of God; 2 Peter 1:3-4); we also see echoes of the sacrificial lamb of the Passover (Exodus).

> *"He who eats my flesh and drinks my blood lives in me, and I in him. As the living Father sent me, and I live because of*

> Bible Quotes are Word English Bible (WEB) except where noted.
> *the Father; so, he who feeds on me, he will also live because of me. This is the bread which came down out of heaven—not as our fathers ate the manna, and died. He who eats this bread will live forever." (John 6:56-58)*

Almost all cultures know of these blood covenants even today – *except Western European and North American cultures*; That is, *us*. The United States is known as the foremost "freedom and independence" culture in the World; this is because even the president is (theoretically) bound by a law that is higher than the king.

We here celebrate independence – and mutual commitment has been eclipsed by a notion of *freedom* that eventually enslaves people and *betrays* them; it leaves them … *alone* (John 12:24).

But Christ calls you back into union with God – with the utmost peace and rest and joy, with protection and provision. That is the Good News.

So, we see that the Blood of Christ is not merely about forgiveness, but about the enactment of the New Covenant; and the Covenant **_in turn_** brings far more benefits than forgiveness alone. A Covenant with God, with Christ as the mediator of that Covenant, fully meets every need a human has, only beginning with reconciliation with God and the restoration of our nature (Eph 4:24).

And yet again – *Blood Covenant* is <u>one more element</u> at the center of the Gospel – at the heart of Christianity itself … but I myself never heard of it *in "church"*. This underscores how far "cultural Christianity" has drifted from the true and full Gospel.

If we are "in Christ" we are surrendered to do the will of God and we are first fully washed – forgiven of all past sins – at the point of our surrender, our turn of allegiance. Then, we get foot-washings by Christ – as needed. We have the power of Christ in us to put sin to death. It is *possible* to *never sin again* once we are born again and filled with the Spirit of Christ…

… but that never happens.

When we *follow* Christ, we are walking in a *process* – our spirits are already perfected, but we are *dismantling* the sin residue in our souls by *His power* (that's how it is grace, 2 Peter 1:3-4). It is not automatic! No true believer practices sin, but we all during this process will fail in weakness. We confess our sin and Christ is faithful to forgive us and to *cleanse us from all unrighteousness*. That is the continuing advocate work of Jesus Christ the Righteous (1 John 2:1). The spilling of Christ's blood as a legal act ratifying the New Covenant (Matt 26:28) and the destruction of His body (with our sin packed into it) – *both happened "once for all time"* (Heb 7:27; 10:10), but the application of it proceeds.

To eat of the body of Christ and drink of His blood is to be nourished in body and soul by them, as an ongoing way of Life. When we discover this "bread that satisfies" (Isa 55) we will "proclaim (publicly announce) His *death* until He comes" (1 Cor 11:26)!

Bible Quotes are Word English Bible (WEB) except where noted.

The Hour Has Come
For Union – *"One as We are One"*

(John 17:1-23) Jesus said these things, and lifting up his eyes to heaven, he said: "Father, the time has come. <u>Glorify your Son, that Your Son may also glorify You</u>, ...

15 I pray not that you would take them from the world, but that You would keep them from the evil one. They are not of the world, even as <u>I am not of the world</u>.

[JF: This is the Second mankind; no more a sinner by essential nature]

<u>Sanctify them in your truth. Your word is truth</u>. *As You sent me into the world, even so I have sent them into the*

world. And for their sakes I sanctify Myself, <u>that they themselves also may be sanctified in the truth</u>. ...

20 "Not for these only do I pray, but for those also who will believe in me through their word; <u>that they may all be one, as You, Father, are in me, and I in you; that they also may be one in us</u>, that the world may believe that you sent Me. **<u>The glory which you have given me I have given them,</u>** *that they may be one even as we are one: I in them, and you in me; that <u>they may be perfected into one</u>, and that the world may know that sent me, and have loved them even as you loved Me. "Father, I desire that they also whom you have given me <u>may be with me where I am, that they may see my glory which you have given me</u>;*

for you loved me before the foundation of the world. Righteous

*Father, the world hasn't known You, but I knew you; and these knew that You sent Me. <u>I made known to them your name</u>, and will make it known, that the love with which you loved me may be in them, **<u>and I in them</u>**."*

Sown in Weakness and Shame

Fully at Peace,
But with Staggering Implications

This passage is worth "careful and prayerful" consideration, study, and meditation, Because Jesus Christ (not just "Jesus") is describing the nature of our union with the Father and its relationship to peace and joy and power and **glory**.

Yes, church!! I said that last word; hear it rightly and clearly (Romans 2:7). The *glory* He calls us to is not the wicked personal pride of mere-humans (1 Cor 3:1-3); Rather it is that of those that have been borne of God and are manifesting His nature (2 Pet 1:4) having escaped the corruption of the contaminated lineage.

Notice the glorifying that is happening, and it is not just between the Father and Jesus. The Lord Jesus sanctifies us (sets apart for service to God) by sanctifying Himself, and He "has glorified" man.

But what are the Father and the Son – by the Spirit - really doing? I believe Jesus is saying – among other things – that:

1. They are "enjoying" fellowship (Gen 2; 1 John; Rev 22).
2. They are "enjoying victorious battle" crushing the head of the enemy (Luke 10:19; Psalm 8:6; Hebrews 2:6).

Without knowing where we sit in the unseen (Eph 1:20-23), what I am telling you would be nonsense; But it's there. I thought it was foolishness until I experienced it firsthand in my daughter's constructive miracle. This occurred when I was given a 5-second dream showing wholeness and joy; I awoke and spoke: "I want that". I have not "mastered" this walk by any stretch; Nevertheless, I have "Tasted of the powers of the age to come" (Heb 6).

Imagine the joy of *routine victory as we grow strong*. We never see Christ stressed out over anything except over anticipation of the crucifixion, the bearing of our sin and sickness and death (Isa 53) – actually *becoming Sin* – and being *Forsaken* by the Father. Accordingly – The New Covenant provides that we would be restored to *Union with God* and *become His righteousness*. It is to be what we are. NOT "poor sinners" any longer!

The walk of Christ was the walk of a victor at all times, as John G. Lake described:

Bible Quotes are Word English Bible (WEB) except where noted.
"God's son, man's servant, and the devils master"[5]

… and we are all called to brow up into the _measure of that stature_ (Eph 4:13).

The Old Testament saints did exploits by the power of God "upon them" or "with them", but not "in" them. But as we just saw in John 14, the fullness of God is – finally – "in us". What will we do with so great a salvation?

It is the mystery hidden through the ages. It is the ambush of all time, and we are invited to step into it and enjoy it as our own; We are also commanded – and nevertheless _privileged_ – to announce to all that they are welcome to participate.

The dance is a joy to the strong; but many spend their lifetimes in Bible studies alone, waiting to be ready. A student when He is fully **_trained_** (not just indoctrinated) will be like His trainer (Matt.10). Bible study is good, but if it is a lifestyle that is "instead of obeying the command to go and make disciples", it is simply advanced disobedience dressed up as religiousness. I know, I've been there! It had me sidelined or defeated for decades.

Let me say this another way: Training and learning is good, but if my "Bible study" is **_instead of undoing the work of the enemy in real life_**, then I am deceived.

"But _we're only human_, and Jesus was _God_, right?" Wrong.

A Christian has been born of God (John 1:14) and is no longer a mere human (1 Cor 3:1-3); Christ emptied Himself of his inherent divine powers (Phil 2:6) to become truly man by constitution… He operated as "a man in whom the fullness of God was pleased to dwell". That is the "Second Adam", right there (1 Cor 15)!

> _(Col 2:9) For in Him dwells all the fullness of the Godhead bodily; and **you** are complete in Him, who is the head of all principality and power._

The ... Dance

I've been aware of the "dance" notion of the Trinity (Greek _perichoresis_) in John 17 for a few years; but recently I heard a wonderful elaboration of it by Malcolm Smith[6]. As with a folk dance, different partners take turns sending and

---

[5] John G. Lake. I find no record of anyone in history outside the Bible that walked so plainly as Christ walked. And he did so simply by rejecting the traditions of man (which justified unbelief and disobedience) and by obeying the Word of God.

[6] I believe this was in "Knowing What You Are" part 2 on YouTube (a wonderful series!)

going; they invite each other out; All know the dance; all thoroughly enjoy it; and there is no limit to the energy supply!

Seriously, we know that our part in this dance includes stepping on the neck of the enemy, exactly as Jesus demonstrated (all gospels); authorized (Mt 28:18), equipped (Acts 2), and sent (Jn 20:21). The Father had Christ sit at His right hand until He makes His enemies His footstool (through us, His Body on Earth). If the Spirit of God is in us as we go, we should find that the enemy cannot harm us at all (Luke 10:19). I get the image of those square dancers doing their thing, with different partners stepping forward but also sending forward, … and STOMPING with joy! Regardless of the extent to which the "dance" analogy applies, clearly, we are born to be active, be overcomers, operate in freedom and unity; and our victory brings joy to the Father and to the Firstborn Son.

Suppose a few dozen people of various race and ethnicity simply gather together as sons and daughters of God agreeing with God for the advancement of His Kingdom on Earth. They *bear the image of God* through true surrender to Him and are actively doing His will; not merely as "saved people thanking Him for forgiveness", but as "a people re-presenting God in the face of the enemy"! People will see not only the glory of selflessness – *goodness*; but also, they will see frequent demonstrations of the liberating power of God that the church has in the past demonstrated only "now and then".

Of course, we of the Second mankind are not God – not eternal, omniscient, omnipresent, nor omnipresent. But we don't have to be those thongs to overcome the enemy. We need merely to be seated in authority far above that enemy – and to renew our minds to it – and walk in it.

It's mind-blowing, but true. If we will bring shed our unbelief we will bring on, in the face of the enemy, not just the cloud of witnesses, but the cloud of warriors that know who has sent them. And they will know the joy of battle. Sons of God will *multiply* as their fruit is borne and abides. Converts will mature in months, not years because they know something of the unseen, and they are not bound by tradition; and they are not in it for "fire-insurance". The power of testimony accumulates and their minds are renewed quickly.

The scriptures show that the "dance" of glory has many types of steps – but all of them include a trampling of the enemy. Millions will flock to the true Church in joy as they see it. The Good News we must hear is *a call from God* saying (among other things), "Shall we Dance?". It will be though the Church, when the Church manifests.

Bible Quotes are Word English Bible (WEB) except where noted.

Reuniting Us with God
Completing the Mission

Mary Magdalene was the First witness to what Christ had Accomplished

---

Not Just *Buried* with Him;
Not Just *Raised* with Him;
But *Ascended* and **United** with **God**

Fulfilling

the Central element of the New Covenant

(John 17) Jesus said to her, "Do not hold me, for I have not yet ascended to My Father; but go to my brothers and say to them,

> 'I am ascending
> to my Father and your Father,
> to my God and your God.'"

Sown in Weakness and Shame

"We" Were Raised To "My Father & Your Father"

Notice the Quotes within the Quotes

If the quote marks were not there, then Jesus would be telling Mary to tell the others that He was ascending. But that is in fact not what the passage says. But the quote marks _are_ there – check it out! You can see them in your own Bible. No responsible translator dares to omit the inner quotes.

Because the quote marks are there, we see that Jesus is telling Mary to tell the original Good News _from her own perspective_. After all – Jesus was raised _for "us"_!

The first believers believed – rightly – that they had been disconnected and estranged from God and that the resurrection and ascension of Christ brought us back to union with God. That is the Joy of the Resurrection and Ascension.

If we don't see it, then we go through Easter after Easter saying "He is Risen" with a secret confusion wondering: "but that's _Hiim_ – **what about … US**?".

If we don't see this, we sit defeated, still in prison, trying to get through life staying thankful for forgiveness alone. We must know that Christ carried us.

Ephesians 1:19 combined with Ephesians 2:6 together show that we were ascended and seated with Him. _This is the central fact of our authority in Christ_, yet it is not taught in the vast majority of Western churches.

The High Priestly Prayer of Christ

Note the easy address-memory trick – "17:20" and "20:17" (close enough).

John chapter 20 could be the "heaviest" prayer in the Bible. Here, just before His crucifixion, Christ declares with His mouth the joy that is set before Him; He is bringing squarely before His mind the fact that He shall see the fruit of the travail of His soul and be satisfied (Isa 53). He of course anticipates the joy of _returning_ to the Father, but in particular He is declaring the agreement the Father has made with the Son: _To bring us into the very Union that they enjoyed with each other_.

Christ – by very identity – always was and always will be, God. But in His love for us, He has ensured that Man is also now on the throne – to _reign with and under Him_ (Rom 5:17; Dan 7:27; Rev 22:5; 1 Tim 2:5). Can you handle the depths of His kindness? See His kindness in restoring authority over the work of the true enemy. Come on in! the Water is Fine!

Bible Quotes are Word English Bible (WEB) except where noted.

Finally, With Us in Him
"Seated" ... Where?

(Ephesians 1:18-23) Having the eyes of your hearts enlightened; that you may know what is the hope of his calling, and what are the riches of the glory of his inheritance in the saints, and what is the exceeding greatness of his power toward us who believe, according to that working of the strength of his might which he worked in Christ, when He raised him from the dead and <u>made him to sit at his right hand in the heavenly places, far above all rule, and authority, and power, and dominion, and every name that is named, not only in this age but also in that which is to come.</u>

He put all things in subjection under His feet, and gave Him to be head over all things for the assembly, which is His body, the fullness of him who fills all in all.

(Ephesians 2:5-7) even when we were dead through our trespasses, made us alive together with Christ (by grace you have been saved), and <u>raised us up with him</u>, and <u>made us to sit with him in the heavenly places in Christ Jesus</u>, that in the ages to come he might show the exceeding riches of His grace in kindness toward us in Christ Jesus.

Far Above Every Name
The Ultimate Kindness

Where are you <u>Now</u> Seated? For what Purpose?

Popular Evangelical Christianity always starts with Eph 2:8, but the true Gospel of the Kingdom would never bypass (Eph 2:6-7). The man or woman that can handle this truth falls to their knees in thanksgiving and gets the breakthrough in this life. The full manifestation of that glory awaits the age to come (Rev 19), **but the signs follow <u>all who believe</u> in <u>this</u> age**.

To transition from the "poor sinner", "worm in the dust", begging and pleading – to one who is buried, raised, ascended, reconciled, reunited, and ***<u>seated-far-above</u>*** – is the definitive inflection point of mind renewal. It is the difference between the mind of the first Adam and the mind of Christ. A Christian is one that belongs to the Most High and knows the rights and privileges of being a true Son.

> "Believe" (Greek *pisteuo – look it up*) in most instances should have been rendered "entrust" or "obey" if you want your New Testament to actually make sense. Likewise, "faith" in many places should be "**allegiance**" or "**fidelity**". "Believe" came from Anglo "Be" meaning "to live" and "Saxon "Lefan" meaning "accordingly". See this and the Bible makes much more sense!

This goes to the mission of Christ to restore us to dominion on the Earth. We are seated with Christ as His body, in Christ, at the right hand of the Father. All things are under His feet, and we are His body so, all things are under our feet (Ps. 8). These are all "truths" which will eventually overrun "facts", changing those facts. We renew our minds to the truth, and we increasingly come to be able to demand that things be bound on Earth as they are in Heaven, that is, bound into the visible World as they are in the unseen realm.

No More Begging & Pleading from Earth to Heaven

This is one of the most mind-blowing passages in the Bible. But among other things it is perhaps the one NT passage that goes most directly to our overcoming evil spirits. Those that set out in diligent mind renewal will begin to do exploits, ejecting evil spirits from themselves and from those they love. The dignity of our being seated with Christ obliterates all issues of self-esteem. But the gaining of authority over even the highest-ranking evil spirits means that we are able to *<u>reject</u>* – and *<u>evict</u>* – all anxiety and depression. This is legally based on the standing we gain by the forgiveness of sins, bought by the innocent blood of Christ. But its *<u>purpose</u>* is *<u>peace</u>* by *<u>restored dominion</u>*.

Ambush Completed
Rulers are Coming to Nothing

(1 Corinthians 2:6-8) However, we speak wisdom ... not of this world, nor of <u>the rulers of this world, who are coming to nothing</u>.

But we speak the wisdom of God in a mystery, the hidden wisdom which God ordained before the world <u>for our glory</u>,

... which none of the rulers of this world knew; for had they known,
<u>*they would not have crucified the Lord of glory.*</u>

On Our Behalf,
The Greatest Victory of All Time

Why are the teachings of Christ in the *Gospels*, so seemingly different that the teachings in the *epistles*? Christ had to keep certain strategic truths of His ambush "veiled" until the enemy made the fateful mistake of crucifying Him.

There is "a wisdom" that is the birthright of every Son of God. That wisdom is embedded into the DNA of those born of God. We have the Mind of Christ (1 Cor 2:16). Yet, it is not "being born of God" that brings it to our *consciousness*, but rather this Wisdom is *spoken among the mature*, to those that renew their minds to the whole staggering truth.

God is glorified in His Kindness Toward Us (Eph 2:7)

For what purpose, and for whose benefit, was this wisdom ordained? The passage plainly states that it was established "for our glory". We are to accept it with humility and joy – and be transformed!

The Second Cosmic Class Action Lawsuit

The Consequences of the First Adam's *Rebellion* was applied to us like a class action lawsuit. Likewise, the Awards of the Second Adam's *Obedience* are applied to us like that of a class action lawsuit. The awards of that ruling are the covenant gifts; and these gifts include *His very presence and nature in us!* This particular gift is the mystery hidden through the ages; but it is ours now, to know and to have; to live by forever.

In this consciousness, we know that He shall reign forever and ever, and "we" shall also reign with Him and under Him forever and ever (Dan 7:27, Rev 22). We know our Father; We know the Firstborn Son; and we know that our heritage is to *bring the rulers of this present age to nothing*.

It has already been enacted legally; It is already happening in the unseen; and the first fruits of it were and are demonstrated in the enemy's face on the Earth in this age (which is coming to a close).

Section Summary: That's Where We Are to Follow

Now, we have all the details of what Christ meant when He said, "follow me". Let's take the brief tour again:

Bible Quotes are Word English Bible (WEB) except where noted.

Christ Went Before Us

Representatives – Guarantors, usually sons – in this case Christ on both sides – Son of Man and Son of God.

Consider Christ's death, burial, resurrection, ascension, enthronement, and sending.

Death and Burial

Christ's **_Death_** triggered an unstoppable Journey that became the greatest Ambush of all time – on our behalf. We are to embrace the whole ambush and live from it

Christ's death was the required "Blood sacrifice" of that **_New Covenant_** – the **_"Christ In us" Covenant_**. When Christ died, He was not innocent, because **_He was Us_**. He had *become sin* (2 Cor 5:21a). For legal purposes, it was in fact our blood if we identify with Him. The soul that sins shall die, and He died AS us. Are we OK with that?

He also **died and was buried** with us in Him, breaking the Power of the Sin Nature that was our DNA (Rom 6). He who has died has been freed from sin (Rom 6:7). Just as Pharoah's army perished in the Sea behind Israel, the power of Sin over us is broken and we are transferred into a new jurisdiction.

Resurrection

He also was **_raised_** **from among the dead** with us in Him ("We is Risen!!"). At that time, _we had become the righteousness of God_ (2 Cor 5:21b). When He was raised, the point was not merely to get us back to the surface of the Earth "on our feet". Anyone that stops at the surface of the Earth will be grateful but will certainly not experience reigning in Life" (Rom 5:17).

So still, He had further to go, with Us in Him, but His death had made the way.

Ascension

When He was raised, He had further to go with Us in Him. *He **ascended** with Us in Him*. He carried us to the Father for reconciliation. Can you say along with Mary Magdalene: 'I am ascending to my Father and your Father, to my God and Your God!' (Jn 20:17). That was the original Good News. Will you identify with His ascension?

Still, He had further to go, with Us in Him, because His death made the way.

Upon arriving to the Father, He was **_enthroned_**, seated at the right hand of the Father, receiving all honor and glory – with us in Him (Eh 2:6).

Finally, to Send That Which Was Promised

Many Christians can name some promises, but cannot identify "The" Promise.

Many Christians can name some spiritual gifts, but cannot identify "The" Gift.

Christ and the Father would then *__jointly send the Holy Spirit__* – of Love and Power into those who Entrust their lives into Him-To Walk as Sons and daughters of the living God, to serve Him without fear. We are to Love as he Loved – as man's servant – to continue His ministry on the Earth and a liberator on His behalf, until He returns.

> In sending His Spirit into us His second-born Sons – God in Christ fulfills the New Covenant as plainly stated by Ezekiel 36, Jeremiah 31, and elsewhere.

So, we who have received the abundance of Grace and the gift of righteousness are to reign in life (Rom 5:17), being like Him (1 Jn 4:17). All because He who knew no sin became Sin so that **we might become the Righteousness of God** (2 Cor 5:17). We become image-bearers once again. Notice, this addresses the second half of Romans 3:23 All have sinned and *fall short of the glory of God*. I have seen not a single gospel tract that actually addresses that problem. But God has addressed it. He redeems the sinner not only from what he has done", but also *from what he is*. Glory to Christ, who brings many sons to glory (Heb 2).

Now that we have seen where Christ went with us in Him (if we surrender into Him), we can also see that Communion – more than anything else, is a celebration of *"Union"*! Union not only in His death, but His life!

This life is a life of "first-fruits" that foreshadow the restoration of all things (Acts 3:21) Pet). When all Christ's enemies have become His footstool. Meanwhile, in this age, you and I are called to live as slaves to righteousness – chains of sin are broken, and the yoke is easy. As we shall see, even as we set out to walk with Him, we begin to see God crushing Satan under our feet.

Bible Quotes are Word English Bible (WEB) except where noted.

PART 6:
OUR INITIAL SURRENDER - ENTERING INTO HIM

In this tier "we" are simply choosing to follow Christ NOT to just "get saved" – which is the "rescue" aspect of having past sins wiped off of our records – but also to experience being adopted sons of God; to experience unmistakable companionship with Him, and to become free from all guilt and shame; To have both the desire and the ability to serve God without fear.

In the unseen World, we are merely going <u>where He has gone</u> – through death (being freed from sin, as we shall see), into both resurrection and ascension to **union with the Father**; Only after this will we be able to "walk as He walked".

As with the first tier, I urge you to study the passages and the headings until you can "state" the panel in your own words, rightly dividing the scriptures. Seek to make it "as simple as possible but no simpler" (A. Einstein). Eventually you should be able to naturally state the gist of each of these key passages.

Anyone that has gotten this far in this book is hungry for God; Therefore, I fully expect that as you form your statements, you will become very aware that God – in Christ – is calling you to follow Christ deeper in His death and burial; and higher in His resurrection, so to speak. As we renew our minds into these truths, we experience the times of refreshing (Acts 3:19).

Getting Right with God
Stakes Could Not Be Higher

"Christ in You" Opposes Religious Culture

We humans (a) have a strong tendency to insist that our parents or pastors could not possibly be wrong; and (b) may recoil against the thought of falling out of the graces of our current fellowship. Therefore, for our own sake, we must resist every tendency to morph the scriptures into the narrative of a tradition.

If our tradition is correct, we will see that it is correct and will be glad we were taught correctly; But if it contradicts the plain and pervasive assertions of the e Word of God… Who will we choose? The stakes could not possibly be higher!

A Common and Beautiful Scenario

But the promise of our becoming like Him should overcome our hesitation. If we choose to obey God, not man, then we are *suddenly liberated* and the transformation quickly follows if we will simply cooperate with the promised and delivered power of God – and the mercy of God. We are transformed to the image of the firstborn from among the dead (Col 1, Rev 1).

And then our family and friends will notice it – they will inevitably have to then ask, "what do I want to become? If they then hunger for righteousness – not just amnesty; and the they – like you - will be filled, and never hunger again.

Entering Into Him – Accepting Your Disappearance

To become "In Christ" – to "be saved" - is to reject yourself and be content to belong to this King. In this sense you accept your disappearance and your right to a superior reputation. You do this because Christ has promised that if you do, then you will share in His present indwelling Life and yu will also share in His future glory (Col 3:3).

You will triumph. You will step on the serpent's head and neck even in this life.

If you remain in Him then He remains in you. His Spirit sets you free and transforms you as you learn from Him (Mt 28). You fear melts away as you become a friend of God, and know it.

This panel describes how, in true freedom, we must respond to the love and mercy of God demonstrated in Christ in order to be made right with God.

Bible Quotes are Word English Bible (WEB) except where noted.

A Turn of Allegiance
To Seek the Kingdom of God

God's sons, man's Servants, and devil's masters (John G. Lake)

(Matthew 9:37) Then He said to His disciples, "The harvest indeed is plentiful, but the laborers are few.

(Matthew 10:1) He called ... his twelve disciples, and gave them authority over unclean spirits, to cast them out, and to heal every disease and every sickness ...

7 As you go, preach, saying, 'The kingdom of heaven is at hand!' Heal the sick, cleanse the lepers, cast out demons. Freely you received, so freely give.

Allegiance: The essential "Faith"

Saving Faith (pistis) = Faithfulness = Allegiance. <u>Exchange</u> ... <u>Not Earning!</u>

To Be "In" Christ is to be doing His will in our own name - rather than going our own way in our own name

And you will be hated by all men for my name's sake.

But he who endures to the end will be saved.

"A disciple is not above his teacher, nor a servant above his lord. It is enough for a disciple that he be like his teacher, and a servant like his lord..."

"Everyone therefore who confesses me before men, him I will also confess before My Father who is in heaven. But whoever denies Me before men, him I will also deny before My Father who is in heaven..."

He who doesn't take his cross and follow after me is not worthy of me. He who seeks his life will lose it, and he who loses his life for My sake will find it.

Sown in Weakness and Shame

See His Glory and Make the Trade

If any would come after, let him deny himself (Mt 16:24)

Life-Exchange followed by obedience, is the "Red Pill" of True Christianity (Analogy from *The Matrix*). Neo (New) represents the New Man that will not be enslaved even if the truth is going to destroy all his plans. He accepts the red pill; sees the *illusion* of freedom he has lived under; gets his new operating system and has to install the new apps to renew His mind; and he <u>goes back out to do what he is supposed to do</u>. We are to bear the Image of God once again (1 Jn 4:17) with the same Spirit having been breathed into *us* (Jn 20:22). But somehow, amazingly, many, many millions in America have been trained to expect only forgiveness, and the joy of it souring as we find we need the same forgiveness for the same sin with no actual liberation year after year. That's not Christianity. More to the point – *that's Not the Image of God (and Christ showed us the Father).*

In the Word of God, we see commands and demands that seem very unreasonable, *in fact plainly impossible for mere humans* – those of the First Mankind.

The Good News is that the First Mankind doesn't have to do it. The Love of God gets big here. **Christ crucified and buried was just the massive legal groundwork.**

The Good News is that there is a Second Mankind that desires to obey God and *can obey God* and *derives its Joy and Dignity by partaking in the nature of God*; The Second Mankind finds his intended place of Dominion. It is peace that comes through overwhelming superiority of power. Accept this and your Bible makes sense.

Nobody Doesn't Want Dominion.

All cultures, with the notable exception of America, know exactly what a Blood Covenant is. It is the strongest bond of commitment man can conceive of and can make to another man or tribe; it is the means by which the weak gain the alliance with the strong, and by which the strong obtain the allegiance of the weak.

We intuitively know that man should have authority on earth, but somehow, man got locked into a trajectory of death. We were all born losers as regards inevitable decay. None of us in our right minds, doesn't want dominion restored; We seek the restoration of that dominion, of that glory, looking for a strong one that invites alliance in exchange for our allegiance.

Now, let me clarify – many, many Americans now indeed have learned what a blood covenant is, but they are sworn to secrecy of it, under the wrong priest.

Sadly, the church has been taught – by omission – to be silent on the "Gospel of the Kingdom" and the High Priest of its Blood Covenant. But Christ's invitation stands.

Our Motive: To Regain That which was Lost

We have seen the glory of the one and only; the Firstborn Son of God, and He invites us to not merely "believe" in Him for forgiveness; He invites – even requires – that we come after Him (Matthew 16; Mark 8; Luke 9).

More than any two-word phrase, He said "Follow Me".

He is seeing the fruit of the travail of His soul (Isa 53). He is no longer the *One and Only* (Heb 2).

If you gaze into the truth of that invitation, and see it for what it means. Then you understand "the hope in which you are saved" (Romans 8:24).

Yet the real question is: "Will you make the trade?"

The Catch – the Stumbling Block for Some

The catch is, the New Mankind is *obtained only by exchange*, that is, the exchange of the First Mankind for the Second Mankind – a conversion of our innermost nature. Not an exchange of *our souls* (our personalities), but of *what we are*. Our redeemed personalities emerge afterwards, re-growing from the converted man.

For the proud, the trade-in requirement is *bad news*. If I am proud of my achievements, my wealth, my power, my reputation, then I – I my blindness – "have so much to lose". If I have invested my life to attain these things, then it is the "sunken investment" fallacy. It is the lie that says the value of thing equals what you have spent on it. No! If my life is divorced from the life of God, then it *is not life at all*.

Knowing that will set you free as soon as you realize you get to trade it in.

Therefore, *the humble hear it and are glad* as they have nothing to lose! If the Son sets you free, you are free indeed (Jn 8:36). Let's receive freedom, and use that freedom to serve God without fear. Let's serve Him with the fulness of His own strength, dignity, and joy.

Bible Quotes are Word English Bible (WEB) except where noted.

If Any Man Would Come After Me ...

*(Matthew 16:24-27) ... "If **anyone** desires to come after Me, let him **deny himself**, and take up his cross, and follow Me.*

For whoever desires to save his life will lose it, but whoever loses his life for My sake will find it.

For what profit is it to a man if he gains the whole world, and loses his own soul? Or what will a man give in exchange for his soul?

For the Son of Man will come in the glory of His Father with His angels, and then

He will reward each according to his deeds.

Let Him!
Jesus Has Said It Plainly

God is Love personified. God is the Father of Lights, in whom there is no darkness at all.

The Lord Jesus is the image of the Father, and has made Him known. If in God there is no darkness but only light, then I suggest we believe Jesus when He says "if *any* man"!

What to "Believe" to Be Saved

In exactly the same way that *pistis* has been erroneously translated to "faith" nearly everywhere it occurs, the verbo form of the same word, *pisteuo*, has been erroneously translated "believe" nearly everywhere it occurs.

But there are a few correct translations of pisteuo to "entrust to", or "commit to". Here is one:

> *2 Timothy 1:13 ... I ...am persuaded that He is able to keep what I have committed to Him until that Day.*
>
> *Romans 4:18-21 Who ..., in hope believed, so that he became the father of many nations, ... and being fully convinced that what He had promised He was also able to perform.*

To Follow Christ is to Commit Ourselves to Him

This is another massive Puzzle Piece Drop! Consider "Follow Me".

These words of Christ are the most quoted in the Gospels and the least Quoted in false churches. See Matt 4, Matt 8, Matt 10, Matt 16, Matt 19, Mark 1, Mark 2, Mark 8, Mark 10, Luke 9, John 1, John 10, John 12, John 13, John 21.

It is actually the truth that makes us free! Who would want to suppress this? The answer should be obvious.

Bible Quotes are Word English Bible (WEB) except where noted.

The Way to Glory
Passes through Self-Denial

I realize that our flesh can be desperate to deny this, but it is the Word of our Lord. Therefore, I will not dance around it as nearly all of today's bible tracts do.

For I consider that the sufferings of this present time are not worthy to be compared with the glory which will be revealed toward us.

(Romans 8:18)

Hope-Based Faith Overcomes

But we can take heart, because God has produced for us "hope" that is sufficient to overcome even the very hardest decision points.

We can seek to save our lives, the going of our own way, the doing of our own wills; But we will then lose it all. But without receiving His nature inside us, every "good" thing we try to do is still fruit of the wrong tree, and utterly unacceptable to God.

Now here is the response Christ seeks from us; I will say it from a few different angles.

Self-Will Resists!
But His Death Made a Way

By the grace of God that has appeared (Titus 2; John 1) we can recognize our core problem of *self-will* that is at our core. We can cast ourselves before His mercy, and trade in our futile lives for His wonderful nature. A true salvation is a transfer of allegiance from self (and the lineage of rebellious mankind) to the Second Man, the Last Adam; the King of Kingdom that shall not be destroyed.

Every human will have either retained his own fallen nature and done evil, or exchanged their lives for the Life of God inside them and practiced obeying His command to love.

We must trade our defeated lives for His life of strength. In the Greek, the term beneath "Lose" (*Luo*) means to "destroy" or "kill". Gal 5:24 tells that those that are "In Christ" have crucified the flesh with its selfish desires – Identifying with John 3:**14**. It is losing your life *to become like Him* (1 Jn 4:17).

It yields a life of peace and joy because if we set out to obey Him, we obtain His life inside us and we get to see Him and know him (Ezek. 36:25-27; Jn 14:19,23).

When Christ returns, He will reward every man for what He has done – and this passage – the most-repeated words of Christ "lose your life to find it" – tell us what we must do. But we do this with an act of *identification*; See John 3;16 and John 3:31, but only after seeing John 3:14-15 and 2 Corinthians 5:21. We are to see ourselves crucified with Christ and ***become the righteousness of God*** in innermost constitution.

Bible Quotes are Word English Bible (WEB) except where noted.

The Way is Now Open
to Escape & Partake

What is the "Free Gift" of Romans 6:23?
Answer: Everything We Need for Life and Godliness

(2 Peter 1:3-4) Seeing that his divine power has given to us all things that pertain to life and godliness,

through the knowledge of Him who called us by his own glory and virtue,

by which he has granted to us his precious and exceedingly great promises, that through these

---

you may become partakers of the divine nature, having escaped from the corruption that is in the world through lust.

Sown in Weakness and Shame

Greatest Promise
Never Heard In Most Churches
Many Sell Fire Insurance; Many Buy It

But Christ provides both power and desire – New Spirit, New Heart, Indwelling!

If Christ only purchased our forgiveness, then sadly we would experience relief *only until our next irresistible sin*. But the good news commonly omitted, is that Christ **purchased our escape from the power of sin**, and He purchased for us the right to become the Sons of God, partaking in His very nature.

If a Christian has escaped the power of sin, they will have the massive dose of dignity that changes everything. This level of Freedom is your "death-right" (to escape the chains of sin) and your birthright (to live the Zoe life of God).[7] If a Christian has begun experiencing partaking in the divine nature, they will never, ever again have a self-esteem problem.[8,9]

Christ is the Firstborn from among the dead, not the only-born (Col1:15), bringing many Sons to Glory, and He is not ashamed to call you and me His brothers (Heb 2:10) if you have been born of the same Spirit.

Called By His Glory and To His Glory

He calls us "by" His glory and virtue. Some manuscripts actually say "to" (Greek "Eis") His glory and virtue; It doesn't really matter, because as we see, verse 4 shows *both* to be plainly true. Christ calls us *to His glory by His glory*.

Note that, for a seed to germinate it must be planted. God doesn't "add" salvation to us. The tense of 2 Peter 1:4 ("having escaped") resonates with Rom 6:1-4 showing that freedom from sin must occur "going into the water", before righteousness can emerge.

The "escaping of the corruption that is in the World" occurs before the "partaking of the Divine Nature", exactly as one has to die before rising, and must lose their life to find it (Matt 10, 16; Lk 9; Mk 8; John 12). And repentance precedes conversion (Acts 3). The truth of God and the Word of God are wonderfully consistent, showing His strength.

---

[7] I experienced this escape in 1999, in a moment.
[8] It wasn't until 2018 that I discovered the partaking part.
[9] It didn't discover either one "in church". But I had no excuse – it had always been there in plain sight.

Bible Quotes are Word English Bible (WEB) except where noted.

The Important Opening
Of Peter's Pentecost Sermon

"Brothers, I may tell you freely of the patriarch David, that he both died and was buried, and his tomb is with us to this day.

Therefore, being a prophet, and knowing that God had sworn with an oath to him that of the fruit of his body, according to the flesh, **he would raise up the Christ to sit on his throne,** *he foreseeing this spoke about the resurrection of the Christ, that his soul wasn't left in Hades, and his flesh didn't see decay.*

This Jesus God raised up, to which we all are witnesses. **Being therefore exalted by the right hand of God**, *and having received from the Father the promise of the Holy Spirit, he has poured out this, which you now see and hear.*

For David didn't ascend into the heavens, but he says himself, 'The Lord said to my Lord, **"Sit by my right hand, until I make your enemies a footstool for your feet."** *'*

"Let all the house of Israel therefore know certainly that **God has made him both Lord and Christ,** *this Jesus whom you crucified."*

(Acts 2:29-36)

The passage continues on the next two-page spread.

The King of Glory
... Calls for Your Allegiance

This frame is not on the poster, but goes along with that of the next spread.

"Believing In" a Deliverer-King

Millions of churchgoers have been conditioned to see the Gospel as centering on their personal salvation. Of course we should care deeply about that!!

But *the Gospel is the announcement of a coming King and His Kingdom.*

Every message of personal salvation should be presented in light of this, because salvation is the restoration of dominion lost and an invitation to become a citizen of that Kingdom even in this age.

Promised to King David – His Dominion Would Never End

At this Pentecost sermon - Before Peter even began speaking of the refreshing and the indwelling of Christ in us, he reminded the hearers that Jesus was the descendant King that was promised to King David.

Seated at the Right Hand of God

Many Israelites, of course, simply wanted a political King or military leader that rescue them from the oppression of the Rome. But this King Jesus - being seatd afar above every other name that is named – also came to rescue us from the oppression of evil forces. It may be popular right now to ignore these evil forces that oppress us and our families, but at the time I am writing, many, many people are admitting the realities of these beings as they themselves or their children are oppressed by them.

But Jesus is Up There ... How Does That Help?!

In the unseen world, we are also there and we walk in the physical world here. We are in Him and He is in us! We will look at this more closely later in this Panel and the one that follows.

His Enemies (and Ours) Become His Footstool - and Ours!

Peter did not set aside the Kingship aspect of the work of Christ to simply preach about "getting saved to go to Heaven someday". He announced that the King of Kings and Lord of Lords had arrived, and He calls on everyone everywhere to make this turn of allegiance.

We will see more and more of this as we go!

Bible Quotes are Word English Bible (WEB) except where noted.

In Hope, I Forsake Sin
To Follow the Firstborn

(Acts 3:18-21) But those things which God foretold by the mouth of all His prophets, that the Christ would suffer, He has thus fulfilled...

Repent *therefore and* ***be converted****, that your sins may be blotted out, so that times of* ***refreshing may come from the presence of the Lord****, and that He may* ***send Jesus Christ****, who was preached to you before, whom heaven must receive* ***until the times of restoration of all things****, which God has spoken by the mouth of all His holy prophets since the world began.*

Baptism is Surrender
A True Pledge of Allegiance

Every phrase speaks of fulness of "grace". Anyone who loves God wants the Life of God. Anybody truly "receiving salvation" is _seeking all of what was promised_, and Peter lists these things in this passage.

If we are in our right minds, then we will only be satisfied with the escaping of the corruption that is in the World; the Partaking of the divine nature (2 Pet 1:3-4). But we obtain it only by repentance, which is the forsaking of "the going of our own way" to invest in something far, far better (metanoia = changed thinking).

Peter, after administering healing to the lame man near the beautiful gate of the temple, summarizes _salvation_ to the onlookers that wondered what just happened. He does so in six verses. In the name of Jesus, Peter calls them not to just "_believe_ and be _forgiven_", but to "_repent_ and be _converted_". He then adds "_so that_", Peter then states the consequences of the conversion:

(a) Forgiveness of sins;
(b) Times of refreshing from the _presence_ of the Lord;
(c) God the Father _sending_ The Lord Jesus Christ (the ultimate objective)

The new "temple" ... is "us"! (Col 1:27; Ps 24). If I surrender my selfish independence – _because it's not working for me!_ – and been reconciled to God, I ask for, and receive His life in me!

Tell of this Life of God

The Angel that freed Peter from prison told him to go and tell others, not primarily of forgiveness, but of the _life that Christ brings_. The Good News spoken by Peter is that the same Christ that lived in and through him (that brought the healing) is ready to live in and through each of us. Naturally, each hearer brings their own history; their own perception of reality, and their own questions; Nevertheless, there are "core-essential" elements that need to be present in a gospel invitation.

Not just the words, but power as well. Peter also "led" with something every single human understands and appreciates – the healing of their human body. If that person were oppressed of a devil, Peter would have of course dealt with it, just as Jesus had taught and commanded (Mt 10:1; Lk 10:19; Mt 28:11, Mk 16:15). Our witnessing and our living are the demonstration of the first fruits _in the face of the enemy_, the preview of the _restoration of all things_. We are to demonstrate and explain _a new kind of life_.

Bible Quotes are Word English Bible (WEB) except where noted.

I Am Recreated In My _Innermost_ Being

(2 Corinthians 5:17) Therefore if anyone is in Christ, he is a new creation. The old things have passed away. Behold, all things have become new...

(Ephesians 4:24 NKJV) For you were created after the pattern of God, in righteousness and true holiness

(Romans 5:17) For if by the trespass of one, death reigned through the one, much more will those who receive <u>abundance of grace</u> and of the <u>gift of righteousness</u> <u>reign in life through the One, Jesus Christ.</u> ... by one Man's obedience <u>many will be made righteous</u>.

The Last Adam, The Second Mankind

Just as If We had Never Sinned

As most Christians are aware, when we surrender our lives to God, our past sins are utterly removed and forgotten (Rom 3:27), and we are reconciled to the Father. We are "made right" with God!

But there is Much More that Happened

But we also need the power to *stay right*, and *grace includes that too*. We are to see and know not only our sins forgiven but also the enemy destroyed and ourselves, in fact, *risen as the righteousness of God. Church, let's just accept this. Yes, it's mystical, that doesn't mean we skip it.*

> *(Numbers 21:9) Moses made a serpent of brass and set it on a pole. If a serpent had bitten any man, when he looked at the serpent of brass, he lived.*

Note the Context – which 99% are unaware of – for the most well-known verse in the entire Bible:

> *(John 3:14-15) As Moses lifted up the serpent in the wilderness, even so must the Son of Man be lifted up, that whoever believes in him should not perish, but have eternal life.*

What was crucified and buried was <u>*sin itself, not **sins***</u>; All of our **sin** was packed both on and into Christ; so thoroughly that He "became" sin. Exactly why did He do that? To forgive us? Answer: Far beyond that, He became sin for us, that we might <u>***become the righteousness of God***</u> (2 Cor 5:21).

If we have surrendered our rebellion to do His will rather than our own, then we were also raised with Him. *Salvation is forgiveness with **<u>conversion</u>*** (Romans 5:10-11; 6:2-4; 10:9-10). A converted one has power to persevere.

Bible Quotes are Word English Bible (WEB) except where noted.

Low self-esteem? "Just a Sinner saved by Grace"?

By all means, be humble, but don't accept that "poor sinner" as your identity. *Before* your *conversion*, you were indeed a poor sinner. But very sadly, many people take that phrase as if they are *still* poor sinners, but now *saved*. If you are still one of the first mankind, then you are not even saved; you are still bound in sin. But as long as you breathe, the offer is available for you.

On the other hand, if you have accepted your death and burial with Christ – the forsaking of self-will (AKA sin), then you have been converted to the second mankind, and you are "saved".

There is no "club membership" or covenant that is more important than the new creation (Gal 5:16). We trade a futile, enslaved, oppressed, defeated, and condemned life for the life of the Son of God. We must see that the problem is in our *nature* – not just our *record*!!!; and that Jesus Christ offers us His own nature and mind; *and then things change*.

If you have surrendered your rebellion and forsaken sin, then He forgives your past sins and converts you into the Second Mankind. When we fail in weakness, we have an advocate (1 John 2:1) That is the Gospel!

The Sin in your Soul is No Longer You

But you must know that the sin that is still in your "soul" (not spirit) is no longer you, and you can now remove it. In ignorance of this fact millions of Christians live in defeat. Steve Backlund rightly said: "If you believe you are a sinner, you'll sin by faith".

Bible Quotes are Word English Bible (WEB) except where noted.

Freed From Sin
To Turn from it & Serve God

(Romans 6:3-22) Or don't you know that all we who were baptized into Christ Jesus <u>were baptized into His death</u>?

We were buried therefore with him through baptism into <u>death</u>, that just as Christ was raised from the <u>dead</u> by the glory of the Father, so we also might walk in <u>newness of life.</u> For if we have become united with him in the <u>likeness of His death</u>, we will also be part of <u>His resurrection</u>, knowing this, that <u>our old man was crucified with Him</u>, that the body of sin might be done away with, that we would no longer be slaves of sin.

For he who has died has been <u>freed from sin</u>.

But <u>if we died with Christ</u>, we believe that we will also <u>live with Him</u>, knowing that Christ, being raised from the dead, dies no more. Death no more has <u>dominion</u> over Him! For the <u>death</u> that he died, he died to sin one time; but the <u>life</u> that He lives, He lives to God.

Thus, consider yourselves also to be <u>dead</u> to sin, but <u>alive to God in Christ Jesus our Lord</u>...

---

21 What fruit then did you have at that time in the things of which you are now ashamed? For the end of those things is death. But now <u>being made free from sin</u>, and having become servants of God, <u>you have your fruit of sanctification, and the result, everlasting life</u>.

Bearing Fruit of Holiness and Its End ... *Eternal Life*

Some traditions, despite the plain teaching of the Word of God:

- make salvation simply "going to heaven someday".
- make the grace of God simply synonymous with forgiveness.
- make obeying God simply a "rewards" issue.

But the scriptures are so clear on this particular matter of holiness that it truly takes a theologian to make such distortions plausible. They are only plausible to the extent that we don't study the scripture or ourselves; or we are somehow blinded by man-made narratives or by religious spirits. For one or more reasons, **we *cannot see what they actually say*.**

One might think that it would be "bad news" that holiness is required for salvation, but just the opposite is true! It is "good news" that God is not fickle – He doesn't go back on His word "the soul that sins shall die" (Ezek 18:20); Sounds like bad news, but ...

(a) We died! (John 3:14; Rom 6:3-4).
(b) He who has ***died*** has been ***freed from sin*** (6:7). This is the "Free indeed". It is the ***relief from "what we were"***. A true salvation is, after all, a "conversion" by "rebirth". Many of the most joyful conversion testimonies speak of this.
(c) Becoming like Him casts our fear (1 John 4:17)
(d) Experiencing the presence of God and His love and care changes everything.

Just as the first Adam's sin brought sin and death to us. In the same manner – the Second Adam's righteousness brings righteousness to us. That's wild! But it is true. I can attest that in a moment in 1999 I was reading Romans 6; I saw that I had died; and I immediately felt the chains of sin drop. Christ makes us free indeed, and then it is up to us to use that freedom to put on holiness.

A Salvation Matter?

This is not popular, but Romans 6:22 at left is plain that Holiness is a salvation issue.

We must use our freedom to serve God. The good news is that by the Life and companionship of Christ in us, we can serve God with joy. When we see this, everything changes; and the Holy Spirit is ready to show it to you. Tell the Lord Jesus –

Bible Quotes are Word English Bible (WEB) except where noted.

"Yes, I need to make the exchange; You can have my life; *I will forsake sin; I want to live entirely from your Life inside me"*. *I will put my sin to death.*

Every man must decide whether they will please God, or please man. Dear brother or sister, do the right thing! Your joy is waiting nearby on this very matter.

For His Part, it is Finished. Will we enter into it?

He had finally become Sin, as Us. His form was marred beyond recognition as Human, bearing zero of the Image of God, and manifesting the full hideousness of Sin – *personified*. He was finally ready to take it down into the "sea" – the burial that everybody knows is final.

Our declaration in Baptism is that we see the glory of Christ and we see enough ugliness of our fallen natures that we know **we belong in that transaction**; The good news is that we are invited to surrender to the Love of God and be part of that transaction, including its resurrection in newness of life (Rom 6). "Chains" are a metaphor, but deliverance for sin is not poetry. You will feel them break, not just gradually weaken. You will suddenly be able to resist sin. You will be free indeed.

The "surrender" is that *we would no longer be going our own way* (Isa 53), but instead, we would practice obedience to His command to love others. But we know that due to **what we are** we cannot do it – and of course He knew that! So, God did what man could not (Rom 8:3-4). Christ died and was buried, carrying the Man of Sin down and is raised with the Life of God so that we, in Him might become the Righteousness of God 2 Cor 5). He who does the Will of God endures Forever; The Good News: We Now Can!

If the Son of Man be lifted up, He will draw all men to Himself (John 12:32).

The transaction of Christ was a class-action event; Those that feel they "don't need it" can stand back and scoff. But those that will accept the burial with Him get to share in His New Life, they shall have been freed from sin (v. 7) and sin shall no longer be their master (v. 10).

By and large, the church seems to nearly always zoom in on "verse 23" **bypassing the significance of the entire salvation chapter**. The church has:

- Omitted or twisted the essential meaning of Baptism (v. 3)
- Omitted, the requirement of holiness as a salvation matter (v. 21-22)
- Omitted, amazingly, the very means of that holiness (v. 4-7)
- Omitted, the command to use our freedom to purify ourselves (v. 12-

17)

This chapter never sees the light of day in many churches, simply because Verse 17 mentions the "O" word (obedience). Yet it is the life of Christ in us that meets the requirement! It is the Obedience of Faith" – the Introduction and the conclusion of the entire Epistle; Yet if we can see our burial ***and rising***, <u>there is nothing more welcoming and wonderful</u>!

We need only admit our futility; deny our self-righteousness *enough to trade our lives in* to do His will instead.

Bible Quotes are Word English Bible (WEB) except where noted.

I Ask & Receive
Power to Overcome the Enemy

> (Acts 1:8) But <u>you shall receive power</u> when the Holy Spirit has come upon you; ...

(Acts 2:4-18) They were all filled with the Holy Spirit ... everyone heard them speaking in his own language. ... "What does this mean?" But Peter, standing up with the eleven, lifted up his voice and spoke out to them, "... this is what has been spoken by the prophet Joel:

(Joel 2:28-32) "... I will pour out My Spirit on all flesh; Your sons and your daughters shall prophesy, Your old men shall dream dreams, Your young men shall see visions. And also on My menservants and on My maidservants I will pour out My Spirit in those days...

> (Luke 11:13) ... how much more will your heavenly Father give the Holy Spirit to those who ask Him!"

Not the Same as Conversion/Regeneration

Several passages show the Baptism of the Holy Spirit occurring "after" conversion itself. It is Jesus Himself that sends it (Mat 3:11; Acts 11:16);

> Acts 8 in Samaria - Acts 9 in Damascus – Acts 19 in Ephesus

... that we might *have Life* and ***have it more abundantly*** – Jn 10:10

Sown in Weakness and Shame

Christ *in You*
Restoring that which Was Lost
Union, Righteousness, Dominion, Peace, and Joy

It is all of what was promised by the prophets and bought by the Christ; the High Priest of the New and much better Covenant. The manifest presence of God; The desire to do what is right and the power to do it; Naturally fulfilling what God requires – loving Him and Loving mankind; Gaining ascendancy not over God; not over man; but over the enemy of our souls.

Not with power to create galaxies; but *<u>far above the true enemy</u>*, putting an end to oppression in me and making me one that sets captives free in His name. It is the confident hope of becoming "Like" Christ, in this life (Eph 4:13; 1 John 4:4); It is exactly the glory Christ came to get back into man. It is the Zoe Eternal Life of God through the ages (John 3:16); It is "glory, honor, and immortality" (Rom 2:7). It is the glory of the victor receiving the crown of Life (Rev 3:14).

It is all that – every bit of it. But very importantly, the <u>*Life*</u> – with its overcoming power – is for <u>*now*</u>; But the <u>*crown*</u> – the final and complete manifestation of the victors (plural because we receive them together and jointly) – is for <u>*later*</u>. At that time, we will <u>*glorify the one*</u> that gave us of His Spirit, to bring it all about.

> In short, this is Restoring that which was lost.
> Bearing the *<u>image of God</u>* once again; regaining *<u>dominion</u>*.

Why do So Many Resist the Main Course?

The tendency of popular Christian culture is to "get saved" (passive) and then do Bible studies as we wait for the rapture and give thanks to God as we and our families *continue in defeat*. This passivity destroys marriages and it is an "anit-witness" to our children and to others. But Christ purchased actual victory!

It's almost as if some entity desperately wishes he had not crucified the Lord of Glory (1 Cor 2:6); but still knew that God's people could still be defeated through lack of *that particular knowledge that would make them free*: Thinking: "Even if <u>*many*</u> Sons are *born*, at least I can keep them from ever growing strong; I can keep them off the battlefield – or better yet – <u>*on the field*</u> but <u>*without strength*</u>. Then they will retreat and live in their camps and do Bible studies. I can keep them from remembering what they are and who is in them. They will remain defeated; and they will have nothing to witness about.

Bible Quotes are Word English Bible (WEB) except where noted.

Craving Righteousness
Desiring to Be ... *a Son of God*

(Matthew 5:3-5) Blessed are the poor in spirit, for theirs is the <u>kingdom</u> of heaven.

Blessed are those who mourn, for they shall be <u>comforted</u>.

Blessed are the meek, for they shall <u>inherit the earth</u>.

Blessed are those who hunger and thirst after <u>righteousness</u>, For they shall be <u>filled</u>.

(Matthew 5:7-10) Blessed are the merciful, for they shall <u>obtain mercy</u>.

Blessed are the <u>pure in heart</u>, for they shall <u>see God</u>.

Blessed are the peacemakers,

For they shall be called <u>children of God</u>.

Blessed are those who have been persecuted for righteousness' sake, For <u>theirs is the Kingdom of Heaven.</u>

Hungry for ... *This*?
If So, You *Shall* be *Filled*

This passage is <u>*not a list of suggestions of the attitudes we should adopt*</u>. The fact is, before we are converted into the Second Mankind, we cannot. Rather, the passage is a statement of the invitation to enter the lineage of the Second Mankind – following the Firstborn – and receiving the entitlements of the Sons and daughters of God. If we read it as such it makes plain and perfect sense.

Throughout the whole list we see ... Forgiveness? No – we see the restoration of Psalms 8 – <u>*Glory and Dominion.*</u> The Dominion is both inward and outward.

Right in the middle of them we see Ezekiel – the New Covenant – the Righteousness of God "filling us". Notice regarding verse 10 ...

If I am selfish and I am proud of all my accomplishments; proud of having gotten myself to the top of the "food chain", and then a <u>*restarted*</u> human race <u>*gets promised dominion*</u> and <u>*it's not me*</u>; If I will not humble myself and renounce it all; then I will want to *keep that new species* ***down*** by any means possible.

That's what happened in the first century of this age, and that's what will happen in the last century of this age.

But the Christians of the first few centuries enjoyed the manifest presence of Christ and worked battle exploits against the true enemy. They considered it a joy and an honor to be counted worthy to be placed into the battle. The last-century Christians will enjoy the same.

The church is to be the community of those being transformed from glory to glory, and trained for battle in the liberation service of mankind; Announcing and demonstrating Kingdom authority over all the power of the enemy.

If we read without tinted lenses, we see that this is simply what Christ trained and commissioned.

Bible Quotes are Word English Bible (WEB) except where noted.

PART 7: ABIDING IN HIM, BECOMING LIKE HIM

Let's briefly review Matt 16:24: We see that Jesus has gone somewhere – and we saw this in detail in the top line of the three center panels.

He had given the open invitation to *anyone* that will choose to accept it…

We see that there is a required life-exchange "surrender" **_event_** – to abandon our lives of selfish independence and *enter the walk of companionship of God*. We saw this explained in the middle of the three center panels.

Finally, we see that there is also – as a salvation matter, a requirement to take up our cross (dying to self-will, putting to death the works of the flesh), and follow Him. This is a **_process_**. If we are committed into a tradition that says our *final salvation is sealed at the time of our conversion*, then we are going against the plain words of Christ. There is too much at stake to settle there.

Doctrines of total depravity and arbitrary predestination originated with the "Gnostics", whom the apostle John called "deceivers and antichrists" (2 Jn 7). Their teaching is not Christianity.

> *(Matthew 16:24-27) Then Jesus said to his disciples, "If anyone desires to come after me, let him deny himself, and take up his cross, and follow me. For whoever desires to save his life will lose it, and whoever will lose his life for my sake will find it. 26 For what will it profit a man, if he gains the whole world, and forfeits his life? Or what will a man give in exchange for his life? For the Son of Man will come in the glory of his Father with his angels, and then he will render to everyone according to his deeds.*

The phrase "obeying" the Gospel occurs in several places in the New Testament but you will not hear it in 99:9% of churches. Not only is obeying God the saving response to the love of God; but it is also very, very dangerous to put off our "obeying the gospel" because after enough stubbornness, our hearts can turn callous and hardened.

Sown in Weakness and Shame

The Salvation Rescue Event and the Process

As a kid you probably heard, "if you're good, you go to heaven; if you're bad to you go to hell". In his introduction to his letter to the Romans, Paul plainly affirms that it is ... true!

> *But according to your hardness and unrepentant heart you are treasuring up for yourself wrath in the day of wrath, revelation, and of the righteous judgment of God; who "will pay back to everyone according to their works:"*
>
> *to those who by perseverance in well-doing seek for glory, honor, and incorruptibility, eternal life;*
>
> *but to those who are self-seeking, and don't obey the truth, but obey unrighteousness, will be wrath and indignation, oppression and anguish, on every soul of man who does evil, to the Jew first, and also to the Greek.*
>
> *But glory, honor, and peace go to every man who does good, to the Jew first, and also to the Greek. For there is no partiality with God.*
> *(Romans 2:5-11)*

If you have grown up under Reformation theology, you might wonder how Paul could say such a thing. Or maybe he didn't really understand grace until he wrote chapter 4? Let's sort this out! There are some critical caveats to make sense of it:

1. We must publicly acknowledge and accept the forgiveness of past sins that was purchased by the innocent blood of Christ;
2. To escape the power of sin, we must die and be born again as the *Second Mankind* that Christ initiated; and
3. To produce the kind of good that is accepted, we *must receive and utilize the indwelling life of God*; We must *renew our minds* to the truth that makes us free. It is not automatic. As we stay the course, we have

a merciful High Priest.

In our initial salvation – our conversion" we were saved from our "past sins" and given a new start but with the power – and His companionship – now to work with us. The freedom, strength, dignity, and joy that we obtain, in this life alone make the journey so very worth it!!

It is worse than fatal to theologize away the requirement; we can train people to be blind to the words of Christ, but the requirement doesn't go away. The irony is that by walking with God according to *His* method, we quickly find a kind of freedom that the world can never find.

The Bottom-Central Panel

In this bottom tier of the large central group – we see we are required to persevere in the "process" of using the indwelling power and companionship of God to put sin to death in our souls; and that we are restored under the mercy of Christ if when we fail in weakness.

Some traditions teach that, if there is any requirement at all on us, then we are "trying to *earn* our salvation". But this is not "earning" anything; The practice of obedience is merely a *condition* of salvation. We must all believe the *Word of God* over our traditions, and we must embrace the *entire* Word of God.

Provision of Everything We Need

Grace includes "everything we need for *life* and *godliness*, not just forgiveness" (2 Peter 1:3-4). The New Spirit and the New Heart (Ezekiel 36:25) of The Second Mankind has – in his innermost constitution – both the <u>desire</u> and the <u>ability</u> to serve God. This is *exactly* how the yoke becomes easy and the burden becomes light (Matt 11:28).

If you will "lose your life to find it", and set out to renew your mind, then you will not only experience the emergence of the mind of Christ into your own mind with its enormous peace and dignity (1 Cor 2:16); but you will also begin to "taste of the heavenly gift (the Holy Spirit) and the powers of the age to come (Heb 6:5). These powers include all the dominion powers that Jesus demonstrated before the multitudes and then trained into the Apostles (Matthew 10; Mark 16; Luke 9; Luke 10).

The "powers of the age to come" didn't "die out with the Apostles because we now have The Bible!!". If we are honest with ourselves we know that this is nonsense.

If we are hanging out with a power-denying church, then we will not be able to live – much less share - the Gospel *of the Kingdom* (Luke 24:14). But once we successfully administer an instant healing sickness or cast out an evil spirit – in the name of Christ – it will be simply settled for us; Life will take on an entirely new and wonderful hope! Need to see some testimony? Check out "the Collected Works of John G. Lake". I read this *for 90 minutes per evening for a year*. My faith changed so radically – and became so clear – that I commanded and received a constructive miracle. Half of all believers in South Africa today can trace their churches back to Lake's work in 7 years at the beginning of the last century. Want to be trained? I recommend John G. Lake Ministries – jglm.org, overseen by Curry R. Blake.

"Lose your life to find it" is the most repeated command of Christ. It's worth it!!

Bible Quotes are Word English Bible (WEB) except where noted.

Let Go and Let God?
Good! ... if *Rightly Understood*

(James 4:6-8) ... "God resists the proud, but gives grace to the humble." ... Draw near to God, and he will draw near to you. **Cleanse your hands***, you sinners; and* **purify your hearts***, you double-minded.*

(Heb 2:1-3) Therefore we ought to **pay greater attention** *to the things that were heard, lest perhaps we* **drift away***. For if the word spoken through angels proved steadfast, and every transgression and disobedience received a just recompense; how will we escape if we* **neglect** *so great a salvation ...*

(Romans 8:13) For if you live after the flesh, you must die; but **if by the Spirit you put to death the deeds of the body, you will live.**

(Genesis 3:6) ... she took some of its fruit and ate; and she gave some to her husband with her, **and he ate it, too.**

(Proverbs 6:10-11) A little sleep, a little slumber, a little folding of the hands to sleep: 11 **so your poverty will come as a robber, and your scarcity as an armed man.**

(Romans 6:22-23) ... being made free from sin, and **having become servants of God***, you have your fruit of* **sanctification***, and the* **result** *of eternal life. For the wages of sin is death, but the free gift of God is eternal life in Christ Jesus our Lord.*

(1 John 2:15-17) Don't love the world or the things that are in the world. If anyone loves the world, the Father's love isn't in him. For all that is in the world, the lust of the flesh, the lust of the eyes, and the pride of life, isn't the Father's, but is the world's. **The world is passing away with its lusts, but he who <u>does</u> God's will remains forever.**

Sown in Weakness and Shame

Passivity is Deadly!
Saving Faith Is Allegiance

It is so important that it bears repeating that the New Testament makes no room for "Once-and Done" salvation doctrine. It is perhaps the single greatest factor in the passivity of today's popular Christianity. See Heb 6:4-6; 2 Pet 2:20-22; Mat 24:10-13; 1 Cor 9:27; 1 Cor 10:1-6; Gal 5:19-21; Heb 10:26-27; Rev 3:5; 2 Tim 2:12; John 15:6; Luke 8:13; Rev 2:10; 1 Jn 2:24-25; Col 1:22-23.

Come Out of the Forgiveness-Only Gospel (the "FOG")

Many readers at this point may experience fog, sleepiness, anxiety, or headache; tempted to put the book down or entirely out of sight. I know this because I went through it myself for many years! But I promise that if we press into the *truth of the Word of God* - even if it means we find ourselves at odds with brother, sister, mother, father; long-time friends – we will find a wonderful refreshing and break through into freedom and boldness. We will find our way to a new kind of fellowship with God as we find the power to overcome the enemy as He intended.

We find that indeed, God is not the cruel one, unilaterally predestining most of mankind to eternal torment. Rather, we find that He is truly loving.

How Passivity Came to The Mainstream

In David Bercot's Historical Faith Series, he shows clearly how the worst heresies of popular Christianity moved from their Gnostic origin into the early Roman church in the 400s, and then again in the 1500s into mainstream Protestant Evangelicalism. Today's popular Christianity reflects the very passivity that the "unilateral" predestination doctrines *inevitably* breed.

In his Commentary on Paul's Letter to the Romans Bercot also brings out the unanimous testimony of the Early church writers to clarify exactly what the traditionally misinterpreted passages such as Romans 9 are saying. A correct understanding of Romans 9 can occur only when we take off the happen if It's key to know that the letter addresses the Jews (Rom 2:17), insists that the salvation of True Israel is not by genetic lineage or birth order, but a matter of surrender; that <u>we</u> are called to make ourselves into vessels for honorable use (2 Tim 2:20-22). Bercot's commentary is simply excellent and makes this all crystal clear! Get those glasses off!

A very important event occurs when we discover that a "sovereign" God sovereignly chose to give man free will (Gen 1:26-28; Psalms 8; Psalms 115); and has given us everything we need for life and godliness (2 Peter 1).

Bible Quotes are Word English Bible (WEB) except where noted.
Even Christ suffered out of love, not as a matter of programming.

We realize that it was not just a cynical trick for Christ to say that He "makes us free indeed" and then says "Follow Me". Rather, it was a supreme act of love.

Thus we all have a measure of real freedom, even if it is only the freedom to see His love and *exchange our life for His life*; We see that in response He gives us the desire and the power to serve Him with joy. If this is the crossroads you are facing; please turn the corner! Besides, many among your family and friends – the ones you think you are *alienating* - will see the joy and peace that is in your new smile and be astonished; They will want it. They will hunger and thirst not just for forgiveness, but for righteousness – and they shall be filled as well!

Then you and your loved ones can grow together into the image of the Firstborn.

Abandon Self-Will
Follow Him to His Kingdom

It is absolutely true that to be saved we begin by trusting in the righteousness of Christ to redeem us from our debt of past sins "committed beforehand" (Rom 3:25).

It is also absolutely true that "as we practice obeying Christ", we shall have points of failure and we depend on His restoration when we confess these (1 John 1:9-10; 2:1).

But nothing in the scriptures teaches that we are irreversibly forgiven for all time at the point of our reconciliation. But God gives us everything we need for life and godliness, then expects us to walk in *that* grace. We are back to the garden, with His very life in us, making the burden light.

Beginning way back with Augustine in the fourth century, a teaching got into the Church that was vehemently opposed by the early church until then.[10] This is the teaching that all events are pre-determined by God and everything that happens is God's will because He is "sovereign"; Today this translates to the "Let go and let God" passive mindset.

Most of us can see the effects of passivity in both believers and unbelievers; Not only does it result in poverty and destroyed marriages, but entrenches souls into downward sowing and reaping and oppressions. Passivity leads us – and those we love - into the ways of the world and to ultimate destruction. Passivity sidelines or even destroys true believers that God wishes to form into the image of His Son and then send as ambassadors.

(Hosea 4:6) For lack of knowledge, God's people are destroyed.

But What if "Grace" works "with" Freedom?

Naturally, if we have been taught that grace means we simply get saved because we were predestined to get saved – and "grace" requires that there can be no cooperation, then passivity is the natural conclusion and we consider this as being "spiritual".

But what if "grace" lies in His providing everything we need, for life and godliness – re-establishing a mankind that was lost? What if both love and

---

[10] David Bercot's Historic Faith Commentary Series quotes church writers 100 A.D. forward

freedom truly exist? *We must abandon not only self-righteousness – but also self-will*. This is the only *true and saving* repentance.

"Foreknowing" Our Response to Him is Not "Causing" It

The "golden chain" begins with *foreknowledge* – not with predestination (Rom 8:29-30). God indeed gives grace to the humble (James 4:6). He knows beforehand who will respond to His mercy; He displays His goodness; we respond in humility; He gives us to Christ who makes us free; we use this freedom to serve Him without fear.

Bible Quotes are Word English Bible (WEB) except where noted.

Abide in My Love
By Keeping My Commands

*(John 15:1-24) "...Every branch <u>in me</u> that doesn't bear fruit <u>he takes away</u>; every branch that <u>**bears fruit**</u> he prunes, that it may bear more fruit..."*

*Remain in me, and I in you. ... "<u>I am the vine. You are the branches</u>. He who remains in me, and I in him, bears much fruit; for without me you can do nothing. <u>**If anyone doesn't remain, he is thrown out**</u> ...*

If you remain in me, and my words remain in you, you will ask what you desire, and it will be done for you. In this is my Father is glorified, that you bear much fruit; so, you will be my disciples...

<u>**Remain in my love.**</u>
<u>**If you keep my commandments, you will remain in my love**</u>*, even as I have kept my Father's commandments and remain in His love."*
"I have spoken these things to you that my joy may remain in you, and that your joy may be made full.

12 This <u>is my commandment, that you love one another even as I have loved you.</u> ... You are my <u>friends if you do whatever I command you.</u> No longer do I call you servants, for a servant doesn't know what his lord does; but I have called you friends, for everything that I heard from my Father I have made known to you. You did not choose me, but I chose you and appointed you that you should go and bear fruit, and that your fruit should remain, that

<u>whatever you ask the Father in My name</u> He may give it to you. These things I command you, that you <u>love one another.</u>"

Sown in Weakness and Shame

But This is Possible ...
Only in Dying to Self-Will

If we have been taught that our salvation is unconditional and automatic, then John 15 – and hundreds of other chapters of the Bible – will cause a headache – because *choosing* is commanded everywhere. To an unconverted person desiring simply "amnesty", the numerous obedience passages are effectively redacted as "misinformation" and the theologians are dispatched to *explain them away*.

But if we are in the *New Covenant*, God has not only given us everything we need for life and godliness; and the Spirit of God has born witness to our spirits that we are the Sons of God; We are united with God in an amazing bond of love – no chains.

If we can accept all this, then all the hardest chapters in the NT are not a stumbling block (v22) but a footstool! Everything God commands He empowers, *and the resulting victory is joy*.

The enemy is SELF WILL. We are called to *reject independence for the joy of Union*. That's exactly why Paul in Ephesians 5 likens Christ and the Church (us) to a ***marriage***. A marriage in which there is any agenda of independence is headed for failure. But those in which both are surrendered to serve God are drawn close to Him and are at peace with each other as an intended effect. All are to know we are Christians by our love.

The Sons of God have their spirits redeemed; mingled and joined with the spirit of God. Yet in their souls, to various degrees, carry a residue of selfish independence; It still at times demands its way but it is now easy to put down. The Sons of God are dismantling that residue (Rom 8:14). As they cast down lies (2 Cor 10:4), the soul gets filled with the mind of Christ (1 Cor 2:16) and the power of God (Jn 14:12); This mind and power become increasingly available for whatever needs to be said and done as a Centurion for the Kingdom of God. We are the Body of Christ continuing His work of setting other captives free.

If we are reborn, God by His Spirit gives us the wonderful awareness of His presence; The awareness of practical knowledge that we need for the day; and at the right times He lovingly points out the next counterfeit of the soul that we are to discard. As we are aware of our soul's weakness, we operate instead by spirit.

Bible Quotes are Word English Bible (WEB) except where noted.

Let's renounce independence, *the going of our own way* – which is rebellion, the original sin. Let us give our lives to be bound with Christ; Hidden with Him in the will of God and walking by spirit. When He appears, we also will appear with Him in Glory.

Bible Quotes are Word English Bible (WEB) except where noted.

We Persevere To ...
Glory, Honor, and Immortality

(Romans 2:5 NIV) ... the righteous judgment of God, who "WILL RENDER TO EACH ONE ACCORDING TO HIS DEEDS":

...

To those who by persistence in doing good seek glory, honor and immortality, he will give eternal life.

See Also ... Numerous Other Passages!

The passage above is immensely important! It is the key to understanding the Book of Romans. It is the verse that exposes the false theology – even of traditions that claim they *uphold the authority of the Bible*. Such traditions will also ALWAYS avoid the following chapters that describe not only the necessity of choosing to obey God, but **_even the very means of overcoming the enemy_**. If you are immersed in such a tradition, you should know that it is not Biblical Christianity.

> *Rom 6:16; Rom 8:5-7, 13; Rom 11:21-22; Gal 5:19-21; 2 Cor 5:10; Eph 5:5-6; Col 1:21-23; Gal 6:7-9; 1 Tim 4:16; 2 Tim 2:12; Heb 5:9; Heb 6:4-8; Heb 10:26-30; Heb 10:36; Acts 10:34-35; Jas 2:21-24; Jas 4:4; 1 Pet 4:17-19; 2 Pet 2:20-21; 1 Jn 1:6-7; 1 Jn 2:3-5; Rev 20:12-13; Jn 5:28-29; Mt 7:21-24; Mt 13:40-42; Lk 21:34,36; Mt 25:31-36.*

On the other hand, if we see that there are two stages of salvation – *faith* followed by *faithfulness* – then the New Covenant and our entire New Testament all make perfect sense. The FOG clears; we find a new kind of peace; boldness appears, because we see that **_God is both loving and just_**.

Sown in Weakness and Shame

He Makes Us Free
Providing Incentives and Power

Quite appropriately Paul, in introducing his most detailed and systematic statement of the theology of salvation itself, defines Eternal Life in Romans chapter 2. Yet most of our churches today not only ignore this plain but glorious truth; they provide a severely reduced salvation that leaves many millions living in defeat. How much glory has God gotten from that? Popular Christianity now makes room for "getting saved" and *going your own way* – and most do exactly that. The effect is that those people that *will not study the Word of God for themselves* are destroyed for lack of knowledge or perish for lack of vision. Even if they surrendered to do the will of God (despite false teaching), their **ignorance of the way of victory** leaves them mostly **in defeat**.

Without being aware of the powers of the New Covenant (Ezekiel 36), Christ's command to Obey Him (esp. John 13-17) invariably causes people to react: "Hey - That's not Grace!". They then turn away from direct Bible-reading and live another defeated decade with the gnawing subconscious awareness that something is wrong.

His Divine Power is His Life in Us

Christ has one "New" command for us – to *Love as He Loved* (John 13). It includes loving the Father and loving others; Moreover, it is a different kind of love – and He makes it all possible by *implanting His own life into those that will receive Him*.

We are to Seek after Glory, Honor, and Immortality

We will see that Christ has initiated a Covenant with us, to provide everything we need both for life *and for godliness*. He took upon Himself not only our sins and the death penalty that was rightly ours, but He even took upon Himself **our sinfulness itself** and **buried it by planting His own body**, so that we *partake in His nature*. Therefore, if we surrender to do His will rather than go our own way, He will not only forgive our sins, but He will also recreate our spirits and hearts with His own divine nature (Eph 4:24), so that serving Him is not only *possible*, but by our perseverance it becomes *natural*. We practice loving others by the power of His own righteousness in us, and *He will reward us with glory, honor, and immortality*. Let's focus on ***hope***, because faith and love spring from it (Col 1:3)! Salvation works by *freedom and bestowed power;* To the humble, this is good news!! Knowing the end of it, they *follow the Firstborn*.

Bible Quotes are Word English Bible (WEB) except where noted.

I Put on the New Man
Overcoming Sin by *His Power*

(Eph 4:22-24) that you put away, as concerning your former way of life, the old man, that grows corrupt after the lusts of deceit; and that you be renewed in the spirit of your mind, <u>and put on the new man, who in the likeness of God has been created</u> in righteousness and holiness of truth.

(Colossians 3:9-10,14) you have put off the old man with his doings, and have put on the new man, who is being renewed in knowledge **<u>after the image of his creator,</u>**

...

Above all these things <u>walk in love,</u> which is the bond of perfection.

Sown in Weakness and Shame

When He Appears
_We'll_ Appear _with Him_ in _Glory_

Christ – the Lover of your soul, calls us to step into the Second Mankind. Christ Himself is its Firstborn, and He came to bring many sons to glory (Heb 2:10).

Conceived in the First Adam

The First Adam _**took us where we did not want to go**_; and we could do nothing about it! We were laden with guilt, shame, fear, and despair. Still today, in America where many people _understand "independence" to be "freedom"_, they observe their decay as time marches onward. If you still have life and breath, however, there is hope!

Another Adam Appeared...

But another Adam came along; and the grace of God [that brings salvation] appeared to all men (Titus 2). Today we see Christ in those that are being transformed. We can look at Him and say… "I want to be like that … Or better … I want to BE that. But we must be careful here – wanting to "be like Him _apart from Him_ is what brought us death (Genesis 3). So – having forsaken sin, we are called to be satisfied with our life _in union_ with Christ, hidden with Him in God (Col 3:3).

...With Us in Him, Having Gone Where We Need to Go

Each one of these "stops" is a glorious truth, but I will just list them.

If you have loved the Lord Jesus and believed that the Father sent Him as an acceptable ransom then by **His Blood** _You_ – Already – have been:

Ransomed – with debt paid in full

But that's just the foyer of the palace of salvation. He did much more:

Was Scourged, Crucified, and Buried

This is freedom – It is the breaking of chains and the sprinkling we all needed. He could not just raise us; He had to become SIN that we "might" - have the right to, and the means to - become the righteousness of God.

Raised, Ascended, Seated in Him and with Him

… far above the jurisdiction or power of any and every enemy. These all become ours in experience if and as we renew your minds to handle them. He did this that we might become not only become _like_ Him but to be "with Him forever". Hallelujah!

Bible Quotes are Word English Bible (WEB) except where noted.

I Confirm ...
My Election with All Diligence

"Grace is not opposed to effort – but to earning"

- Dallas Willard

(2 Peter 1:5-7) For this very cause, adding on your part all diligence ... to supply goodness; ..., knowledge; ..., self-control; ... perseverance; ..., godliness; mutual affection; and ... love.

... For he who lacks these things is blind, having forgotten the cleansing from his old sins.

Therefore brothers, be more diligent to make your calling and election sure. For if you do these things, you will never stumble.

How Long Will Theologians Spoon-Feed Us?

2 Peter 1, Romans 6, and Romans 8 are among the most outrageously wonderful good news passages ...

... that almost nobody in popular Christianity *has ever heard*. Why are they suppressed? Because just like we all now know about "Fake News", there is also a "Fake *Good* News". It is the promise of salvation without surrender, without forsaking sin; and all in the name of ... "grace"!

Who is Most Qualified to Interpret the New Testament?

If we read the writings of the direct disciples of the Apostles and the ministering companions of the Apostles[11], there is no mistaking how they interpreted the New Testament - and it matches the plainest reading of the Bible. But their interpretation is very, very different than that of Augustine and the two that resurrected him eleven hundred years later (Luther and Calvin). Who is more qualified to interpret it?

If we accept faulty translations or if we just take the pastor's word for everything *without reading for ourselves*, we are vulnerable to this error because we *do not realize how much has been omitted* from sermons and Bible studies programs. Unfortunately, many people who have been indoctrinated in this error **_cannot even see_** the fifty – I am not exaggerating – passages to the contrary. The FOG is obscuring them.

There is Therefore Now No More Contradiction

I was under that FOG for decades. I read the Bible thinking: "how can there be so many terrible contradictions??!!". But once I saw that there are two phases of salvation and that forgiveness is simply the first-step component of salvation, I got free indeed – in real, practical, reality; and so much fell neatly into place. I am writing this book so that others can avoid the contradiction or get free from it if they are already under it.

The true Gospel lays out the hope (Christ in you, the hope of glory), and states the requirements. Back to 2 Peter 1. The passage at left shows plainly that we ourselves – *have the power to make our calling and election sure.*

In Romans 8:29 we see that God's "knowing" precedes His *predesting*. He "saw" who will be humble before Him, and gives grace in many ways to them.

---

[11] David Bercot's Historic Faith Commentary Series quotes church writers 100 A.D. forward. The Romans commentary lists the fifty passages.

Bible Quotes are Word English Bible (WEB) except where noted.

The early church leader's writings unanimously affirm our true free will… until Augustine arrived to popularize Gnosticism in about 400 A.D.

God is sovereign, … and He *sovereignly* chose to *make man free*; and He *sovereignly* chose to *give grace to the humble*. When man rebelled and lost his life-source he then had only one essential freedom left – to "make the trade"; to die to rise; to lose his life to find it; To surrender and to do the will of God.

It's the same challenge each of us has faced and will face until our last breath.

If a man will plant himself as that seed, so to speak – dying to self-will and putting it to death, then he will see a wonderful thing emerge in its place. This is the only arrangement that affirms and preserves both the justice and the mercy of God, and it is what the scriptures plainly teach.

So – shall we confirm our calling and election? He gives us everything we need for it (this is grace, verse 3)! How can we ignore so great a salvation?

Bible Quotes are Word English Bible (WEB) except where noted.

No Eye has Seen
What God has Prepared ...

Old Covenant:

(Isaiah 64:4 NKJV) For since the beginning of the world Men have not heard nor perceived by the ear, Nor has the eye seen any God besides You,

Who acts for the one who waits for Him.

New Covenant:

(1 Corinthians 2:9-10 NKJV) But as it is written: "EYE HAS NOT SEEN, NOR EAR HEARD, NOR HAVE ENTERED INTO THE HEART OF MAN THE THINGS WHICH GOD HAS PREPARED FOR THOSE WHO LOVE HIM."

But God has revealed them to us through His Spirit. For the Spirit searches all things, yes, the deep things of God.

But God
Has Revealed Them By His Spirit

God shows us the glorious things that are to come; things to come in this age, things to come in the Millennial reign of Christ, and finally, the "Restoration of all things" (Acts 3:21; Phil 3:21; Rev 3:21). Looks like a countdown (3-2-1), doesn't it? I'd like to say "When Jesus returns, we go to Heaven!", but there is an age before that; It is an age of restored justice, but it is not the "final state".

Taken together, Revelation 19-21 and Psalms 110 show us that the next age is a 1000-year physical reign of Jesus Christ "on the throne of David", in Jerusalem. At the return of Christ, we shall receive our *glorified bodies* (1 Cor 15); and the governments of the earth will all be brought into subjection to Christ. The enemy will be released for a short time near the end of that age.

Revelation 22 then shows us the World to come, re-formed through fervent heat; The enemy taken out of play forever, and every tear wiped from our eyes. Every promise will be entirely fulfilled. Simply reading it is very good for us.

Meanwhile, we enjoy the first fruits of every ultimate covenant blessing. God saw fit to make it "work" as follows"; Exactly as with forgiveness and conversion, we obtain the subsequent blessings by "turn-of-allegiance" faith (pistis); This faith is the unwavering, undoubting asking and receiving; It is coupled with active service. As we renew our minds, we begin to get supernatural results; this is "tasting the heavenly gift and the powers of the age to come" (Heb 6).

What are the limits of it? Christ tells plainly that we will do greater works than He did once we are back in union with the Father (Jn 14:12). Just as the Father sent Jesus, so Jesus sends us (John 20:21). This understanding of faith – authority to "re-present" the sender – is what moved Christ to commend the Centurion for a faith He had not seen "in all of Israel". I estimate that only a small fraction of the church affirms this; the rest deny the power.

But each of us can have it, and live by it, and enjoy it to the extent that we will do the work to renew our minds (Eph 4:23; Rom 12;3). We are here to Re-present Him, bearing His image in this age and undoing the enemy's work. We step out in obedience to love others after the manner in which He loved us. (Jn 13, 15). This is not "sympathy", but *power* to set captives free in Christ's name. The early church demonstrated it; Today's true church is finally beginning to once again "manifest" as Sons of God, causing His enemies to scatter.

Bible Quotes are Word English Bible (WEB) except where noted.

1st Mankind Sees 2nd:
Two Possible Responses

(John 15) "If the world hates you, you know that it has hated me before it hated you.

<u>If you were of the world</u>, the world would love its own. But because you are not of the world, since I chose you out of the world, therefore the world hates you. Remember the word that I said to you, 'A servant is not greater than his lord.' If they persecuted me, they will also persecute you. If they kept my word, they will also keep yours. But they will do all these things to you for my name's sake, because they do not know him who sent Me.

22 If I had not come and spoken to them, <u>they would not have had sin</u>, but <u>now they have no excuse for their sin</u>. He who hates me hates My Father also. _If I had not done among them the works which no one else did, they would have no sin; but now they have seen and hated both Me and My Father."

An Issue of Dominion:
Who Shall Reign Forever?

Different people have diametrically different responses when they see the Glory of the Firstborn Son – or any other Son of God. He has given us His glory (Jn 14:12; Jn 17:20) and united us with Him and sent us to re-present Him in both love and power. Christ was the Firstborn Son of God, but out of His love He is no longer the only Son born of God… <u>*He came to bring **many** sons to Glory*</u>. Nearly all the Vision passages we have seen prove that very fact – and we must deal with it. <u>*It **IS** the New Covenant*</u>!

Dear reader – if you have not seen this before, please now know, that the Lord Jesus invites *you to become a Son of God*. He will not be ashamed to call you His brother or sister, because you will be born of the same Spirit of the same Father. Your rest, your joy, your strength – will all appear (Rom 5:5; Rom 8:17).

But Others have a Different Response

If you have identified with Christ (Rom 6:7), then you are free from the power of sin, and no one that knows God continues to practice sin (1 John 3).

But others will be ***outraged*** because He who sets us free from the sin nature **removes their excuse** *for sinning (v22)*. Desperate to protect their worldly power, selfish sensual pleasures, and reputation, they have one response to the appearance of the New Mankind – *destroy Him* or at least disparage and isolate Him. As true ambassadors of this Kingdom, we *demonstrate* the Kingdom as we speak of it. If our witness is only of forgiveness, then we <u>have not *witnessed* the rebirth</u>, nor have we tasted "the" Heavenly gift or the powers of the age to come (Heb 6). If there were no power in a true believer's witness, <u>***there would be no persecution***</u>. But if the Spirit of God indeed dwells in us, ***there is both power and persecution***. And His joy has us covered.

God Provides the Power to Endure; But It's Not Automatic

In verses 20 forward we see the dynamic we will face. Jesus is reminding them what he told them, as also recorded in Matthew 10 (one of the several "endure to the end" passages). Yet every son of God, by the joyful witness inside him of the hope that awaits, has the power to endure even unto death. God meets the need of any and every moment. Remember, <u>it is His life</u> in you! We need only obey His command to set our minds rightly (Rom 12:1-3; Eph 4:23; Col 3:3). If you are gazing into the truth of the Word of God, then you are doing that right now. See the Glory of God and you can endure whatever comes.

Bible Quotes are Word English Bible (WEB) except where noted.

Walk According to Spirit
... and Live

(Romans 8:1-14) There is therefore now no condemnation to those who are in Christ Jesus,

<u>who don't walk according to the flesh, but according to the Spirit</u>.

For the Law of the Spirit of life in Christ Jesus made me free from the Law of sin and death...

He condemned sin in the flesh; that the righteous requirement of the <u>Law might be fulfilled in us</u> <u>who do not walk according to the flesh</u> but according to the Spirit

For <u>if you live after the flesh you must die; but if by the Spirit you put to death the deeds of the body, you will live</u>. For as many as are led by the Spirit of God, <u>these</u> are <u>children of God</u>.

Sown in Weakness and Shame

The Life of a True Follower: "No Condemnation"

Paul summarizes salvation theology in light of what he has just shown. (Rom 5) Just as Abraham *entrusted* himself to God (Hebrew *heymunah*, Greek *pisteuo*) and it was credited to him as righteousness, likewise our setting out to follow Christ (faith and repentance) is *credited to us as righteousness* even before any actual true and acceptable righteousness appears in our souls, words, and deeds.

According to Romans 6 we were buried with Christ in Baptism and raised to life with Him in His rising. He who has died **has been freed from sin** (verse 7)! Given this freedom, we must choose to no longer be slaves to sin. We then have our actual fruit to righteousness, and its reward, eternal life (verse 22). Those that have been striving in vain to obey God against our sinful natures have been living lives of misery. But by burial and resurrection with us in Him, Christ has rescued us from it. If we now obey Him, we are *In Him*.

No More Condemnation ... For those who Walk ...

Walking, of course, is about *behavior*, not "standing"! I emphasize it at risk of sounding harsh, but this is *an eternal destiny matter* for every person. Romans 8 is such a terrible chapter for the old man, but a wonderful chapter for the New Man. A true Church embraces Romans 6 and 8 as marvelous and precious, while a "religious institution" hates the chapter because it levels the field (all are Sons of God) and ruins the marketing plan of those that seek personal glory.

The "no more condemnation" is ***not*** merely "to those that *are forgiven by the blood of Christ*, but rather, to those that *use their newfound freedom* – gained by burial and resurrection – *to walk no longer according to the flesh, but rather put the deeds of the flesh to death (verse 13)*. Scripture tells us this is not difficult to one that knows he has died, been buried, **and has been freed from sin** (Rom 6:7). When you see it in your heart (not your feelings but in the seat of your will), ... *you will feel it break*.

If we now step out to live by the Spirit of God that is now within us, then *unmistakable* fruit begins to appear immediately, even if not much; Wonderfully, the same spirit that raised Christ from the dead will give life to our "mortal" bodies, that is, to these bodies – on this earth.

> Our simple **turn** to "follow" – is credited to us as righteousness (Rom 4). Our **actual following** (Rom 8) by His power (Rom 6) keeps us in His love.

Bible Quotes are Word English Bible (WEB) except where noted.

He Perfected Man
Our Conscience Finally at Peace

(Hebrews 9:14; 10:9-18) ... how much more will the blood of Christ, ...

<u>*cleanse your conscience* ... *to serve the living God? ...*</u> *For the Law, having a shadow of the good to come, ... can never ... make perfect those who draw near. ... because the worshippers, once purified,* **<u>would have had no more consciousness of sins...</u>**

<u>*He takes away the first that He may establish the second*</u>*. ... But he, after he had offered one sacrifice for sins forever,*

sat down on the right hand of God, from that time waiting till His enemies are made the footstool of his feet.

For by one offering He has perfected forever those who are being sanctified.

But the Holy Spirit also witnesses to us; ...

"This is the covenant that I will make with them: 'After those days,' says the Lord, 'I will put my laws on their heart, I will also so write them on the mind;' ...
"I will remember their sins and their iniquities no more."

(1 Cor 2:16) But we have the mind of Christ.

Sown in Weakness and Shame

To Be His People
Living by His Life In Us

When we have sins forgiven, the power of sin broken, the presence and power of God indwelling, we are free! But this freedom is not freedom to go our own way as in, *independently of God*. This **selfish independence** is <u>**the very definition of sin**</u> that scripture provides (Isa 53:8); and it is the mode of living that is mass-propagated by forgiveness-only gospels.

Rather, being "in" Christ brings us the freedom to go "<u>***our***</u>" way together as a body:

> Living and moving <u>*with God and with His People*</u> in perfect unity,
>
> Operating with the Faith – the understanding of Authority that the Centurion had …
>
> but in the Name of the *Highest King* and the *Greatest Power*.
>
> Our Joy is made complete,
>
> We shall ultimately, reign with Christ and under Him – forever and ever.
>
> John 1:12; Mark 9:35; 1 John 4:4

Even now, we are:
God's son, man's servant, and the devil's master
(John G. Lake)

Bible Quotes are Word English Bible (WEB) except where noted.

Some Jews were Jealous!
But *God* Sees and Chooses

Millions have been misled by an erroneous interpretation of Romans chapter 9. The teaching has led them to doubt the very goodness and justice of God. With sadness many see their grown children leave the faith and say, "I guess they were just not elected for salvation". It bears repeating that, unlike the Gnostics, whom the Apostle John branded as heretics, the early church writers from 100-400 A.D. unanimously affirmed the true free will of man to humble himself before God or not.[12] The fact that God "sees" all history at the same time (from outside of time) does not mean He pre-programs the *choices* of man. He sovereignly chose to extend mercy to those that would walk humbly before him; and by His own Son's blood He achieved both justice and mercy.

> *(Romans 8:29) Those whom He **foreknew** he predestined ...*

The Heirs of Promise were Not the "Physical" Firstborns!

> *Romans 9:6-33 ... they are not all Israel, that are **of** Israel. Neither, because they are Abraham's offspring, are they all children. But, "your offspring will be accounted as from Isaac." That is, it is not the children of the flesh who are children of God, but the children of the promise are counted as heirs. ...*

He Sees the Humble Beforehand

> *11 For being not yet born, neither having done anything good or bad, that the purpose of God according to election might stand, not of works, but of him who calls, it was said to her, "The elder will serve the younger."*

He Extends Mercy as He Alone Sees Fit

> *Even as it is written, "Jacob I loved, but Esau I hated." What shall we say then? Is there unrighteousness with God? May it never be! For he said to Moses, "I will have mercy on whom I have mercy, and I will have compassion on whom I have compassion." So, then it is not of him who wills, nor of him who runs, but of God who has mercy.*

---

[12] David Bercot's Historic Faith Commentary Series quotes the early church writers

Not by Bloodline
Nor Rituals, Empire, or Society

Perhaps you have been told that God, in a private meeting in eternity past, decided to create 8 billion people but arbitrarily program 7 billion to eternal torment. If you believed it, then honestly, what is your opinion of the goodness of God? *This false teaching has done massive damage to the reputation of God!* Honestly, is it hard to see who would be behind such a story? But if we see that foreknowledge comes before predestination, then we can make sense of the roughly 1600 points in scripture where man is urged to "choose" to obey God.

He Sees the Proud Beforehand and Resists Them

17 For the Scripture says to Pharaoh, "For this very purpose I caused you to be raised up, that I might show in you my power, and that my name might be proclaimed in all the earth." So then, he has mercy on whom he desires, and he hardens whom he desires.

God Shows No Partiality

20 But indeed, O man, ... What if God, willing to show his wrath, and to make his power known, endured with much patience vessels of wrath prepared for destruction, and that he might make known the riches of his glory on vessels of mercy, which he prepared beforehand for glory, us, whom he also called, not from the Jews only, but also from the Gentiles? As he says also in Hosea, "I will call them 'my people,' which were not my people; and her 'beloved,' who was not beloved."... What shall we say then? That the Gentiles, who didn't follow after righteousness, attained to righteousness, even the righteousness which is of faith; but Israel, following after a law of righteousness, didn't arrive at the law of righteousness. Why? Because they didn't seek it by faith, but as it were by works of the Law.

Striving in the Law of Moses rather than Surrendering Pride

... even as it is written, "Behold, I lay in Zion a stumbling stone and a rock of offense; and no one who believes in him will be disappointed."

Bible Quotes are Word English Bible (WEB) except where noted.

Becoming Like Him
This Hope Does Not Disappoint

(Ephesians 4:13) until we all attain to the <u>unity</u> of the faith and of the <u>knowledge</u> of the Son of God,

to a full-grown man, to the measure of the stature of the fullness of Christ;

(Romans 5:5) and hope doesn't disappoint us, because God's love has been poured out into our hearts through the Holy Spirit who was given to us.

(John 4:17) In this love has been made perfect among us in this: that we may have boldness in the day of judgment; Because <u>as he is, so are we in this world.</u>

No Fear
As He Is, So are We in This World
Casting Down the New Lie of the Enemy

Firstly, as long as we retain the Old Adam in our innermost man, we will bear unacceptable fruit; we will have sin-consciousness in our souls; and we will fear death. But millions of *truly born-again converts and their loved ones* are defeated by the lie that they are still "Just a Sinner" (saved by grace). That lie was crafted by the enemy to "deny" the New Covenant Itself.

But when we make the life-surrender, the life-exchange, we gain a witness inside that we are a Son of God (Rom 8:17); Furthermore, we obtain the witness on the outside – This is the good fruit of the good tree. We see it and we will sense His smile as He sees it. This is how we obtain rest, peace, and joy in this life. Like the child knowing he is secure in his parents' love (see back cover!).

Dignity: Like Him in This World

We take Joy in the Fruit that naturally grows from our lives. It brings peace and casts out fear, because we are living His own life; and He is living through us. True righteousness is the fruit of our lives, and we know it is naturally pleasing to Him. Popular Christianity proclaims "Forgiveness Now and Heaven Someday". The catch never mentioned is that it is the one who "sets out to follow" that shall receive what was promised. This is:

- The faith of Abraham – "go where I will lead you".
- The central salvation teaching of Paul (Rom 2:7, 6:7,21, 8:1-4).
- The command of Christ ("Follow Me – whoever seeks to save His life will lose it").

We are called to know Christ and the power of His rising (Phil 3:10); and becoming like Him, Living His life, and living it from Heaven to Earth while we are on the Earth.

This is **unspeakable dignity**

Nobody doesn't want Freedom, Strength, Glory, Honor, and Dominion.
The Love of God in Christ has ***paid for all these***;
But most of the church **doesn't even mention them**. We settle for forgiveness.
Will you?
Seek the Holiness without which no one will see the Lord (Heb 12:14).

Bible Quotes are Word English Bible (WEB) except where noted.

A Mature Son of God
I Overcome, and Yes - I Tread

(1 John 4:4) You are <u>of God</u>, little children, and <u>have overcome them</u>, because <u>He who is in you is greater</u> than he who is in the world.

(Luke 10:19) Behold, I give you the authority to tread on serpents and scorpions, and over all the power of the enemy. Nothing will in any way hurt you.

I Walk as He Walked

> **"God's Son**
> **Man's Servant, and the devil's master"**
> **- John G. Lake**

JON FARMER FOLLOW THE FIRSTBORN

Advancing the Kingdom
On Earth as it is in Heaven

On the pages that follow, we will see plainly what our purpose in life is to be. I appeal to you to search these scriptures *for yourself* – to see "which is it?":

1. We are called to "let go and let God" until He returns; or
2. We are called to persevere in allegiance, loving as He loved, in compassion and power; exactly as He demonstrated, trained, and commissioned.

Our High Priest stands ready to convert you into a Son of God, and to turn your fear into strength and joy. Read on, because God is Good! He always provides the Hope from which faithfulness and love will spring (Col 1:3-5).

The Blood of Jesus bought our access to the Father. It is the truth that makes you free, and it is the truth by which you overcome the enemy.

I believe God gave me the analogy for this. A week ago, I dreamt that a housecat (like our cat Indie, but it was not him) was standing in the foreground, conscious only of himself, preening. Close to him, but slightly to the background stood a large Lion. The outline of the Lion matched the outline of the cat perfectly except for the mane that was not on the cat. The cat didn't even seem to know the Lion was there. With human eyes the Lion was looking intently to the small cat. I understood that He was waiting for it to dawn on the cat that it was of the same nature as Himself. That was a week ago. This early morning, I sat down to write the intro to this tier based on:

> (John 20:21) Jesus said to them again, "Peace to you. As the Father has sent Me, even so I send you."

As if to give me fuller perspective, our cat walked into the room as he always does at 5 a. He knows it is my job to feed him, and he kindly but confidently calls on me for a refill. He knows that he has access in and out of the house by his portal. He climbs onto my lap to rest secure at any time; If I speak a simple kind word to him, He then purrs with contentment for a few minutes. That's all very good.

> But that's *not all he does*.

After this meeting he goes outside and dominates his world; In rest and strength he Dominates, with all (those) things "under his feet; He tramples anything he finds creeping on the ground. His joy is complete. And Christ is the **_Lion_** of Judah!

Bible Quotes are Word English Bible (WEB) except where noted.

Until the Day
With Christ as He Returns

*(Rev 19:6-16) I heard something like the voice of a great multitude, and like the voice of many waters, and like the voice of mighty thunders, saying, "Hallelujah! For the Lord our God the Almighty reigns. Let's rejoice and be exceedingly glad, and let's give the glory to him, for the marriage of the Lamb has come, and his wife has made herself ready; it was given to her that she would **array herself** in bright, pure, fine, linen; for the **fine linen is the righteousness acts of the saints.***

I saw heaven opened, and behold, a white horse, and he who sat on it is called Faithful and True. In righteousness he judges and makes war. His eyes are a flame of fire, and on his head are many crowns. He has names written and a name written which no one knows but he himself.

He is clothed in a garment sprinkled with blood. His name is called "The Word of God".

<u>And the armies which are in heaven</u> followed him on white horses, clothed in white, pure, fine linen.

Out of his mouth proceeds a sharp, double-edged sword, that with it he should strike the nations. He will rule them with an iron rod; <u>he treads the wine press of the fierceness of the wrath of God,</u> the Almighty. He has on his garment and on his thigh a name written, <u>King of kings</u> and <u>Lord of lords</u>.

Sown in Weakness and Shame

But there is a Treading For This Age

Vengeance against man is not for man. But vengeance against the true enemy – according to the Word of God – certainly is.

We were saved because we surrendered our rebellion; we persevered in following Him rather than going our own way. All this is to be "In Christ".

In this Age we enjoy the first fruits, as Paul writes in the conclusion of his letter describing sound and true salvation theology:

> *(Romans 16:20) And the God of peace will quickly <u>crush Satan under **your** feet.</u> The grace of our Lord Jesus Christ be with you.*

Precious souls reading this: Please see the elements that together form the backbone of the Word of God, from Cover to Cover:

The Steadfast Love of God;

The New Covenant and the New Man, The Second Mankind, The Restoration of Dominion to Man on Earth – the Kingdom of God

Those In Christ – doing the will of God, have the privilege of *going everywhere Christ goes*. In the timeless unseen He has already gone there, but in the material world the final battle has not arrived, ***<u>but it certainly shall</u>***.

> *(Matthew 16:2-28 RSV) For what will it profit a man, if he gains the whole world, and forfeits his life? Or what shall a man give in exchange for his life?*

> *For the Son of man will come in the glory of his Father with his angels. and then <u>he will render to everyone according to his deeds.</u>*

Bible Quotes are Word English Bible (WEB) except where noted.

Life is Very Different If We Actually See Christ

If we are surrendered then we see Christ; This is not just theology or poetry – but fact! I attest that I have seen Christ many times. It's promised right there to those that will surrender self-will and entrust themselves to Him; to do the will of God.

> *(John 14:19-21) Yet a little while, and the world will see me no more; **but you will see me**. Because I live, you will live also...*
>
> *One who **has my commandments, and keeps them**, that person is one who loves me. One who loves me will be loved by my Father, and **I will love him, and will reveal myself to him**."*
>
> *(John 16:16) A little while, and you will not see me. Again **a little while, and you will see me.**" ...*

This is one more instance of a wonderful, real, truth that never sees the light of day in most churches. Even more – once we see Him, the nature of our faith changes radically; There is much less doubting and wavering; we begin to conquer the true enemy as a way of life. We are not only clothed in His righteousness but are also complete with His conquering life in us (Col 2:9).

In every age – there are some Sons of God manifesting, but in the conclusion of the Age of the Gentiles, we will be revealed as Sons of God (Rom 8:21).

Bible Quotes are Word English Bible (WEB) except where noted.

Freed by His Death <u>As</u> Us
Not Only *Buried* with Him

Christ Died not only "For" us, but "As" us; So Chains Break

> If our rebellion is laid down; if our *will* is aligned with His, then we are In Christ; Everything He is, has, and has done; and everything appointed to Him – becomes ours as well.

Isaiah 52:13-14 Behold, My Servant shall deal prudently; He shall be exalted and extolled and be very high. 14 Just as many were astonished at you, So <u>His visage was marred more than any man, And His form more than the sons of men</u>;

Numbers 21:9 So Moses made a bronze serpent, and put it on a pole; and so it was, if a serpent had bitten anyone, when he looked at the bronze serpent, he lived.

John 3:14-15 And as Moses lifted up the serpent in the wilderness, even so must the Son of Man be lifted up, that whoever believes in Him should not perish but have eternal life.

2 Corinthians 5:14-21 For the love of Christ compels us, because **we judge thus: that if One died for all, then all died;** *and He died for all, that those who live should live no longer for themselves, but for Him who died for them and rose again... Therefore, if anyone is in Christ, he is a new creation; old things have passed away; behold, all things have become new. ... For* **He made Him who knew no sin to be sin for us, that we might become the righteousness of God in Him.**

Romans 6:6-8 knowing this, that <u>our old man was crucified with Him, that the body of sin might be done away with</u>, that we should no longer be slaves of sin. 7 For <u>he who has died has been freed from sin.</u> Now if we died with Christ, we believe that we shall <u>also live with Him</u>, ...

6:22 But now <u>having been set free from sin</u>, and *having become slaves of God*, <u>you have your fruit to holiness, and the end, everlasting life</u>.

Sown in Weakness and Shame

But In the Unseen,
We Were Also *Raised* with Him

*Ephesians 1:20-21 which he worked in Christ when he raised Him from the dead and <u>made him to sit at his right hand in the heavenly places</u>, far <u>above all rule, and authority, and power, and dominion</u>, and every name that is named, **not only in this age but also in the age to come.***

*Ephesians 2:5-6 ... made us alive together with Christ ... and **raised us up with him**<u>, and made us sit together in the heavenly places in Christ Jesus</u> ...*

John 20:17 ... say to them, "[Notice the quote marks! As Mary is instructed to say, as herself] <u>'I am ascending</u> to My Father and your Father, to My God and your God.'"

Hebrews 2:10 For it became him, ... <u>in bringing many children to glory</u>, to make the author of their salvation perfect through sufferings.

*Romans 8:4 He condemned sin in the flesh, that the righteous requirement of the Law might be **fulfilled** in us who do not walk according to the flesh but according to the Spirit.*

Col 1:13-23 who delivered us out of the power of darkness, and translated us into the Kingdom of the Son of his love, ... And you, ... He has reconciled in the body of His flesh through death, to present you holy and without defect and blameless before him— if you continue in the faith, ...

2 Peter 1:3-4 ... his <u>divine power has granted to us all things that pertain to life and godliness,</u> through the knowledge of him who called us by his own glory and virtue, 4 by which he has granted to us his precious and exceedingly great promises, that through these you may become <u>partakers of the divine nature, having escaped from the corruption</u> that is in the world by lust.

*1 John 4:17 ... love has been made perfect among us in this: that we may have boldness in the day of judgment; because **<u>as he is, even so are we in this world</u>**.*

Bible Quotes are Word English Bible (WEB) except where noted.

Part 3 Revisited:
The Body of Christ, Growing

Hebrews 12:1-2 Therefore let's also, seeing we are surrounded by so great a cloud of witnesses, lay aside every weight and the sin which so easily entangles us, and let's run with perseverance the race that is set before us, looking to Jesus, the author and perfecter of faith, who for the joy that was set before him endured the cross, despising its shame, and has sat down at the right hand of the throne of God.

*Revelation 3:1-5 "And to the angel of the assembly in Sardis write: ... "I know your works, that you have a reputation of being alive, but you are dead. Wake up, and **keep the things that remain, which you were about to throw away**, ... **Keep it, and repent.** If therefore you won't watch, I will come as a thief, and you won't know what hour I will come upon you. Nevertheless, you have a few names in Sardis that didn't defile their garments. They will walk with me in white, for they are worthy. 5 He who overcomes will be arrayed in white garments, and I will in no way blot his name out of the book of life, and I will confess his name before my Father, and before his angels.*

Shall We Join Them?
The Remnant in White Robes

Here we turn the discussion back to the poster panels 3c & 3d again – these are the bottom-right and the right-edge portions of the Glory & Dominion "smile" (⌞ ⌟) that runs along the edges of the bottom half of the poster.

Glory and Dominion await us; They are the Hopes that give rise to faith and love (Col 1:3). They "spring" from it!

We see – at the right half of the bottom edge – there is a growing and unstoppable flux of citizens of Heaven, hidden with Christ in God, with a Spirit of power, love, and a sound mind. They held fast even through the great falling away. They all varied as to *how much* of the image of God they presented; but in every case there was *fruit of the right tree* still being borne, and their testimony of allegiance to Christ was intact.

They have sown themselves, planted themselves, to be buried with Christ in order to be raised with Him (Rom 6:4). The have enjoyed the first fruits, and they shall have neither fear nor shame at the Second Coming of the Lord Jesus Christ.

And they shall inherit all things; They shall reign with Him and under Him forever and ever.

Now, please carefully devour Revelation 19 through 22. You will see the Millennial reign of Christ and the Restoration of all things. But for the remainder of this age, we who are surrendered into Christ are to be seated with Him in the unseen as we do battle … both inwardly and outwardly.

Inwardly and Outwardly

If and as we overcome the work of the enemy in our own souls, it is also our assignment to overcome the work of the enemy around us. Even the demons are subject to us. But there is no dominion – no *re-presenting Christ* – without denying ourselves.

And "we bear one another's burdens, fulfilling the Law of Christ" (Gal 6;7).

The Kingdom of God is not for cowards. The Kingdom permits violence, and the violent enter it by force. They shall indeed enter, because the breaker, the Messiah, has gone before them (Micah 2:13). It is this breaker that calls to us and says "Follow Me".

Bible Quotes are Word English Bible (WEB) except where noted.

PART 8: THE ROMANS CENTER-LANE

Paul's letter to the Romans wasn't written primarily to correct some bad teaching that was afoot. It turns out that this very same false teaching has persisted through the centuries and has strangled the life of the Church to this very day in the American popular Gospel.

I include the explicit passages wherever needed to be accurate and precise as regards areas where unscriptural teachings have crept into widespread acceptance.

Romans 1: For the Obedience of Allegiance

Our reconciliation to God comes by faith in the sacrifice of Christ; It purchases the forgiveness of our past sins (Rom 3:27). But the overall, higher purpose of the Gospel is not to proclaim "faith *instead of* obedience". An honest and complete amplified Bible true to context would expand the full definition of pistis: "… for the "obedience of [faith, faithfulness, loyalty, fidelity, solidarity, and allegiance]. This is still all *by grace* in that we accomplish this by diligently utilizing His powerful provisions.

In the Gospel, the **righteousness of God** is revealed in a believer[13] to the next person that sees and *hungers* (because he in turn believes)[14].

We cannot see "faith", but we can all see its obedience in others. I emphasize this point only because many millions have been misled in this area and their breakthrough awaits.

> *Romans 1:5 NKJV Through Him we have received grace and apostleship <u>for obedience</u> of faith among all nations for His name,*

---

[13] 1 John 4:17 As He is, so are we in this world; Matt 10 When trained, will be like His master
[14] Rom 1:16-17 In the Gospel, the righteousness of God is revealed from faith to faith

Romans 2: Everybody Wants Glory, Honor, & Immortality[15]

God will Render According to Deeds. Eternal Life is the reward, not merely for getting past sins forgiven, but by living to do the will of God (definition of In Christ", the central concept of all of Paul's epistles) *by the power of God after conversion*. More specifically, the issue is, how to obtain both the desire and the ability to restfully serve God, doing good?

> *Rom 2:5-8 ... the righteous judgment of God, who "will pay back to everyone according to their works": to those who by perseverance in well-doing* **seek after glory, honor, and incorruptability**; *but to those who are self-seeking and* **do not obey the truth**, *but obey unrighteousness—will be wrath and indignation, ...*

Romans 3: Sins Committed; Image of God Lost

Not only have we all sinned and "need our record of sins erased"; but unredeemed mankind *also **no longer bears the image of God*** – this is simply "that which was lost"[16]. As regards "dominion", the earth and the enemy do not obey us if we do not bear the image of God[17].

> *Romans 3:21-23 But now apart from the Law a righteousness of God has been revealed, being testified by the Law and the prophets, even the* **righteousness of God** *through faith in Jesus Christ,* **to** *all and* **on** *all those who believe. For there is no difference; for all* **have sinned** *and* **fall short of the glory of God**,
>
> *being justified freely by his grace through the redemption that is in Christ Jesus; ... through the passing over of* **prior sins**, *in God's forbearance.*

Romans 4: No more Guilt of what We've Done

The record of sons committed is purged for those for those who come out from idolatry (serving created things) and turn in faith to obey God. Abraham did not merely "believe that His sins were paid for". In this chapter we see exactly what He believed:

---

[15] Rom 2:7 To all who through perseverance in good seek after ... He rewards w/ Eternal Life

[16] Luke 19:10 The Son of Man came to restore that which was lost. Note the Son of Man.

[17] Ge 1:26-27 Let us make man in our image (Hebrew Tselem. Re-presenting)... Dominion.

Bible Quotes are Word English Bible (WEB) except where noted.

> *Romans 4:20-24 Yet, looking to the promise of God, he didn't waver through unbelief, but grew strong through faith, giving glory to God, and <u>being fully **assured that what he had promised** he was also able to perform</u>. Therefore it was "credited to him for righteousness".*

Forgiveness is wonderful! But it is only the first phase of the grace of God; as we shall see, we also need actual righteousness; that is, fruit from the good tree[18].

Romans 5: Two Adams, Two Mankinds ... Choose!

> *Romans 5:17 For if by the trespass of the one, death reigned through the one, much more those who receive abundance of grace and of **the gift of righteousness** will reign in life through the One, Jesus Christ.)*

- We must **Be born to the lineage of the *Last* Adam and *Live*** – Any man can only go where his or her selected Adam has gone

Romans 6: No More <u>Shame</u> of What We <u>Are</u>

Popular Christianity teaches that Gospel simply announces the means of forgiveness. Sadly, it does not even address people's <u>*deeper*</u> need for <u>*dignity*</u> and the power to stop sinning[19].

> *Romans 6:7 For he who has died has been freed from sin.*

In all the above, please do not read the word "righteousness" and think "forgiveness", since scriptures do not say that. Without the chains broken[20], we have no true witness[21]. But by identifying with both the death[22] and the rising – and ascension and seating and sending[23] – we not only get the "chains broken", we are given constitution of Sons of God[24]; Not only have we escaped the corruption, but we are also partaking in the divine nature; And we have an unspeakably glorious inheritance.

---

[18] Rom 10:10 ... believes and is justified; confesses *Jesus as Lord* and is saved
[19] 1 John 3 No one that is born of God continues to sin - enslaved or actively practicing
[20] Luke 4:18 He has sent me to proclaim liberty to the captives
[21] 1 Timothy 3:5 ... a form of godliness; holding the form of religion but denying the power
[22] John 3:14-16 (context for John 3:16) We must see our sin crucified, not just forgiven
[23] Eph 1:20ff Seated far above ... every name named... Eph 2:6 and *raised us with Him*
[24] Eph 4:24 For you were created in righteousness and true holiness after the pattern of God

As we have seen throughout this book, many Christian traditions do not mention these hugely important passages and their precious truths. As true disciples, we are to proclaim the main entrées – freedom, power, and fellowship with God - not just the appetizer and the dessert. As long as we sell the gospel short, God will not honor it with His power.

> *Romans 6:8-11 But if we died with Christ, we believe that we will also live with him, knowing that Christ, being raised from the dead, dies no more. Death no more has dominion over Him! ... Thus consider yourselves to be dead to sin, but alive to God in Christ Jesus our Lord.*

Eternal Life is the result of holiness, and holiness comes from deliverance, rebirth, and obedience: This is a "stumbling block of the proud" but beautiful to the humble:

> *Romans 6:17-22 But thanks be to God, that you became obedient from the heart to that form of teaching to which you were delivered.*
> ***Being made free from sin,*** *you became servants of righteousness...*
> *so now present your members as servants to righteousness for sanctification... But now **having been set free from sin**, and having become servants of God, you have your fruit of sanctification, and the result of everlasting life.*

Romans 7 – No More Misery, No More Hypocrisy

Rule systems entice those of the First Mankind, still enslaved.

Paul celebrates the truth of Romans 4,5, and 6 here, because the power of God liberates the "pharisee" – one that has sought to obey God without *surrendering* to God, seeking to be justified and righteous *in his <u>own name</u>*.

> *Romans 7:23-25 But I see a different law in my members, warring against the law of my mind, and bringing me into captivity to the law of sin which is in my members. What a wretched man I am! <u>Who will deliver me from this body of death? 25a I thank God—through Jesus Christ our Lord</u>!*

Despite Romans 4 (forgiveness), 5 (identification), 6 (deliverance and rebirth), and *<u>this entire chapter up to verse</u>* 25, many teachers nevertheless use verse 25:

> *Romans 7:25b So then, with the mind I myself serve the Law of God, but with the flesh the law of sin.*

Bible Quotes are Word English Bible (WEB) except where noted.

… to prove that Christians **should expect to remain powerless** in overcoming sin. But in light of the surrounding chapters Paul in verse 25a was simply *recapping the misery of living from self-righteousness* (from the First Mankind, not born again).

Romans 8: Now to Put Sin to Death by His Spirit in Us

Romans 8 is the *conclusion* of Paul's theology of salvation, echoing key truths of chapters 1 through 7. It describes the freedom, life, power, and hope of a Son or daughter of God. The chapter begins by defining "In Christ", and by stating *who it is* that is no longer under condemnation:

> *Romans 8:1-4 NKJV There is therefore now no condemnation to those who are in Christ Jesus, who don't walk according to the flesh, but according to the Spirit. For the Law of the Spirit of life in Christ Jesus made me free from the Law of sin and of death. For what the Law could not do in that it was weak through the flesh, God did, sending his own Son in the likeness of sinful flesh and for sin, he condemned sin in the flesh, that the ordinance of the Law might be fulfilled in us who do not walk after the flesh but after the Spirit.*

In popular preaching, we hear only the **_first half_** of the **_first verse_**, out of context:

> *Romans 8:1a There is therefore now no condemnation for those who are in Christ Jesus*

This is why we must state the gospel as simply as possible but no simpler! Without deliverance, rebirth, and the indwelling spirit of God, the following verse would be dreadful – so _seeker unfriendly_!!

> *Romans 8:13 For if you live after the flesh you must die; but if _by the Spirit you put to death the deeds of the body, you will live._*

But with the full Grace of God – everything we need for life and godliness[25] – and with the Hope supplied – it is wonderful:

---

[25] 2 Pet 1:3 By His divine power He has given us everything we need for life and godliness

Romans 8:18-19 For I consider that the sufferings of this present time are not worthy to be compared with the glory which shall be revealed in us.

Bible Quotes are Word English Bible (WEB) except where noted.

Two Mankinds, Two Lineages, Two Laws

We now have both: the Right and the Power to Choose

*(John 1:12) But as many as received Him, to them he <u>gave the **right** to become God's children</u>, to those who believe in His <u>name</u>:*

*(Romans 8:2) For the Law of the Spirit of life in Christ Jesus has made me **free** from the Law of sin and death.*

*(2 Peter 1:3-4) ... his divine power has granted to us all things that pertain to life and godliness, through the knowledge of Him who <u>called us by his own glory and virtue</u>, by which have been granted to us his precious and exceedingly great <u>promises</u>, that through these you <u>may</u> become **<u>partakers of the divine nature, having escaped from the corruption</u>** <u>that is in the world by lust</u>.*

Free Indeed! ... Now the Do-Over: Our Choice: Sow to Flesh, or Sow to Spirit?

*<u>(Galatians 6:7-8) Don't be deceived</u>, God is not mocked; for whatever a man sows, that he will also reap. For he who sows to his flesh will from the flesh reap corruption, but **<u>he who sows to the Spirit will from the Spirit reap everlasting life</u>**.*

Sown in Weakness and Shame

The Romans Center Lane: In "Three-Up" Format

Romans chapters 1-8 contain the most detailed statements of New Covenant salvation theology we have been given! Therefore, with care we can see the full terms of it. I include the explicit passages in areas where I myself have seen unscriptural and oversimplified teachings dominate popular Christianity.

Notice in particular, that in Christ, God has given us the ***right to become*** Sons of God. Nothing happens without reconciliation; So, the Blood of Christ wipes away our record of past sins. This is the "legal groundwork" for our entrance into the Kingdom of God.

Salvation itself is bigger (and better) than forgiveness alone. Forgiveness erases guilt, but it does not erase shame. So even our conversion requires an actual turn of allegiance (Romans 10:10); We set out to obey His commands – to Live as He lived, and to Love as He loved – all by His power.

If we have camped on overly simplified teaching; but will accept this small but hugely important expansion, then this will be a **<u>huge breakthrough</u>** for you as it was for me.

Bible Quotes are Word English Bible (WEB) except where noted.

Romans 1, 2, 3
For Obedience to the Faith

As I mentioned previously, the purpose of the Gospel is not to proclaim faith "instead" of actual obedience - except for forgiveness of *past sins* Rom 3:27), but that we might possess His nature (righteousness) and bear His image (glory) by His provisions. In the Gospel, the **righteousness of God** is revealed from believer to in a believer to the next person that sees and hungers (believes).

> *Through Him we have received grace and apostleship for obedience of faith among all nations ... Rom 1:5*

Reward for Doing Good: Glory, Honor, & Immortality

God will Render According to Deeds. Eternal Life is the reward, not merely for getting past sins forgiven, but by living to do the will of God (definition of In Christ", the central concept of all of Paul's epistles) *by the power of God after conversion*. More specifically, the issue is, how to obtain both the desire and the ability to restfully serve God, doing good?

> *Romans 2:5-8 ... the righteous judgment of God, who "will pay back to everyone according to their works": to those who by **persevering in well-doing seek for glory, honor, and incorruptibility, eternal life**; but to those who are self-seeking and do **not obey the truth**, but obey unrighteousness, will be wrath and indignation.*

Sins Committed; but Also, The Image of God Lost

Not only have we all built a record of sins; but unredeemed mankind *also **no longer bears the image of God*** – this is simply "that which was lost". We had it, and lost it, and no "religious rules" will fix this. But God fixes this for those who will acknowledge their need and then forsake sin by His power.

> *Romans 3:21-23 But now apart from the Law, a **righteousness of God** has been revealed, ... even the righteousness of God through faith in Jesus Christ to all **and on all** who believe... for all **have sinned** and **fall short of the glory of God**.*

The Bible clearly teaches that we have all "fallen short of the glory of God", but only man's revisions teach that we are "totally depraved" being unable to even grasp a rope while we are drowning in sin. It is not pride or programming, but rather *humility* that reaches for that rope!

Romans 4, 5, 6 ...
Fixing Shame of What We <u>Are</u>

The record of sons committed is purged for those for those who come out from idolatry (serving created things) and turn in faith to obey God. Abraham did not merely "believe that His sins were paid for". Let's look at what He believed:

> *Romans 4:20-24 Yet looking to the promise of God, he didn't waver through unbelief, but grew strong through faith, giving glory to God, and <u>being **fully assured that what he had promised, he was also able to perform**</u>. And therefore it also was "**credited** to him for righteousness."*

Rom 5:10-11 and Rom 10:9-10 both show that a "Justification" *event* is not synonymous with our ultimate Salvation – as much as we would wish it. There is no getting around the fact that reconciliation to God (initial salvation) and our eternal destiny (ultimate salvation) rests on whether or not we will <u>*actually forsake sin*</u> and practice righteousness, by cooperating with God's power.

If – and only if – we accept this, the *apparent* contradictions in the Gospels and Epistles finally evaporate and you finally know you got it right (2 Pet 1:3-4).

> Forgiveness is not "instead" of obedience. Rather, being united with God and living under His Mercy - makes faithfulness both possible and enjoyable.

The *immediate* results of this are joy and boldness. You no longer need theologians to interpret (spin) passages for you. The entire Old and New Testaments makes sense because you see how a believer under the New Covenant meets the requirements of the Law of Moses (the righteousness requirements of it); and you also see the pathway to glory and dominion. You know exactly how you can overcome (Eph 4:22-24; Rev. 2).

Forgiveness is wonderful! We obtain it when we see and embrace the News that God raised Christ from the dead – accepting His payment for our sins; Nevertheless, forgiveness alone is far from "everything we need for life *and godliness*" (2 Pet 1).

We escape sin's power by identifying with the death of Christ, and we confirm our calling and election by utilizing the power of the Spirit of God in us to put sin to death (2 Peter 1:10; Rom 8:13). In this way, the burden of Christ is light.

Can you see the puzzle pieces now finding their place into the backbone of "The Kingdom of God" of "Dominion"? He equips you to "overcome".

Bible Quotes are Word English Bible (WEB) except where noted.

Two Adams, Two Mankinds ... Choose your Lineage

> *Romans 5:17 For if by the trespass of the one death reigned through the one; so much more will those who receive the abundance of grace **and of the gift of righteousness reign in life** through the One, Jesus Christ.*

Any man can only go where his or her chosen Mankind (chosen Adam) has gone.

Deliverance from *what We Were*

Simplistic Christianity teaches that the Gospel simply announces the means of forgiveness. It fails to mention the need for ***the actual power to stop sinning***:

> *Romans 6:7 For he who has died has been freed from sin.*

But by identifying with both the death and the rising, not only do we ***escape the corruption***, but we also ***partake in the divine nature****! This is the central benefit of the Gospel.

> *Romans 6:8-9 But if we died with Christ, we believe that we will also live with Him, knowing that Christ, being raised from the dead, dies no more. Death no more has **dominion** over him.*

Eternal Life is the result of holiness, and holiness comes from deliverance (as we have seen, from the power of sin), rebirth, and obedience:

> *Rom 6:22 ... being made free from sin, and having become servants of God, you have your fruit to holiness, and the result of eternal life.*

Sown in Weakness and Shame

Bible Quotes are Word English Bible (WEB) except where noted.

Romans 7, 8
No More Sinner by Constitution

Paul celebrates the truth of Romans 4,5, and 6 here, because the power of God Romans 6 Deliverance) liberates the "religious" from the misery of frustration:

> *Romans 7:23-25 But I see a different law in my members, warring against the law of my mind, and bringing me into captivity to the law of sin which is in my members. What a wretched man I am!* <u>*Who will deliver me out of the body of this death?*</u> <u>**25a I thank God through Jesus Christ, our Lord**</u>*!* *25b ... with the mind I **myself** serve the Law of God, but with the flesh the sin's law.*

Romans 7 (a) celebrates the fact that Romans 6 freedom from sin is the end of a Pharisee's misery; (b) establishes that is freedom now our responsibility – by an act of our mind, to put to death the sin that *<u>is no longer "us"</u>* but is merely *<u>in us;</u>* and that Christ has made the way for it. Or, as most of the church has done for fifty years, we can pretend chapters 6 and 8 are not there, and refuse to renew our minds in the name of "grace"; and hope for the best. *That house* is built on *sand*.

Despite Romans 4 (forgiveness), 5 (identification), 6 (deliverance and rebirth), and <u>*this entire chapter up to verse*</u> 25, many teachers nevertheless use verse 25b to prove that Christians **should expect to remain powerless** in overcoming sin, but in light of the surrounding chapters plus verse 25a, we see that Paul was simply describing the life of the Pharisee, **living without deliverance from the power of sin**. It's "religion".

Because Christ sets us "free indeed", we can now we can see exactly who it is that is no longer under condemnation – and it makes perfect sense…

Sown in Weakness and Shame

As a Salvation Matter:
Put Sin to Death by His Spirit

Romans 8 is the *conclusion* of Paul's theology of salvation, echoing key truths of preceding chapters. We saw how by God's provision we live in the freedom, life, healing, power, and hope of a Son of God.

The conclusion begins by stating specifically *who it is that is* no longer under condemnation:

> Romans 8:1-4 There is therefore now no condemnation to those who are **in Christ Jesus**, who ***don't walk according to the flesh, but according to the Spirit***. For the law of the Spirit of life in Christ Jesus has made me free from the law of sin and death. For what the Law couldn't do in that it was weak through the flesh, God did, sending his own Son ... He condemned sin in the flesh, that the ordinance of the Law might be fulfilled in us, **who do not walk after the flesh but after the Spirit.**

Without deliverance, rebirth, and the indwelling God, the following verse would be dreadful:

> Romans 8:13 For if you live after the flesh you must die; but if by the Spirit you put to death the deeds of the body, you will live.

But with the full Grace of God – including deliverance, it is wonderful:

> Romans 8:18-19 NKJV For I consider that the sufferings of this present time are not worthy to be compared with the glory which shall be revealed in us.

Bible Quotes are Word English Bible (WEB) except where noted.

Chapters 4-8
In One-paragraph Summaries

Chap 4: Justified by Believing the Promise – No More Guilt

*Rom 4:20-24 Yet, looking to the promise of God, he didn't waver through unbelief, but grew strong through faith, giving glory to God, and being fully assured that what he had promised he was also able to perform. And therefore it was "**credited** to him for righteousness".*

Chap 5: Transferred to the Second Adam and His Destiny

Rom 5:17 For if by the trespass of the one death reigned through the one, so much more will those who receive abundance of grace and of the **gift of righteousness** reign in life through the One, Jesus Christ.

Chap 6: Empowered for Holiness – and Its Reward

*For **he who has died has been freed from sin**. Now if we died with Christ, we believe that we shall also live with Him, knowing that Christ, having been raised from the dead, dies no more. Death no longer has dominion over Him. ... now present your members as slaves of righteousness for holiness... But now having been set free from sin, and having become slaves of God, you have your fruit to holiness, and the result, eternal life.*

(Rom 6:7; 18-22)

Chap 7: Relief from the Life of Defeat under "Religion"

... Who will deliver me from this body of death? I thank God through Jesus Christ our Lord! (Rom 7:25)

Chap 8: No More Condemnation for those who Walk ...

Rom 8:1-2 There is therefore now no condemnation to those who are in Christ Jesus, who don't walk after the flesh, but after the Spirit. Rom 8:18 For I consider that the sufferings of this present time are not worth comparing with the glory which will be revealed toward us.

PART 9: THE WAY OF HOLINESS
Cover Photo Analogy

My hope is that you are seeing more clearly than before, the "Way" that Christ made is "beautiful"; very unlike what it is commonly understood to be. It is joy, peace, and beauty!

This is a very short "part" of this book, but a picture is worth a thousand words, and I believe that you will be strengthened to see the Way of Christ with this very scriptural analogy.

The Cover Photo, though it is heavily cropped, speaks of the strength of the elevated, beautiful, and immovable Highway. I chose it as a depiction of the King's Highway. Please consider the following correspondences to the Vision Passages.

Notably, one month before this book was published, I was on a driving trip in the Appalachian Mountains ... and found myself driving over this very bridge!

The Bright Stripe

The center lane is the "straight and narrow" which is simply to do what is right by the power of His righteousness. We do this knowing that He is with us, in us, and for us. We are walking in the company of the redeemed, we see the lights of the witness ahead that have gone before us, with Christ at the very head; for He Himself created this _**way**_. Jesus – both Lord and Brother – is bringing many sons to glory (Heb 2).

Notice that from a distance it looks like one strip in the middle. It is really the Firstborn Son of God and His brothers that are "in Him". We are united with God because Christ carried us there (Col 3)!

The Mountain

The Rock, which is underneath; at your side; behind you; and going before you, is God Himself. He is one being yet three persons in perfect unity. It is the

Bible Quotes are Word English Bible (WEB) except where noted.

Good Father, in whom there is no darkness at all; It is Christ our High Priest, who has shown us the love of the Father; Christ is the Mediator of our reconciliation and also our advocate for the entire journey. His innocent Blood established the New Man, the Second Mankind, our wonderful new constitution and lineage. That blood never stops speaking on our behalf if we simply persevere. The Holy Spirit conveys the Life and Power and presence of God into our beings, and into our real experience.

The Rails

In *The Kingdom that Turned the World Upside Down*, David Bercot explains the ditches – the chasms on either side of the narrow way:

> On the one side, there is the chasm of laxity and worldliness. Most professing Christians fall into this chasm. The kingdom walk is too stringent for them. They want an easier road. And there's no shortage of preachers who will tell them that they don't really have to obey Jesus' teachings. Those same preachers will also tell them they don't really have to be separate from the world.
>
> On the other side of the narrow way is the chasm of pharisaism. This is the abyss of self-righteousness. If we don't fall into the first chasm, we're likely to fall into the other.
>
> The way is not easy.

The Rails are the "checks". Dozens of passages show that we are free to disobey God. If we have not seared our consciences by persisting in disobedience, then when we are compromising, the Spirit of God brings it to our awareness. If we are in Christ, this is simply the way of life we have chosen when we first surrendered: If we confess, we are forgiven and cleansed (1 Jn 1:9; 2:1).

The Pillars

All the Strength we need is ours by the steadfast love and forbearance of God, and the New Covenant in the Blood of Christ; By these, God brought about the Second Mankind (2 Cor 5; Rom 5; 1 Cor 15) and has restored Dominion (Dan 7; Rev 22); and our inheritance as Sons of God. We obtain it all when we see His love and surrender our rebellion (Mt 16:24). By life exchange, we are converted and we live His life. We now desire to do His will (Mt 16:26) and we accomplish it by His power (Eph 1:17-19).

The Water Below

Christ not only died "for us", but "AS" us (1 Cor 1:20; Rom 6:1-7)! The water below is where the Old Man was buried, and we have been freed by His death (Rom 6:7).

The Water Above

The Water Above is glistening and refreshing, charged with Life; It flows from the throne of God (Rev 22). After we are submerged in the water below, we rise and are filled and refreshed from this living water. We hunger and thirst no more (Matt 5:6).

The Pavement

The pavement is a light and welcome path, level and beautiful and full of confident hope. This highway takes turns to unforeseen seasons and situations. Nevertheless, we walk on it restfully, because we have been freed by His death (Rom 6; Mt 11:28). This pavement is massive strength under our feet because we are also Strong by His Righteousness, alive and working in us and through us (Ezek 36; Jeremiah 31; Joel 2; Gal 2:20). He has indeed provided everything we need for Life and godliness (2 Pet 1:3-4) so we are not only joyful, but also responsible and diligent (2 Pet 1:5).

We, having escaped the power of sin, walk no longer after the flesh but according to the spirit, and there is now therefore no more condemnation for us (Rom 8).

There lies ahead a restoration all things (Acts 3:21), when the Kingdoms of the World are given to the people of the Most High (Psalm 115:16; Psalm 8:6; Dan 7:27). He not only bore our sins and our sicknesses; but the day is coming when He shall divide the spoil with the strong (Isa 53).

The Light

The Light is the Dawn – the perfectly real and sufficient Hope; the Joy of the love of God arising on our hearts; and the knowledge of our unspeakably beautiful inheritance. We were saved in this Hope; and in this hope we purify ourselves (1 Jn 3:3). We have no fear of judgement because in this world, we are Like Him (1 Jn 4:17).

The light of God also represents power. This same power will remake the earth itself with fervent heat, and the sea will be no more – and we shall inherit that world.

Bible Quotes are Word English Bible (WEB) except where noted.
Above it all, we are seated with Christ, far above the adversary. We are to rule with Christ and under Christ (Jn 20; Eph 1:17; Eph 2:6), bearing His image once again (Gen 1:26).

PART 10: SECOND MANKIND GOSPEL SUMMARIES

By selecting and prioritizing passages from this vision collection, we can train ourselves to be ready to share the Gospel accurately, with no salvation-relevant omissions. When we speak to a captive and offer "Christ In You – the Hope of glory" (Col 1:27), we will get a response. Whether they run to it or from it is up to them, and God *knows* their pride or humility in advance, but it is *up to them*.

Our assignment is to be true and honest witnesses. God's job is to confirm the Word with signs accompanying (Mark 16:12-20).

Obviously, if you have read this far, you are "of the light" and have run to it so that the World would see that your works are of God; because you rightly desire dignity; God wants you to want it if your plans are not selfish. This is *healthy* glory and *healthy* dignity!!!

God foreknew you would enter the light (Rom 8:29), and you are being conformed to image of the firstborn from the dead. You are being transformed by the gift of His very power; you are working out your salvation (Phil 2:12-13), putting sin to death (Rom 8:13), and being transformed from one degree of glory (the manifest presence of God in you) to the next (1 Cor 3).

You are the Proof; You are the Witnesses

Bible quotes are for shining light - Not for "Proving". The Word is the message, but just as Christ was the bodily proof in the First century, you are now the bodily proof to the end of this age. Speak the Word of God as His ambassador – not to "prove", but to relay *Words of Hope* to meet their need of deliverance from any and all oppression. Invite them to become citizens of the Kingdom that shall never end.

If you do not have a personal testimony of your own transition from weakness to strength and overcoming – with supernatural power, you simply are not a witness yet.

If you cannot tell of an appealing Kingdom, then you do not have an appealing King. If this is you, surrender your life to Christ as explained in the pages that follow – be born of God and then be filled by His Spirit. Then you will know for sure that you are a son or daughter of God (Rom 8:17), and you will be both *free indeed* and a *witness indeed*.

C. R. Blake: "Start with the Character and Nature of God"

Any presentation of the Gospel must begin with a statement of who God is. Wikipedia (at least at this moment) gets it right:

> "In Christianity, God is the supreme creator of the Universe and everything in it. He is one being in three persons; He is everywhere present; He is all-knowing; He is all-powerful; and He is Love."

As regards the essentials of the Gospel – if you have studied the vision passages then you of course know the essentials by now, and you have seen the scriptures that expose the disastrous omissions that have been made by man in the fourth century (the Gnostics and Augustine), and the fifteenth (Luther and Calvin). Even within in these traditions, millions have given their lives to Christ; Nevertheless, many of these have been defeated in their personal lives and defeated when they attempt to help others. Secretly, many doubt the power or the goodness of a God that leaves them enslaved. Their children notice as well. This is why the current growth rate of heathenism far exceeds that of Christianity.

But what passages – if you "focus" on them – will enable you to always have at the tip of your tongue the essential benefits that God invites man to enjoy, and the conditions upon which we may receive them? I suggest the following:

1. Master some key passages from *each* panel – so that you won't miss important elements. Do not skip salvation-requirements passages.
2. Focus on conveying the ***Hope***, before you state the ***conditions***.

For example, Ezekiel 36:25 plus Jn 14 meets both these needs. Jn 14 keeps you from skipping the requirements.

Dominion Appeals to Everyone

Nobody doesn't like freedom, dignity, strength, joy, and overcoming. But the Dominion that Christ came to restore is not over other humans. If you are witnessing to a gang member, for example, you must offer them not only the ability to overcome evil spirits and gain protection from evil; you must also offer to them the dignity of becoming a Son of the Most High God.

Most gang members are gang members because they have been betrayed; Perhaps they were raised without a Father or in a situation of abuse. Most typically members joined the gang either for a sense of belonging; or because somebody got them addicted to drugs; or because they need to get a paid gig even if it is crime.

In cases like these, they are not likely to care very much about forgiveness of sins, unless you are also showing them a real solution – God's solution – to the hurts that got them where they are. So – you will do better to offer them, on behalf of Christ – freedom, deliverance, immeasurably superior belonging; dignity ... and yes – dominion on a whole different scale.

Starting Points of Sharing the Gospel

The above goes to prove that the way we present the Gospel will be very, very different depending on where the hearer "is at". Let's look at how this would impact what you might select to emphasize.

But even with variations in emphasis, it it should be very clear by now from the scriptures we have seen, that the salvation requirement is not just to "believe" the fact of the atonement!

Do Not Omit the Terms and Benefits of the New Covenant

It is disloyal to Christ to omit the "seeker-unfriendly" fact that Christ requires us to renounce selfishness, forsake sin, and then resist sin for the remainder of our natural lives. But this "downer" is more than offset of we will simply include the wonderful provisions of the New Covenant itself, such as:

- The Joy of reconciliation and companionship of God.
- The breaking of the power of sin (Rom 6:7) so that we can resist it;
- The power of the indwelling Spirit of God to overcome the enemy

Now let's look at how our Gospel presentatons might be adapted to different audiences; that is, to people whose mindsets are at different "starting points".

But two things all unbelievers have in common:

1. all unbelievers are oppressed or at least deceived by the enemy
2. all desire dominion – they want to "win" against those that oppose them;even if they are severely deceived as to who this is.

Starting Point = Shame and Despair

In my first witnessing excursion after I embraced the dominion gospel, a small group of us witnessed to young men that were homeless; literally released from prison that very day. They knew that they were bad, and they had very little dignity and hope. The were thinking, "I am what I am, so I am going back". There were three that I spoke to that night.

Bible Quotes are Word English Bible (WEB) except where noted.

I introduced myself with my name; but then immediately identified myself as a son of God, with an invitation for them to become one. Right there I went to the heart of the Good News. They saw my boldness and my own dignity, and they heard also my compassion. They knew that I myself was a glad and grateful to God for it; They also saw that I had no fear (you saw why that is, in 1 John 4:17).

I offered them dignity ... the full benefit program, starting with the glorious but inferior OT benefits (Ps 103) progressing to the New Covenant benefits – Christ in us, the Hope of Glory (Col 1:27); the *desire* and the *power* to live right.

I was two for three that night.

Anthony and Marcus didn't just "get saved". They saw God's mercy, yes; but they also saw *what God was calling them to **become***; and they gave their lives to Him.

Forgiveness of sins alone was not sufficient, and for good reason. What appealed to them was: Bearing the Image of God, partaking in the Divine nature – with the Dignity and Freedom that come with it. No longer needing constant forgiveness (see 1 John chapters 1 and 2; Heb 9 and 10).

In other words, **this was how they would not simply end up back in prison**. And that's what makes the New Covenant better than the Old:

> *(Romans 8:2-4) For the law of the Spirit of life in Christ Jesus made me free from the law of sin and of death. For what the law couldn't do, in that it was weak through the flesh, God did, sending his own Son in the likeness of sinful flesh and for sin, he condemned sin in the flesh; that the ordinance of the Law might be fulfilled in us, who walk not after the flesh, but after the Spirit.*

If you take any popular "Romans Road" Gospel tract as truth, then you will be *badly misled* and you will not experience freedom; But if you understand the above passage, and you <u>*did not gloss over Romans 6:7-22*</u>, then your Bible will make way more sense, and you will know the truth that sets you free!

Starting Point = Broken Conscience

If the recipient's conscience is not working (seared by sin, or blinded by a spirit) and you start proclaiming *forgiveness of sins*; then you will be disappointed in their lack of enthusiasm. Even though you have already prayed for souls before you went out to witness, you should in such a case, pray briefly for the Holy Spirit to bring conviction.

Acknowledge that "hurt people hurt people". It's important for them to know that you know it and are trying to help them deal with their burdens and regrets (Gal 6:2).

If we have been beaten down by life long enough, we despair and we ourselves start to "hurt the world back" very naturally, even to obtain a cynical sense of justice. Ask if they remember the innocence and joy of their childhood. Perhaps they didn't even get a joyful childhood; but Christ is sufficient to set them free nevertheless.

Then ask them how they have been hurt in life; and how their lives are leading to their own enslavement or producing injury to others.

Starting Point = Hyper-Grace Christianity

As you share the full Gospel with "*cultural* Christians", you will eventually encounter some – even pastors – that believe that "grace" means *no longer any requirement to obey God as a salvation matter*". In truth, as we have seen, the Gospel is, among other wonderful things:

1. The forgiveness of past sins (Romans 3:27 omitted from tracts).
2. The power to Obey God (Rom 6:21-22 omitted from tracts).
3. The salvation requirement to then practice obeying God (Rom 8:1 always included but cut short).

4. Glory, honor, and immortality as the definition of Eternal Life and the hope if it being our prime motivator (Rom 2:7 omitted from all tracts).

In sharing with persons from a hyper-grace tradition, we must be gentle and loving, but nevertheless we must protect the integrity of the Gospel. You should show from the scriptures that "Grace" is not only forgiveness of past sins, but also the desire and the ability to do what God expects, including putting sin to death by His power (Ezek. 36; Rom 6. Rom 8).

I am always careful to state two things.

1. I am careful to state that our obedience is by the action of our wills, but it is "by his power" so it is clear that even though we are required to practice overcoming the enemy while we have life and breath, it *is entirely by God's grace that we can do so*.
2. I am also careful to state that even if we do sin, we have an advocate –

Bible Quotes are Word English Bible (WEB) except where noted.
Jesus Christ the righteous (2 John 1). We can confess our sins and be fully restored.

Before any evangelistic conversation, we should call on the Holy Spirit to do His work in the recipient, convincing and convicting of sin, righteousness, and judgement as we share the hope of the Gospel.

First, note that "unbelief" in the Greek is not "failing to believe"; rather it is *"actively not heeding"*. Unbelief is the condition of stubbornness. But the one that wants their heart to be softened (Ps. 51) is ready to hear what you have to say.

Repentance is a Turning of Loyalty from Self to God

Unlike a duplicitous politician, God doesn't have a "public stance" that contradicts his "secret will". So, we are to proceed as Christ did, declaring the Kingdom of God to all, *knowing the actual and true will of God* is that He *desires* all men to be saved (1 Tim 2:4; 2 Pet 3:9).

It should go without saying that love cannot exist without true freedom, and God is Love. In other words, God is not honored *by robots that submit to Him*. Just as God has sovereignly assigned the earth to man; God has also sovereignly made man free to accept Him or reject Him. God foreknew our response long ago and calls accordingly now. Therefore, His foreknowledge doesn't excuse our responsibility to surrender to Him!

Be aware that *it is not given to us to know who will come into the light when they see it*. Our job is to obey Christ and cast the seed.

Evangelism is Kingdoms at War

It is true that some people we encounter have – with full knowledge – already entrenched themselves in an agenda to gain power over other humans. Exactly as the First Adam they have – with full awareness of the love and power of God – sold their souls seeking *independent dominion*. Precisely as the Lord Jesus demonstrated, some will not come into the light even when a superior power appears. If such a person does not gladly surrender to the merciful but just King that you represent, then their knees will be forcibly bent at a time to come (Phil 2).

So even when we manifest both love and power, we will encounter persecution. We can kick out sickness or demons from those people and they might simply invite them back as they walk away. Christ has (and grants) authority over all the power of the enemy. Even in Nazareth "there were a few sick, *and He healed them*."

God Confirms the Gospel of the Kingdom with Signs Accompanying

Nobody in their right minds will truly settle for a "forgiveness with defeat" package if they know that freedom, recreation, reunion, indwelling, and dominion are also available. If you don't know this then you have no business doing evangelism.

But if we are *ex*-captives set free indeed an know it; and if we are *ex*-sinners made sons of God and know it; if we are offering glory, honor, and immortality on behalf of Christ; and we ourselves are bearing even a degree of the genuine image of God – and power – the results will be different.

They will want the joy and dignity of power, love, and a sound mind (which is very rare nowadays); They will *want the intruder evicted*. Millions – even in the church, are oppressed and are afraid to mention it.

If they see the Second Mankind, the mankind that will stop ruining their own lives and those of others, then they will NOT want forgiveness alone; They will trade what they are for what God has created you to be. They will want to be the Second Man and they will want it Now.

Starting Point = Simply Ignorant of What Christianity Is

This recipient might not even have a concept of "sin" as a *word*. My opinion is that only a "cultural Christian" needs fixed definitions of theological words.

Everybody ten years or older (your kids' mileage may vary), if not deluded by a blinding spirit (which we can evict), understands well enough what rebellion, selfishness, and independence are; and **nobody doesn't want freedom and strength.** All unbelievers are captives of the enemy and are enslaved, and every youth or adult understands what oppression is.

Starting Point = Forgiveness-Only Churchgoer

In my forty years of observation in Evangelical Christianity, it appears to me that *even most true Christians* nowadays have never even been told how to actually escape the corruption of evil desire, and how to actively partake in the divine nature (see, well, the 200 outrageous passages I just shared, from the Word of God).

This is simply because salvation has been reduced to the Romans Bypass, which <u>*systematically omits*</u> the scriptural requirement of repentance and holiness; giving a chopped-short definition of repentance (acknowledge need of forgiveness) and entirely excluding the means of holiness. Every single passage of the Romans Bypass is a violation of context designed to be the lowest-cost salvation bargain on the market.

This has filled the church (or what we call the church) with people that have been told *they are still sinners*. These precious people are tormented in an unnecessary shame; Believing they are sinners, they "sin *by faith*" as Steve Backlund has said.

No Christian (or preacher) should spend their lives "protesting" Catholicism. I don't do that, so I do not call myself protestant. But I do protest the "Romans Road" gospel that systematically removes our true responsibility to to utilize the power of God to overcome the enemy. Traditions built on this are home to many respectable but chronically-defeated people; and is precisely why the divorce rate among Christians for sixty years has matched the divorce rate among unbelievers (George Barna 1995- present).

How did it happen? The answer is very simple: Millions have been sold a severely reduced gospel emptied of all power and infected with unbelief and human tradition. Teachers and preachers – and I say this with all due respect – *change your message if you need to*. You will **find refreshment from your burn-out**; you will yourself and your congregation being renewed; You will see "Christ being fruitful and multiplying", bringing many sons to glory. I witness this transformation in my local body of believers *continually*.

I'm 65. I'd been there in the deception for forty years, and *now I'm here*. Here is not only scriptural, it's better!! Give me a day to tell you about it. I will answer your questions and minister – by God's promises and God's power. It is for me to simply I obey. As Dutch Sheets put it, He is the producer, I am a distributor.

Ambassadors Bearing the Image of God

We are to approach an unbeliever not as church recruiters, but actually knowing fully that *we are in fact **ambassadors of a Kingdom***, inviting people to be recreated as a far superior being; reborn as a Son of their maker; standing to inherit all things if we continue in faithfulness; in allegiance to this particular King.

When an ambassador speaks, he or she speaks on behalf of the one that has sent them; the pronouncement stands; the hearer must consider the resources of their own kingdom. They must either enter covenant now or be soundly destroyed at a later time (Rev 19).

But on the other hand, some – if they see righteousness; the fruit of a curiously and beautifully different tree – will hunger for it. Blessed are those!

In summary, if you are bearing the image of God – in both love and power (not just bringing doctrine), then they will want what you have. If you are not, then they won't – and it really is that simple.

Starting Point = Demon-Oppressed

If the recipient will not make eye contact and/or has an odd nervousness then this might indicate that they are oppressed of a demon (I never say possessed, since nine times out of ten it's not the case, and the word freaks people into despair). Bind the spirit and bring the real person to the conversation, and then ask them if they want to be free. If they don't, then they are still not in their right mind. Try again. Then call them to freedom and they will want it!

Contending for the Faith

Please hear me now: I hate to be this blunt but many readers need to hear it again. *We must never, ever, omit the salvation requirement of "practicing obeying His command to love as He loved".* Romans 2:7 is a good self-test to see if you are out from the stronghold in the mind and free of the spirit of religion. If you are still making salvation unconditional, or are making Holiness optional or automatic, then there is still a stronghold in your mind that you will need to deal with (2 Cor 10:4).

But I sincerely hope that you now know that Christ came to set captives free; that He makes you "free indeed" to serve the living God without fear; that we were alienated by rebellion but that we are reconciled by a true and sustained surrender.

Now – let's look at some Gospel summaries.

The Original Great Commission

To mankind – us – God granted authority on the earth as its stewards, to <u>bear His own image</u> and to subdue it, even everything that creeps on the earth. God granted us glory and honor and placed us over all the work of His hands; and <u>placed all things under our feet</u>. This is the Great Commission, and it has not been retracted.

God is love, and Love cannot exist without true freedom. Therefore, God did not intend for rebellion to occur, but He fully intended for us to have freedom indeed.

Underlying the entire history of mankind – past, present, and future – is the loss and restoration of *union*, *image-bearing*, and *dominion*; all built on the *covenant love of God in Christ*.

Bible Quotes are Word English Bible (WEB) except where noted.

We Forfeited Dominion; No Longer Bore the Image of God

The first Adam, affecting the entire First Mankind, used his freedom to go his own way seeking after *personal* glory, *personal* honor, and *personal* dominion apart from God. In doing so He disconnected his entire lineage – all of us – from the very life of God. Man's innermost constitution was contaminated and both death and decay entered. The enemy, the thief, became free to invade unopposed, and infected the entire cosmos so that every child, though innocent at birth, absorbs the mind of *self*-will, the mind for selfish independence. Having a dead spirit, we were powerless to resist it. The Law of Sin and Death reigned.

The entire OT is the story of the fundamental law of sowing and reaping – by individuals and by Nations; choosing obedience or rebellion by degrees. Surrendered individuals obtained the Life of God "upon them" or "with them", but not "in them", much less to remain in them forever. But many were justified by faith just as Abraham was. God also showed Abraham Christ's day, and he was glad (John 8:56).

Precious Promises of God

The Prophets foretold of the promised solution for reuniting Mankind with God. He would cleanse man, forgive him, and give him not only the desire to do what is right (His law on our hearts) but the ability for it as well (by His spirit in us). Moreover, He would produce millions of sons of God by an ambush that would reverse the entire curse of the First Mankind. He would once again be our God and we would be His people. In Union with Him we would not only be at complete peace with Him; we would regain glory, honor, and immortality. And we would reign on the earth.

If we go our own way then we are defeated and destroyed; but if we align our actions on earth with His will in Heaven then we Overcome and inherit the promises.

The "STEP OUT" Acrostic

In the pages that follow I present a simple way to remember how hope translates into joyful surrender and perseverance.

- S   See His Glory
- T   Trust His Promises
- E   Entrust yourself into Him; Escape the Corruption
- P   Partake in His Nature; Put on Righteousness

- O   Overcome the work of the enemy
- U   Unload counterfeit
- T   Tread on the Enemy

I find this to be a very helpful way to understand - and explain - the way of salvation without over-simplifying it. In witnessing, as real witnesses, we should be able to testify to the reality of every item. I now expand each of these in the paragraphs that follow.

Bible Quotes are Word English Bible (WEB) except where noted.

See His Glory and Trust His Promises

Christ is the fulfillment of "the promise" – not just of amnesty, but of instituting the New Mankind – a mankind *created after the pattern of God Himself.*

He came to restore that which was lost, even though the price was beyond our ability to grasp. He suffered and died on behalf of all of us – literally "as" us – with all the Sin of the First Mankind packed into Himself. By His lacerations, His crucifixion, and the complete shedding of His innocent Blood, He reconciled Mankind to God. Legally and metaphysically, He cancelled both the power and the penalty of sin upon man… for those that are "In Him".

He not only _died_ with us in Him; He _rose_ as the *Firstborn from among the dead*; He would establish the Second Mankind and bring many sons to glory; born of the same Father.

Still more, the Lamb of God is also the Lion of the Tribe of Judah. He not only _rose_, but was _seated_ at the right hand of the Father – and yes – with us in Him. Upon His seating, Christ began _sending_ "The Promise" – His own Spirit – into to those that obey Him (Acts 5:32).

In short, He called us *to His own* Glory, *by His own Glory;* He calls us to surrender our self-will and fallen lineage; to be born of God; and to be united with Father, Son, and Holy Spirit, and to inherit all things. He paid the immeasurable price for it all, and His offer stands to the end of the age; It is available to us *only as long as we breathe*, and only on a trade-in basis.

We gain the Second Mankind only by renouncing and forsaking the First Mankind. The Life of God in exchange for pure counterfeit. That's what baptism meant to the Early Christians. Who knows it nowadays?

Escape the Corruption and Partake in His Nature

We gained death, shame, and fear by *rebellion*; and we gain Life, glory, and freedom only by *surrender*.

In His most repeated words, Christ calls out to all of us and makes the invitation – "if _any man would_ come after me, let Him". The terms are simply … "life-exchange". It is purely Grace, because we trade counterfeit life (death disguised as life) for the Life of God (Greek Zoe).

If we hunger and thirst not just for amnesty, but for the *Kingdom of God* (dominion restored) and *His righteousness* (to become like Him), then we <u>*shall*</u> be <u>*filled*</u>; we <u>*shall*</u> produce the <u>*acceptable fruit*</u>, and <u>*shall*</u> receive with overflowing every true blessing a human could possibly desire.

We are called to gain *His Righteousness* as our innermost constitution, and to bear the *acceptable fruit* of His righteousness; There is no place for personal inherent righteousness; only His inherent righteousness installed in us, and our *choosing to living from it*.

Upon our trusting in the work of Christ, our record of sins is purged, as far as the East is from the West. Then, with our consciences cleared, we make our pledge of allegiance to the King that is not ourselves; *This* is our public confession that <u>*Jesus Christ is Lord*</u>; and the verse tells us that *in this we are **saved***. It is the very first fruit of the righteousness of God – the fruit of the good tree. It is the expression of allegiance, because there is a change of Kings underway.

As did the earliest converts, we seek not merely to have our sins blotted out and to avoid Hell but to experience refreshing newness of life from restored union with God; and to have His life-giving Spirit literally move into us. After all, this was and still is … <u>*the literal heart of the New Covenant!*</u>

Bible Quotes are Word English Bible (WEB) except where noted.

Put On Righteousness
Overcome, Unload, and Tread

There is now neither guilt nor shame, but sons of God, enjoying dignity and freedom. Moreover, we know the glory, honor, and immortality that is promised to those who overcome in fidelity to Christ, but only by His indwelling Life.

> Greek *Pistis* is not just "faith" but also "fidelity"; and only *fidelity* brings *consistency all the scriptures* and the New Covenant as a *covenant*.

With a clear record and exchanged innermost nature, temptation is still present, but we are no longer slaves to sin. We are now able *to overcome*. Shall we go on practicing sin? Absolutely Not!! To be "In Christ" is to have forsaken sin, to have escaped corruption; to be partaking in the divine nature, and be *abiding*: Note again Romans 8 & John 15:

> There is therefore now *no more condemnation* to those *that are in Christ*, who *walk no longer according to the flesh but according to the Spirit*... If you *go on practicing sin you shall die*, but if *by the Spirit you put to death the works of the flesh*, you shall *live*.

> If you obey my commands you will abide in my love.

Wonderfully, *faith and love spring from Hope* – knowing what lies ahead. Note in Romans 8, John 3, John 4, Romans 16:

> The sufferings of this present life are *not worth comparing* to the glory that is to be revealed in us.

> He who has this hope *purifies himself*, even as *He* is *pure*.

> In this we have confidence on the day of judgement, because *as He is, so are we in this world*.

> *And God of peace will soon crush satan under your feet*.

So, we persevere, practicing righteousness to the end; Yet even if we sin in weakness, we have an advocate – even Jesus Christ the Righteous. Can you see how all the scriptures now fall into place?

Looking Ahead in Hope
To Dominion Restored

Many have experienced a profound "relief" that Christ has paid for the sins of the entire world – and this includes us ourselves (1 Jn 2:2; 2 Peter 3:9).

But to stay surrendered, to do the will of God rather than lapse into self-willed independence, we absolutely must have hope. This is why – as we have seen - Paul opens his salvation basis discussion with ***hope***:

> *... the righteous judgment of God; who "will pay back to everyone according to their works:" to those who by perseverance in well-doing seek for glory, honor, and incorruptibility, eternal life; but to those who are self-seeking, and don't obey the truth, but obey unrighteousness, will be wrath and indignation, oppression and anguish, on every soul of man who does evil, to the Jew first, and also to the Greek.*
>
> *But glory, honor, and peace go to every man who does good, to the Jew first, and also to the Greek. For there is no partiality with God. (Romans 2:5-11)*

The scriptural fact is that we endure because we seek glory, honor, and immortality, collectively called "eternal life"; and this is the reward for perseverance in doing good.

Therefore, if we are to be effecctive witnesses, we must impart a real hope that we ourselves actually possess; We must personally experience this hope driving us to continue resisting sin and obeying Christ's command to love as He loved.

In Revelation 2, we saw that "*To Him who overcomes*, Christ will give Him the right to eat from the Tree of Life". In Revelation 22, we saw that "There shall be no mourning, nor crying, nor pain, nor death anymore. He shall be our God, and we shall be His people", and we also saw the ultimate and eternal expression of the kindness of God toward us: "We shall reign with Him forever and ever."

In short, the Gospel announces a do-over opportunity under unimaginably good conditions; By the work of Christ, justice and mercy join hands. How shall we escape if we neglect so great a salvation? Now let's look at one of the passages we opened with. In light of Follow the Firstborn so far, Psalms 24 now makes total sense.

Bible Quotes are Word English Bible (WEB) except where noted.

Will You Ascend?
Gain *Clean Hands* & *Pure Heart*

(Psalms 24 NKJV) The earth is the LORD's, and all its fullness, The world and those who dwell therein. For He has founded it upon the seas, And established it upon the waters.

Who may ascend into the hill of the LORD? Or who may stand in His holy place?

He who has clean hands and a pure heart, Who has not lifted up his soul to an idol, Nor sworn deceitfully.
He shall receive blessing from the LORD,

And righteousness from the God of his salvation.

This is Jacob, the generation of those who seek Him, who seek Your face.

Selah

Lift up your heads, O you gates! And be lifted up, you everlasting doors! And the King of glory shall come in.

Who is this King of glory? The LORD strong and mighty, The LORD mighty in battle...

All That We Need:
No More Guilt, No More Shame

We are approaching the conclusion of Follow the Firstborn. At this point I want to provide a moment to refocus on the two requirements for entering the Kingdom of God – for obtaining Dominion over the true enemy, for overcoming. Please notice that these two things fulfill the promises of the New Covenant (Ezekiel 36 forward and Jeremiah 31 forward).

How to Obtain Clean Hands

The middle tier of the central panel shows the way to obtain the "clean hands". The answer from the Word of God is to get forgiven by the Blood of Christ upon the surrender of our self-will. Merely believing the historical "fact" of the sacrifice of Christ – in our heads, of course, is not "faith". We not only "trust" Christ, but we "entrust" (Greek pisteuo) our lives to Him. We also must declare – aloud with our mouths – our allegiance to this new King.

In the early church, it was normal that a breaking of the compulsive power of sin occurred at the time of our baptism (Rom 6:1). Baptism declares the *burying* of our old lives under the Old Mankind, the First Adam; with its lusts of the flesh; it's greed for things, and the pride of our human accomplishments; its shame, weakness, and mortality. We do this because Christ has promised that what will rise in its place is we are to expect to germinate and grow and rise as the Second Mankind after Christ the Firstborn. Only a self-denying life-exchange is a true and biblical, and no other "faith" is saving faith.

And a Pure Heart

Without this self-denying, life-exchange faith, we will lack the power to keep our hands clean and to purify our hearts – these are our job (Jn 3:3; Rom 8:13; Eph 4:21-22). It is impossible to overstate the importance of this **true freedom**, yet 99% of churches hold a position that says to "cooperate" in our salvation is "trying to **_earn_**" it. This is simply faulty logic and denies numerous scriptures.

We obtain the pure heart by "taking up our cross and following where Christ has gone. In the physical World we serve with Him indwelling and assisting; while we sit with Him in heavenly places in Union with the Father. We are "in Him" because our wills are at peace with God's will (Col 3). The pure heart is the surrendered soul – the will to serve God with desires made right; a clear conscience that stays clear by immediate reflexive confession. As we put to death all selfishness – by the power of God – we are transformed. When we fail, we have the means of restoration and cleansing (1 Jn 1:9-10; 2:2).

Bible Quotes are Word English Bible (WEB) except where noted.

Kingdom & Dominion
Water of Life, Tree of Life

(Luke 19:10) "For the Son of Man came to seek and to save <u>that</u> which was lost."

(Daniel 7:27) Then the <u>kingdom and the dominion</u>, And the greatness of the kingdoms under the whole sky, <u>Will be given to the people of the saints of the Most High.</u>

(Revelation 22:1-5) He showed me a river of water of life, clear as crystal, proceeding out of the throne of God and of the Lamb, in the middle of its street. On this side of the river and on that, was the <u>tree of life</u>, ...

the Lord God will illuminate them ...

Rev 22:5
*And **they** shall **reign** forever and ever.*

Sown in Weakness and Shame

To Him Who Conquers:
Glory, Honor, Immortality

At this point I am revisiting the "motivation" for denying ourselves to following Christ. The passages at left are the kinds you can "gaze into" and feast on. Here are two more passages – the "R-Two-Sevens" are very easy references to remember:

> *Revelation 2:7,11*
> *... To him who <u>overcomes</u>, I will give to <u>eat from the tree of life</u> which is in the paradise of my God. ... He who <u>overcomes</u> won't be harmed by the <u>second death</u>.*

> *Romans 2:5-8*
> *... the righteous judgment of God; who "will pay back to everyone according to their works:" to those who by perseverance in well-doing seek for glory, honor, and incorruptibility, eternal life;*
> *but to those who are self-seeking, and don't* ***obey the truth***, ***but obey unrighteousness****, will be wrath and indignation.*

Both of these show the right understandings of the love of God and the fear of God. Notice that the "good" fear of God is not mere "reverence". It is "fear" that recognizes what is at stake in our practice of obeying Christ. At the same time, our right love of God is rooted in our right and very healthy desire to not just "get saved", but to be like Him.

As we ourselves see the love of Christ springing forth in our hearts (Rom 5:5) – in this life – this fear increasingly melts away. The very fact that "purification works" now as we resist is by God's power – powerfully motivates us to stay the course. We also find that the false "once-saved always saved" debate becomes increasingly irrelevant for us, because we *are following* and are *seeing* God and *hearing* His voice; we see His Kingdom; *Love* has overcome *fear*; We are overcoming both inwardly and outwardly; and we are ***becoming like Him.***

Bible Quotes are Word English Bible (WEB) except where noted.

The Apostle's Creed: The Early Church's Summary

Here is one more Gospel statement – from the Early Church. Maybe they had it right? I would think so! David Bercot writes[26] (italics and bold are mine):

> "The kingdom gospel is so simple, so unattached from complicated theology, that for the first 300 years of Christianity, the following statement of faith sufficed:
>
>> 'I believe in God the Father Almighty, Maker of heaven and earth. And in Jesus Christ ***his only Son our Lord***, who was conceived by the Holy Ghost, born of the virgin Mary, suffered under Pontius Pilate, was ***crucified, dead***, and ***buried***; he descended into ***hell*** [Hades]; the ***third*** day he ***rose*** again from the dead; he ***ascended*** into heaven, ***and sits at the right hand of God the Father Almighty; from thence he shall come to judge the quick and the dead***. I believe in the Holy Spirit; the holy catholic [universal] church; the communion of saints; the ***forgiveness*** of sins; the ***resurrection*** of the body; and the ***life everlasting***.'
>
> The institutional Church didn't grow into a better understanding of Christ once it abandoned the gospel of the kingdom. Rather, it has grown further and further from the real Christ."

---

[26]Bercot, David. The Kingdom That Turned the World Upside Down (p. 149). Scroll Publishing Co.

Christ Made the Way
Forgiveness, Resurrection, Life

The early church clearly understood that the Gospel was to be "obeyed", not just *believed*. This truth – and the seriousness of it – should be worked into any presentation of the Gospel, along with the careful statements of the provisions that God has made for us, that this book has brought out for consideration.

Born of Woman

As mentioned earlier, because God had appointed man into authority on Earth (Ps 8; Ps 115), Christ had to become man (1 Tim 2:5) to enter the realm of authority on Earth (John 10).

Where Did Christ "Go"? Where is He Now Seated?

Notice all the "places" the Lord Jesus traveled (crucified, dead, buried, raised, ascended, seated). If we are in Him – forsaking sin to do His will by His power – then we are with Him now in the unseen where He is seated. When He appears, we also will appear with Him in glory (Col 3:4)!

There is a Healthy Fear of God

We can see that Christ is seated in supreme authority and that He will return to judge the living and the dead. This is not just "reverence" or "awe" after we place our faith in our doctrines. Even those who have truly received Christ and His Spirit can drift into presumption or neglect; Tragically this is a common way in much of popular Christianity. But if we *actively* maintain our surrender to obey His command to love, by His power, then our love is progressively perfected; consciousness of sin fades (Heb 10:1-2), because the New Covenant brings the teachable heart and His own Spirit inside us (Rom 8:1:1-4).

If we obey His commands then we will remain in His love (Jn 15:10).

We Have an Eternal Kingdom to Gain

Notice the very last phrase; "life everlasting". Literally this means "the life of God (Greek Zoe) through the ages". If we belong to Him – having given our lives to Him and remaining in Him – then we will obtain a rich welcome into that Kingdom (2 Pet 1:11).

Bible Quotes are Word English Bible (WEB) except where noted.

The Full-Grace Witness:
The Power of Our Testimony

Here we translate these *core New-Covenant truths* into a "Full-Grace" narrative. We affirm the full provision of God, not only for forgiveness, but also for true freedom, for Dignity and Dominion so that in this life we are manifest as Sons of God in character and nature. Later, we will restate these truths from different angles and in different levels of detail. ***Actual power to become like Christ*** – to overcome the enemy – is of course never "dry theology"! It is the most practical truth there is!!

Dignity and Dominion, Given and Given Away

Because God wanted companionship, He created us to be in Union with Him, with His Spirit in us as the source of our life and joy. We could fellowship with Him because He had given us of His own nature. The Commission of Man was, and is, and will always be, to replicate after the nature of God as the crown of creation (Gen 1:26-27). By God's design – by His "grace" rightly understood, Mankind enjoyed glory and honor, and authority (Ps 8:3-6).

The creeping creature that had already been cast to the earth – persuaded man to seek *personal glory* – a powerful life lived *apart from God* to serve selfish desires and ambitions.

In seeking pleasure over obedience, and independence over union, the First Mankind gave away the dignity and the dominion of sonship. He no longer bore the image of God. From then on, the *fruit* of his life was bad *because his innermost constitution* was infected. Forgiveness alone could not fix this.

The New and Better Covenant Foretold

As the Covenant of Moses proved, deterrents and punishments could suppress evil to a degree but it could never address the *heart* of the problem – which was the *selfish independent nature (SIN)*. Sins are the fruit of sin; so, forgiveness was good, but only until the inevitable *next* sin. Animal sacrifices could point to the coming High Priest that would also be the sacrifice itself.

Glory, honor, and immortality could be restored only if God Himself brought man back into union with Himself; by creating a New Man, a Second Mankind, by *getting His Spirit back into man*.

God is love, and love requires true freedom; God would not be honored or glorified by robots that turned to Him. Rather He would be honored by getting them "back to the garden". He would cancel their debt, set them free; and dwell in them. Having given them everything needed for Life and godliness, He would once again call them to *use their free will to live from it*.

Abraham saw this Covenant from afar, and demonstrated for us all the saving response of *repentance from idolatry* and the walk of solidarity to the will of God. David also knew that he needed a ***new and right spirit within him***, not just *with* him as Moses had. He was *after God's own heart*; He wanted to be like God not just in military or political power, but in *character*.

The provisions of the New Covenant were plainly announced (Jeremiah 31; Ezekiel 36; Isaiah 42; Daniel 7; Joel 2, and as we see in Acts 3 – "all the prophets"):

   a) Forgiveness of sins.
   b) God's Spirit *in us* – not just "upon us" or "with us".
   c) *Union* with Him – the alignment of wills; He would be our God and we would be His people – *bearing His Image as Sons*.
   d) A heart of flesh rather than a rebellious, unteachable heart of stone.
   e) All the rights and privileges of the sons and daughters of God.
   f) Power to overcome the enemy inwardly and outwardly.

After the apostles died and after we had a Bible, the early church demonstrated the actual supernatural *power of God* to do the *will of God*, with His power being *released by their command* – just as many passages describe. Christ works in those who believe (Mk 16:17-18) to "confirm the word with signs accompanying". That's obedience and cooperation! Supernatural results in ministry comes to us only as we discard the leaven of the pharisees – the huge body of unbelief theology that tries to explain why we shouldn't really expect any supernatural results. It is only *The Kingdom of God* we have discarded.

By Diligent **mind renewal** we dismantle unbelief to bring the mind of Christ into the soul (1 Cor 2:16; Eph 1:17ff; Rom 12:1-3; Eph 4:23). Discipleship trains the obedience that the Holy Spirit *works with*. ***The provisions of the New Covenant beyond forgiveness must be restored to our statement of the Gospel.***

The New Covenant Presents the Precious Promises

We are called to embrace and pursue what the New Covenant promises! But there are conditions; If we embrace the hope enough to trade in our lives for it, then we are Christians; and our destiny is to reign with Him forever and ever provided we continue in it.

The Purpose: Restored Union, Freedom, and Restored Dominion
The Terms: Forsake Sin and Obey God ... Through His Death and Into His Life

Bible Quotes are Word English Bible (WEB) except where noted.

The Act of Witnessing
Must Flow from the <u>Fact</u>

In the great commissions, we are not just called to *witness*. Rather, we are called "be" witnesses. The *act of witnessing* absolutely must flow from the *fact* that we are Sons of God. Have we witnessed the power of God? If all we know of is the "teaching" of forgiveness by the Blood of Christ, then there is no strength or true refreshing to be a witness of. But if we have tasted the heavenly gift and the powers of the age to come (Heb 6), then we will naturally but humbly tell of our conversion and our own times of refreshing. We will not be *bragging;* Rather we will simply be obeying the command of Christ, and joyfully; we will be serving man by the love of God in us and the power of God in us.

We will simply be, in fact, witnesses. Telling of it will be our joy.

Awaken their Hunger for Freedom and Dominion Restored

I believe, as John Lake did, that all of mankind has an inner yearning – a desperate hunger – for a *Dominion restored*, even if they cannot consciously remember it, or even identify the enemy that stole it.

The proud seek merely to replace their oppression with *personal power*. But the humble – by definition – are willing to acknowledge their deficiency and their need. They are aware not only of their guilt (what they done), but also their <u>shame</u> – **<u>what they are</u>**.

Yet even the *proud humans* are not "the enemy". The devil and his servants are the enemy. But when a son or daughter of God manifests peace; or joy; or strength; or kindness that "doesn't compute", both the proud and the humble will notice it.

The humble will run into the light and learn to live in the light. God foresees who will respond with humility and perseverance, and He predestines them to be conformed into the image of His Firstborn Son (Rom 8:29). He sovereignly

More than any other two words, we see Jesus, the Firstborn from among the dead, saying "Follow Me". He requires us, not just to accept His precious payment for past sins, but to also ... *follow* Him.

If and only if we practice obeying His command to love as He loved (John 13), we get to see Him (John 14:19; 21; John 16:16). And when we see Him, we become witnesses.

Sown in Weakness and Shame

People Seek
The Meeting of Their Needs

Does it Meet the Need?

If what God offers truly satisfies, and His people are indeed witnesses of being satisfied by it, then success in evangelism should be very natural! More specifically,

If:

1. we are offering the full and true Gospel message,
2. and if we ourselves have been truly satisfied by it
3. and we can attest to and demonstrate the power of God toward man

then:

1. our *joy* will show,
2. the *truth* of our words will be apparent;
3. people will *respond* clearly – in one manner or another

But if we are selling God short, or we have no true witness to God's power at work, then evangelism of course falls flat to any listener.

In all the following – I have drawn boxes around points that will help you keep the New Covenant and the New Mankind in focus.

Christ has Prepared the Table Before Us

The humble have a *healthy hunger* for *glory* (the presence of God), *honor* (dignity), and *immortality* (with the end of fear of death).

In partnership with the Holy Spirit who convinces and convicts, <u>we are to prepare a table before them</u>, even as the enemy watches helplessly (Ps 23).

> In witnessing, we are preparing a table before them in the presence of their enemies.

Bible Quotes are Word English Bible (WEB) except where noted.

On behalf of Christ, We offer <u>Christ in You!</u> – Not Just forgiveness.

Forgiveness without conversion to the Second Mankind *does no good*. According to the Hebrews 4 and Romans 6-7-8, this is precisely why we needed a New Covenant!!! Unless we gain the **pure heart** (*Converted* to the Second Mankind) we cannot **keep our hands clean**. We remain enslaved and we simply rebuild our record of sins. Millions of churchgoers remain enslaved and it doesn't have to be that way.

We Need the Righteousness of God in Us

If we know we are born prone to selfishness and *call out to God for His own righteousness* – with a clear and desperate move of *life-exchange* – then we shall be *rescued* (that's what the word plainly meant); The power of sin is then broken (Rom 6:7) and our record of sins is obliterated. We experience joy!

But there is more. His Spirit witnesses to our spirit that we are sons of God (Rom 8:16), As sons, we then ask for the main course of the New Covenant – to be filled with His Spirit (Ezekiel 36:25; Luke 11:13).

There is battle to renew our minds and put sin – in our souls - to death, but before long, defeats become the exception, no more the rule (Rom 8:13).

<u>As God's Ambassadors</u>

**We are inviting every man to be born of God;
to obtain His Character and Nature –
and the dignity, freedom, strength, and actual victory that comes with it**

If we present to the World the **_credible_** offer to be born into the New Mankind, to share in Christ's dominion; inheritance; and destiny – then we will have the World's attention. But if we don't, then of course we won't; we would simply get more of what we got - "religious culture".

Ezekiel 36 Benefits, Acts 3 Conversion, and Romans 8 Walk

At this point we have looked at the overwhelming record of the scriptures on these matters of Glory, Honor, Freedom, and Dominion. Now I will turn to speak to "you" more personally; I hope you will see the "witness" and "ambassador" mentality taking shape and playing out in your own life.

You should speak of the benefits that you yourself have experienced and are experiencing. Recite the "menu" of salvation: Don't dwell on forgiveness!

Sown in Weakness and Shame

Somebody rightly described forgiveness-teaching as the kindergarten of salvation school. Forgiveness of past sins is the reconciliation that opens the door to all other Covenant benefits; but it is only the *foyer* of the *palace* of salvation. I believe we must embrace the whole package:

- Forgiveness of sins.
- Healing and deliverance from spirits.
- The conscious companionship with God Himself living inside us.
- The factual crucifixion of our old man; The breaking of the sin nature in our innermost being (our spirits) and the ability to purify ourselves.
- Compassion and mercy for when we do fail.
- Power over the work of the enemy.
- Fruitfulness of the work of our hands, to meet our needs.
- the **joy** and **dignity** that comes from all of it.

The Terms

By this point you have read the passages I have presented. You should now have seen the connections and the consistency. You should know now that:

1. Salvation is unearned but it is by no means unconditional.
2. Holiness is required (some fruit of the good tree), but by God dwelling in us, His divine power has given us everything we need for life and godliness, including mercy when we fail in weakness.

First – a person absolutely needs conviction by the Holy Spirit that there is a sin problem in their own innermost constitution – and that they can do nothing about it. They must know they are a sinner, and they must be desperate to escape it.

Bible Quotes are Word English Bible (WEB) except where noted.

Announce the Offer
Keeping Promises & Terms in View

If we internalize the following passages - getting them "into our DNA", then they will ignite breakthrough for us personally and give us the breakthrough in joy and strength. We will never again be at a loss for how to speak – or how to minister - as an ambassador of Christ

> *(Ezekiel 36:25-26) I will cleanse you from all your filthiness and from all your idols. I will also give you a new heart, and I will put a new spirit within you; I will take away the stony heart out of your flesh and I will give you a heart of flesh.*

> *(Acts 3:18-21; 5:20 NKJV) But those things which God foretold by the mouth of all His prophets, that the Christ would suffer, He has thus fulfilled...* **Repent therefore and be** *converted, that your sins may be blotted out, so that times of refreshing may come from the presence of the Lord, and that He may send Jesus Christ, who was preached to you before, whom heaven must receive until the times of restoration of all things, which God has spoken by the mouth of all His holy prophets since the world began...*

> *"Go, stand in the temple and speak to the people all the words of this life."*

> *(Romans 8:1-4) There is therefore now no condemnation to those who are in Christ Jesus,* **who don't walk according to the flesh***, but according to the Spirit.*

> *For the law of the Spirit of life in Christ Jesus made me free from the law of sin and death...*

> *He condemned sin in the flesh; that the righteous requirement of the Law might be fulfilled in us* **who do not walk according to the flesh** *but according to the Spirit*

Sown in Weakness and Shame

As Simple as Possible but No Simpler

Albert Einstein said: "Make it as simple as possible, but no simpler". The last thing we need is a Gospel that omits critical things like the conditions for final salvation. This is the first book I have ever brought to be published because God had to stop me before – at times when I myself had not experienced firsthand both the essential powers and responsibilities of sons and daughters of God. He has not only given me the go-ahead; He even gave me the title "Follow the Firstborn" as a direct instantaneous download – literally while I was asking for it in a short sentence of silent prayer.

Seeker-Friendly Compromises Destroy People

False gospels promise <u>Forgiveness and Heaven without the requirement to forsake sin</u> – and they make this very definition of "grace". Such gospels are so pervasive now that the true church needs to ***explicitly state the whole truth***, solidly substantiated from the Word of God.

In this section, I make no "seeker friendly" compromises. I state the scriptural terms of salvation accurately, precisely, and concisely. It is not flowery or sloppy, because my objective is to be clear. I substantiate each element with a footnote that paraphrases some applicable scriptures.

Not a "Downer" to State the Whole Truth

That said – there is actually a "glory" of God that comes through the true and complete gospel. There is glory in the fact we are *invited* to glory, honor, and immortality if we persevere. There is glory in the fact that we are being transformed into glory by degrees. There is glory in the fact that His promises are enough to motivate us to serve Him without having to be programmed to do so. There is glory in that we come to "crush Satan under our feet" in this life (Rom 16:20).

Here we go! I speak this as to a person, but I provide footnotes with references.

* *

"Grace" is everything we need – for being born of God[27], escaping the corruption that is in the world and partaking in the divine nature[28], for bearing

---

[27] John 12 To all who received Him [inside?] He gave the right to become the Sons of God;
[28] 2 Pet 1 Everything we need for Zoe life and godliness; partaking ... having escaped

Bible Quotes are Word English Bible (WEB) except where noted.

acceptable fruit[29], and for enjoying companionship with God[30] and His people forever.[31]

If we surrender,[32] Christ **makes us truly free** in our **innermost** nature[33], and walks with us that we <u>might</u> **use that freedom to put sin to death** in our thoughts, words[34], and actions[35]. The reward for doing this is Eternal Life[36].

To be **"In Christ"** is to be doing His will rather than our own[37]; Therefore, one *surrenders* to get into Christ and then <u>*obeys Him* to stay there</u>…[38] This is not burdensome because we do this <u>*by His power, **by His very Life in us**.*</u>[39]

---

[29] Rom 2:6 God repays each Mat 16:27 for what he has done; Mat 12:33 Tree good, fruit good

[30] John 14 For all who obey Christ he brings them into Union with the Father, Son, and Spirit

[31] 2 Pet 1:3-4 Everything for life and godliness … escape corruption; partake in divine nature

[32] Acts 3 Repent and be converted, so that times of refreshing … God will send Jesus Christ

[33] Mat 12:33 – make the tree good and its fruit good;

[34] Mat 12:36 By your words you will be justified; by your words you shall be condemned

[35] Eph 4:22-24 put on [righteousness]; Rom 8:16 but if by the Spirit you put to death … live

[36] Rom 2:7 He Rewards with; Rom 6:22 holiness, and its end; Rom 8:1 for those who walk

[37] Gal 5:24 Those in Christ have crucified the flesh; Isa 53 Each has gone his own way

[38] Mat 16:24 The event of taking up our cross; the process of following; see also John 15:10.

[39] Mat 11:28 My yoke is easy and my burden is light; 1 Jn 2 If we sin, we have an advocate

Bible Quotes are Word English Bible (WEB) except where noted.

The New Covenant:
Benefits & Terms

The Gospel of Christ announces the availability of this **indwelling Life** under the **"*New Covenant*" that the prophets spoke of.**[40] The Gospel simply announces the arrival of what was promised[41]. It brings the *desire* and the *power* to do what is right.

To *know the full Gospel*, then, is to *know all that was promised and how to obtain it*:

- Christ – our High Priest of this Covenant – went before us to **make the Way**[42]; He seeks to lead us into every good[43] thing He purchased by His own Blood.[44]
- If – and only if - we *surrender our rebellion*[45] *in hope,*[46] then we are **born of God**[47] with a **new innermost nature not bound by sin**[48]; which is **Christ taking up residence in us**. We are then under the New Covenant.
- If we persevere[49] in allegiance ("faith") then the **results in this age** are dignity[50], freedom[51], strength[52], and power[53] by which we *overcome the*

---

[40] Jer 31; Ezek 36; Isa 42 & 53; Joel 2 Cleansing, New spirit, heart, Union through Exchange

[41] Mat 3 He will bap. you in HS; Jn 7 Rivers of Life; Gal 3: recv the promise; Heb 6 The gift

[42] Jn 20 Magdalene: I am ascending; 1 Cor 2 Ambush complete; Acts 2 Spirit in man

[43] Mat 5:3-10 inh. Kingdom, comforted, inherit the earth, obtain mercy, see God; Sons of God

[44] Heb 9 Christ entered the Most Holy Place once for all by His own Innocent Blood

[45] Mat 16; Luke 9; Mark 8; Jn 10 Most repeated invitation – if any man would follow, *let him*.

[46] Mat 5 Those who hunger shall be filled

[47] 2 Cor 5:17 If any be in Christ he is a new creation; Eph 4 created in righteousness, holiness

[48] Rom 6 Those baptized into … buried and raised; v7 He who has died has been freed

[49] Rom 2 by perseverance in doing good;

[50] 1 Jn 4:17 confidence because as He is, so are we in this world; Gen 1 Bearing His image

[51] Rom 6 He who has died is freed from sin; Jn 8:36 He whom the Son sets free ,,, indeed

[52] Dan 11 Those who know their God [restored union] shall grow strong; Jn 14 Greater works

[53] Mat 5 Sons of God; John 8:36 Free indeed; Rom 8 Glorious liberty; Dan 11 isa 40 Strength

Sown in Weakness and Shame

works of the enemy[54]. Making His ways our ways[55] and His people our people[56] and we obey the disciplines He taught, demonstrated, and commanded.[57] _It sounds impossible, but_ **having exchanged our lives for His Life**[58]**, He leads us in triumph**[59]. By patience and servanthood in hope[60], we **overcome**[61]**,** and the **results in the age to come** are participating in the final victory[62], Life[63], reigning[64], glory[65], honor[66], immortality[67], and the full restoration of Dominion[68] on the Restored Earth itself[69]. Yet even in this age, we taste the *powers of the age to come*[70].

Implications for Leadership

In leadership we should all strive, above all other objectives:

1. to get ourselves deeper into Christ to see Him better, by obeying Him better;
2. to be able to better demonstrate and communicate the reality of this

---

[54] To him that *overcomes*: Eat from tree of Life, not blotted out, Sit with Me in My throne

[55] Mat 28:12 Make disciples … teaching them to obey all that I have commanded you

[56] Ruth 1 Where you go… where you stay … Your people … Your God; Christ: "Follow me"

[57] John 13 Love as He loved; John 15 Abide; Mat 10 Endure; Mat 16 Follow; Mat 28 Go;

[58] 2 Cor 5 He became sin; we become God's righteousness; Isa 53 Described it, explained it

[59] 2 Cor 2:14 He always leads us to triumph; Josh 10: Come, put your feet on the kings' necks

[60] Col 3 When Christ, who is your Life appears, you also will appear with Him in glory

[61] Rom 6:22 Put sin to death … You have your fruit to holiness and its end, Eternal life

[62] Rev 19 He is … the Word of God; The armies of Heaven followed Him … white and pure

[63] Rev 2: The right to eat from the tree of Life; Rev 22 Invitation to eat from the tree of Life

[64] Rom 5:17 having the abundance of grace and the gift of righteousness shall reign in Zoe life

[65] John 17 I have given them my glory; Col 3 you also shall appear with him in glory

[66] Luke 9:26 Whoever is ashamed of me [allegiance], I will be ashamed of him when I return

[67] Ps 8:3-6 Crowned with … placed all under His feet; Dan 7 same; Heb 2 same; Rev 22 same

[68] Dan 7 Kingdoms given to the people of the Most High; Rev 22 They shall reign forever

[69] Rom 8:22 The earth itself seeks the revealing of the Sons of God; 2 Pet 3 Renewed by heat

[70] Heb 6: Having tasted the heavenly gift and the powers of the age to come

Bible Quotes are Word English Bible (WEB) except where noted.
treasure.

To that end, I believe we should do whatever we can to ensure that everyone who visits – wanderer, seeker, believer, teacher, pastor, or preacher – gets quickly introduced to a true and coherent Gospel Statement that ***does not compromise on what grace is and how it works*** (Reconciliation with God and the power to serve Him without fear).

Then – The New Covenant itself – with its true benefits and its true terms – will become simple and bright in the experience and in the witness of everyone whose lives we touch.

Bible Quotes are Word English Bible (WEB) except where noted.

A Time to "Major"
In the Gospel of the _Kingdom_

*And this gospel **of the kingdom** will be preached in all the world as a **witness** to all the nations, and then the end will come (Matthew 24:14 NKJV)*

Evangelism is the announcement - and a demonstration - of a superior Kingdom offered to all who will entrust themselves to its King. This King personally paid for our past offenses and equips us with all we need to serve Him acceptably and without fear, including not only the forgiveness of sins and the breaking of the power of sin, but also His very presence and companionship within us.

If we will actively entrust our lives to Him, we will know Him; and He will live in and through us.

This King will return to judge the living and the dead according to what they have done; But those that love Him enough to practice obeying Him will find that love overcomes fear, and what emerges is freedom and joy.

You are nearing the end of this book. This is a good point at which to review the "Key Truths" introduced at the start of the book. I placed them there so that, at the outset, you would see "what I had hoped to prove" from the scriptures.

Now that you have seen and considered so many scriptures (like a "great cloud of witnesses"), would you now say that the scriptures are clear and consistent – and indeed saying these amazing things?

I hope I have made my case for the radical truth that Christ indeed came to make us like Him, in this world, in this age.

Sown in Weakness and Shame

It Makes Us Free
... If we *Know* It and *Walk* in It

There is a truth that is so important that Jesus called it **"the"** truth. Christ had to keep this "mystery hidden through the ages" veiled (Col 1, Eph 3, Rev 10) it was veiled until the ambush was complete (1 Cor 2:7). This ambush was the bringing of *many sons to Glory* (Heb 2). Will you be one them?

> *(John 8:31-35) Then Jesus said to those Jews <u>who had believed Him</u>, "If you remain in My word, you are truly my disciples. And*
>
> *you will know the truth, and the truth will make you free."*
>
> *33 They answered Him, "We are Abraham's offspring, and have never been in bondage to anyone. How can You say, 'You will be made free'?" 34 Jesus answered them, "Most certainly, I tell you, <u>whoever commits sin is a bondservant of sin</u>. 35 And a bondservant doesn't live in the house forever. A **<u>son remains forever</u>**."*

Christ operated as a man in whom the fullness of God was pleased to dwell. Will we? Now? The central truth of all helpful Christian writing is that Christ made that way for us to walk as He did in this life (1 Jn 4:17; John 3:14; 2 Cor 5:21). Please consider the following, carefully and prayerfully:

> *(Philippians 2:7) rather, <u>he emptied himself</u>, taking the form of a servant [as opposed to "son"], being made in likeness of men.*

Note that He was born of woman, and not bearing the image of God ... until He was baptized and filled. He was without sin, but He was not manifesting until He was. This is why His brothers and friends didn't believe in Him ("is this not the son of Joseph ...?"). This is why we hear almost zero of His childhood, teens, and twenties. The glory was not there until the New Covenant filling was there.

But He was the human in whom the fullness of God was pleased to dwell. By this He made the way for us to do the same. The amount of glory (doxa, the manifest yet unspoken presence of God) that we manifest is a function of the degree to which we renew our minds and put sin to death – all by His power. So yes – it is all by grace "through faith" (pistis, the same word is both "faith" and "faithfulness"). Embrace this truth – do not let a human tradition lock you out of it! – and it will change you.

> *(Colossians 1:19) For all the fullness was pleased to dwell in him; (John 5:19) Jesus therefore answered them: "Most certainly I tell you, the Son **can do nothing by himself**; for whatever things He does, these the Son also does likewise."*
>
> *(1 Jn 4:4) You are of God, little children, and have overcome them, because*
> **He who is in you is greater than he who is in the world.**

As we see plainly here, Christ was not able to overcome the works of the devil "because He was God". To believe that would give us the excuse for our powerlessness; and this is what most of the church does today ("Just a poor sinner").

Rather, He emptied himself of that nature to demonstrate the way that we are called to "follow Him" in. By the Innocent Blood of the High Priest, the central promise of The New Covenant is released: It is simply but profoundly, "**Christ in you**".

Do not make the mistake that has shipwrecked the church! Yes – observe the central trend of today's church – the divorce rate and I believe also the *sin rate* – is statistically the same among most Christians as that of unbelievers, and most "Christian" parents suffer the heartbreak of seeing their children leave their faith as soon as they can. In forty years of ministry, I know this to be true.

Make Your Calling and Election Sure

There is nothing "automatic" about it. There is no room for *worshipful passivity*. This is simply neglect and presumption in disguise.

Since the days of John the Baptist – when Christ was baptized and filled – The kingdom of God allows violence, and the violent take it by force; They crash through the gate by the power of the breaker (Micah 2); Partaking in the divine nature, having escaped the corruption, they make every effort to make their calling and election sure (2 Pet 1:10).

To the Bible Belt: Notice 2 Peter 1 summarizes the most precious truth of God toward man. But, *if your Tradition buries **even that**,* then unless you have forged through the Word of God *honestly for yourself without colored lenses*, you will not see it.

If you have been taken by the FOG – the Forgiveness-Only Gospel – then even if you read your Bible a hundred times, it remains … FOG and headache and sleepiness. Will you accept that Christ seeks to "bring many sons to glory" (Heb 2)? He gives His Spirit to *those who obey Him*. It is all over the entire chapter of John 14 and recapped plainly in Acts 5:32. It "is" the New Covenant itself … but have your teachers mentioned it? If not, then it is more than a "tradition" that has hidden it. I have seen that thing directly. It hates your soul because God has appointed the Earth to man, but Christ is the lover of your soul.

If and when we are reconciled and surrendered, we are then men and women in whom the fullness of God *is pleased to dwell*. We turn to obey God; the power of sin is broken; we ask and receive the promise of the indwelling. Then we set out to grow up into the full measure of that stature (Eph 4).

Bible Quotes are Word English Bible (WEB) except where noted.

Gospel Narrative
In "We and You" Points-of-View

In the last three years, as I have developed both the poster and the book; I have continually sought to bring a simple but accurate Gospel message, making it "as simple as possible, but no simpler" again as Einstein has said. I took a shot at presenting the entire poster narrative as if I were presenting it to "the man on the street", within thirty minutes.

In real life there will be interaction, but not *constant interaction*. If you will come out of the gate with love and power, you will have their ear. If you are offering escape not just from hell, but from sin itself; and you are offering to them rebirth as a different species of man that carries the presence of God and His nature, you will have their ear.

I am not suggesting that, upon first hearing, each and every man on the street will receive the message. But:

1. Before I witness, I pray against any blinding or deaf spirits.
2. When I speak, I am stating the truth that will make that person free.
3. If there is sickness or spiritual oppression, I minister healing and/or deliverance. The Lord will confirm my words with signs accompanying (Mark 16:20). Again, at this point I have their ear. As I become aware of oppressors in their souls, or strongholds in their minds, I speak liberation.
4. Through it all, The Holy Spirit does His work to convince and convict. God knows in advance who – by their truly free will – shall respond with a surrender or not, and when. But for my part – I simply obey as warrior, liberator, and ambassador. It is all in the name of the one that sent me (John 20:21).

In any given conversation I am "planting" or "watering"; If they see the glory of the invitation of God to them, they will want to meet again and move forward. If they don't (yet) then they won't (yet).

Again, I just do my job and obey the commission (Mark 16; Matthew 28).

No Two Cases are Exactly the Same

Naturally, each hearer comes with his or her own experiences, hurts, baggage, mind-strongholds, and perhaps oppressive spirits. We must be discerning, and we must tailor the depth and focus of our words to fit the needs of the hearer.

But in absolutely every case, you are there as a liberator of a captive; you are to awaken their hunger for freedom; You are discerning their oppressions and you are speaking the words of eternal life to them.

Timing

I am giving roughly two or three a minute of narrative for each panel and about a half-minute per frame. The last paragraph of each panel formulates an invitation to those that are "at that stage" and considering their next step or steps toward entering the Kingdom of God or walking in it as both warrior and ambassador.

When I come to a Panel Heading, I put the narrative into "Title" formatting as you see immediately below – as we get started. Also please remember – to the average man on the street, we are to speak the Word of God, *but we do not give chapter and verses references*. The early church didn't even have a New Testament.

I want to Invite you to become a Son of God

I want you to Enjoy Peace, Dignity, Freedom, and Strength; It will all start with the annihilation of your guilt and shame. You will also gain power over any and all the spirits that oppressed and tormented you and the damage they have done will be undone.

(Yes, you start by blowing their mind with something that, deep inside, they've always craved but never dreamt was really possible.)

[You minister healing or deliverance at this time]

Now, there is a World that is coming to an end – most people can see this now! – and there is also a World to come. If you want to know how to escape judgement and live through the ages, it is not going to be five minutes and there will be no simple "repeat after me".

The fact is, it's going to take 30 minutes; but if you really hear, will never be the same.

Here is the Background

We were created for peace, strength, joy and rest. As originally created, we were made to re-present the goodness and power of God on the Earth and to have easy dominion, to reign over all other creatures, including the creeping things that opposed us. Those evil spirits opposed us then and oppose us now. Man originally easily dominate them, but we were deceived and enticed with sensuality, selfish pride, and a demand for independence. We wanted glory "apart" from God.

Bible Quotes are Word English Bible (WEB) except where noted.

Sin entered and death reigned. It reigns on the Earth to this day, except for those that have been reborn into the second mankind, after the pioneering work of Christ; Not only forgiven by Him, but reconciled and **reconstituted** by Him, partaking in His nature. We hunger above all for His *righteousness*.

Christ Himself planted Himself as a seed – becoming man, dying to his own glory to serve mankind – in the knowledge of what would come of it. He planted weakness and shame, knowing that glory, honor, and immortality would appear. This is what He meant by "follow me".

Jesus Christ was the firstborn Son of God, calls us all to escape the corruptions of the World and partake in His Nature, and overcome the enemy's work inside of you and outside of you. He made *the way* for this and said "follow me".

The Popular Gospel is, In Fact, Badly Distorted

Christ made a way not only for us to be "forgiven", but to make us like Him, in *this* World, in *this* Age; The Popular version of Christianity *focuses almost totally on the forgiveness aspect*, but Christ made a way for us to become free from the controlling power of sin and to be reconnected with the Life – and companionship – of God. He even gives us both the desire and the power to live in full peace, freedom, strength, and dignity… And there is far more.

We "are" a spirit; we "have" a soul; and we are "in" a body. In order to understand how God transforms us, it is crucial to know that, when we surrender to Him, we are in fact re-created in our spirits to be a different species of mankind. Once we are recreated, we still have residue (called "sin") in our souls. Fortunately – as I will describe in a moment – we have the power then to dismantle and remove that residue. But it is extremely important for us to not look at our souls and say, "that's what I am". If you are truly "converted", you are a son or daughter of God; like a seed that is planted, a new thing is born but takes time and "gardening" to bring to maturity.

Through many centuries, popular Christianity has come to ignore or discard many of the most important and wonderful aspects of the work of Christ.

The Missing Pieces Have Always Been Right There

The Old Testament on its own shows a lot of "mystery", but the New Testament clearly explains them. Some important basics are:

God is good, all the time! He is absolutely just, and absolutely merciful to those that surrender their rebellion.

The Prophets spoke of the means by which a man can be reconciled and recreated. There is an Old Mankind, and a New Mankind.

The New Mankind lives in union with God; He increasingly experiences dominion over things that would oppress him; He tastes the powers of the age to come; and he lives in the joy of an unspeakably wonderful inheritance.

We Enjoyed Dominion & Fellowship but Forfeited Both

God created us as the crown of creation, reflecting His own "image", with "glory and honor" and with "all things under our feet". But in our desire for self-centered dominion and independent glory, we made God our enemy and death entered; We became subjects of the enemy.

Nevertheless, God had sovereignly assigned the Earth to man. Through the ages, through the prophets, He reasserted this intention, even providing illustrations of His overwhelming military power at work in favor of individuals – or even with Israel as a nation coming out of Egypt – with those that would obey the command of God. That command was, essentially, to love Him and to love others.

Indeed, from cover to cover, we see that "restored glory, honor, and immortality" is the hope of man and the promise of God. Even at the end game – the "restoration of all things", all the Kingdoms of the Earth will be handed over to Christ and to those "that overcome". We must overcome the true enemy – very, very, actively! ... *by the power of God at work in us. That*, is "grace". As we shall see, those that *overcome* in this age will inherit the Earth in the age to come. This repeated all over Revelation 2; Most of the church has entirely lost sight of it. Let's bring it back and celebrate the joy of overcoming.

The Spirit of God brings the power of God. In the early ages, that Spirit would "come upon" mankind, for example Samson for specific exploits; In later times that same Spirit would be "with" mankind, e.g. Moses and the Israelites coming out of Egypt, striking terror into all the nations that were in their path.

In about 1800 B.C. Abraham was led by God to abandon sin, o come out from idol worship in "Ur of the Chaldees", and promised (covenanted) that He would inherit the Earth and that His descendants would be countless. This is "restored dominion" to him who overcomes; but the history of Israel was to be wave after wave of great rebellion followed by only temporary repentances; They were taken captive by the Babylonians and Assyrians.

But the plan of God was not merely to be "upon" mankind; not merely even to be "with" mankind ... His plan was to "make His home in us" – in *as many of us as would receive Him* (John 1:12). This would be to the ultimate glory of God as a demonstration of His kindness to man.

Bible Quotes are Word English Bible (WEB) except where noted.

In about 700 BC the prophets – especially Isaiah, Jeremiah, Ezekiel, Daniel, and Joel – revealed some details of that "New Covenant".

He would put our sins away from us as far as the East is from the West, and remember our sins no more; And *also*:

- He would put *His Own Spirit* "into" us!
- He would take away our hard-hearts and give us the ability to love with His kind of love – truly unselfish.
- He would put an end to the enemy's oppression in us.
- We would provide everything we need; We would enjoy the fruit of our labors; without struggle and without theft.
- We would belong to God, and He would belong to us.

Why do we in America keep on wanting only forgiveness – leaving everything else on the table? Are we still insisting on … independence?

I am Here

When Jesus arrived on the scene in public ministry, much if not most of Israel just wanted freedom from the Romans; always yearning for military dominion, and always "over" other nations of people. But in Jesus' direct earthy ministry, He demonstrated dominion – *but not over* **man**!

He was a man "in whom the fullness of God was pleased do dwell". He was both the *Son of God* and the *Son of Man*. By the Spirit of God that "lived in" Him be brought restored dominion – *over the true enemy* – to His disciples, He demonstrated it to them; he trained them; He sent them ahead of Him; Finally, He commissioned them with the very same dominion task of Genesis 1.

Shortly before His Crucifixion, Jesus explained plainly in John 14 that He came to fulfill the promises of the New Covenant; but he explained there that His indwelling in us was only for those that would obey His commands.

Sown in Shame & Weakness; Raised in Glory & Power

The Spirit of God tells man that man is broken; apart from the solution Christ brings, mankind is hopeless in selfishness and inexorably … dying. New – and transformed life is created only when a seed is planted. Christ made the way and showed it to us. We are to see our selfishness and our futility *compared to His love and His power*. We are to see our shame *compared* to His *glory*.

This "sowing shame to reap glory" is the pattern that unlocks "the Way" of the true Gospel. One you get hold of it, then study the Word of God from that perspective, you will see massive puzzle-piece-drops (PPDs as I like to call them). When the puzzle pieces drop, you grow in joy and boldness.

"Sowing shame and weakness to reap glory and power" occurs in our lives in three phases as follows.

First – Christ is the Second Mankind and the Last Adam

Christ planted the ultimate dead seed, which was Himself when he took upon Himself all our sin and shame – even becoming sin – so that upon His resurrection and ascension and reunion with the Father – we might become, not just carry, the righteousness of God. Christ – The Second Adam – "is" the way, because, if we follow Him, then we are "in" Him.

The Father gave Christ as a Covenant – a profound bond of mutual love and loyalty, to restore to us that which was lost – birth and Sonship, partaking of the nature of God, to live in union with God; and yes – bearing of the image of God.

God seeks to once again crown mankind – *__you__* – with glory and honor; and to put all things back under your feet.

Christ accomplished – for mankind – the ultimate ambush of all time. He went through self-denial to glory so that we could follow Him there – not by our strength, but by our very, very active surrender; by His own righteousness – "rightness" – in us.

In summary, Christ invited all to be reborn – not as mere humans, but with His own Spirit mingled with ours. Christ is the Last Adam we will ever get.

This Jesus Christ offers to live His life in you if you see your desperate need; see both His love and His glory – and surrender "into" Him. You must "follow Him: by sowing your dead life."

Second – We Make the Trade – We Escape and Partake

At the next level is *the only offer of Amnesty that is on the table*. Christ invites us to sow ourselves into Him, to escape condemnation and death; but being buried (hidden) with Him by doing His will – brings to us the sharing of His nature in our rising. We are "converted" – we become those who do the will of God and endure forever. But again, **there is no reaping without sowing**. There must be *germination*. But *if* we die with Him, we are freed from sin; and we shall then certainly rise with Him as Sons of God and fellow heirs; and Christ is not ashamed to call us His brothers. We also ascend and are seated with Him in Union with the Father, and we are seated with Him far above the enemy. This is the basis of restored dominion; but it happens first in the unseen; then as we renew our minds, we learn to exercise that dominion.

Bible Quotes are Word English Bible (WEB) except where noted.

Thousands of churches tell us that "grace" means "there is no sowing". Satan is the author of that lie; he keeps millions defeated, "poor sinners saved by grace".

So – God has shown us all the depth of His love, in packing all of *our hideousness* into His own Son and destroying Him in our place. So, what is our required response?

Many people have a severe response when they see the suffering of Christ; but a conversion does not occur merely "if we see and feel pity" or even "if we realize we need forgiveness"! I believe that the instant and true conversion occurs when we ***see that***:

a) According to God's justice, **we stand rightly condemned**; and
b) According to God's mercy, **Christ died "as us"** – not just "for us".

I know this from direct personal experience. After twenty years of religion, I saw the plain truth of Romans 6, and the compulsive power of sin in me was broken in an instant. I had never heard it in church; I had to stumble upon it on my own.

Another twenty years after that, I discovered the supernatural power of God to undo the work of the enemy, but that it is only ours to use if we will use it to love mankind the way Christ loved mankind. Once again, I had never heard it in church; I had to stumble upon it on my own. That's why I am telling you this.

God Himself is delighted as you uncover the treasures that He has placed for all who follow His beloved Son, the firstborn from the dead. He came to bring many sons to glory. Can we handle that?

Our Transformation - Renewed to Be Like Him

Salvation "begins" when we are born again and adopted as Sons of God.

Upon that definitive surrender, we have been recreated after the pattern of God, and with the Spirit of God in us. As Sons of God, we asked to be filled with His Spirit and we were filled. The power of sin is broken, and we are commanded to use that power.

Now, seeking glory, honor, and immortality, we obey His command to love as He loved. As we do so we are abiding in His love by His power.

We "put on" the New Man; We overcome the sin that dwells in us. The burden is now light, because "sinner" is no longer *what we are*. This is not "earning my salvation", but it is most certainly the requirement.

Here is the secret to getting started. Trust that His power in you finally gives you the power to resist sin; Then resist it. If you step out and obey God, then

God manifests Himself to you. When you know the fellowship of God, everything changes. But our <u>*obedience*</u> – ***now by His power*** – must happen <u>*first*</u>. In both the introduction and the closing of His letter to the Romans, Paul called the gentiles to the "*obedience* of faith". That is faithfulness, allegiance, loyalty, and solidarity. These are simply the other definitions of *pistis*, which is translated as "faith" in far too many places.

In every context that speaks of love and power in action, it is not "faith" but rather "faithfulness". This is why Christ was amazed at the Centurion's faith – it was how He "lived", not just something he agreed was true; and having nothing to do with believing His sins were forgiven. In His day job he was sworn to enforce the laws of Rome, but he understood authority.

Accordingly, we who walk no longer according to the flesh are no longer under condemnation. When we stumble, we confess our sin to God – or to the one offended as the case may be – and we both forgiven and made clean again.

Hope has not disappointed us because the love that is of Christ has been poured into our hearts. Again - it is the main course of the New Covenant! So, we walk without guilt or shame; we are becoming like Him, and we finally cast out fear of the day of judgement.

Until He returns, like a Centurion we are to take and occupy and retain the territory. We once again tread on the enemy according to the original great commission of God toward man. The sons of God are added to the Great Cloud of Witnesses.

If and as we do the will of God rather than serve our selfish ways in this life, we are hidden with Christ in God; When Christ appears, we shall appear with Him in glory.

Bible Quotes are Word English Bible (WEB) except where noted.

Simple Truth
Makes you "Theologian-proof"

> If we are Surrendered into Christ and are abiding in Him,
>
> then we are:
>
> ## Freed by His death
> ## and Strong by His Righteousness
>
> Glory, honor, and immortality – Eternal Life itself
> is the reward for *living from Christ's provisions of Everything
> we need for Life and godliness.*

Conversion is the Restoration of the Life of Christ into Man

We obtain that goodness in our spirits by *converting* from the First Mankind to the Second, breaking the chains and receiving the internal witness of Sonship. As Sons, we ask for and receive the Heavenly gift. It is like a nuclear reactor in us, but it is still subject to our knowledge of it and *it is still subject to our minds and wills*.

Again, "He whom the Son sets free is free indeed" but … Now What shall I do with such freedom? Shall I go on sinning? If I am humble before God and have been set free from sin (Rom 8:21-22) then of course I shall no longer practice sin.

Discipleship is Abiding in Christ by Obeying His Commands

We bear the acceptable fruit in our thoughts, words, and actions by actively and continually putting on the behavior of true Sons, *by the power of the indwelling Christ* – and His commands are not a heavy burden.

Even if we fail in weakness, we have a merciful advocate (2 John 1) that is ready to restore us as we persevere.

Sown in Weakness and Shame

Application
We are Invited to Live that Life

These truths have revolutionized not only my own life; but I also routinely watch the same truth of God transform the lives of many others. The Truth changes us very quickly and effectively if we are diligent not only to set our minds on them, but also to <u>*make the needed changes*</u> in our practical lives. To make this change a reality in our lives, this means entering into discipleship and surrounding ourselves with the right cloud of witnesses.

We must never forget that we are in fact *free by <u>His</u> death* and *strong by <u>His</u> righteousness* (Rom 6). We must not deny the power of God; and finally, we must practice loving as He loved.

As John G. Lake has said:

> "In Christ we become God's <u>***sons***</u>, man's <u>***servants***</u> and the devil's <u>***masters***</u>".

Most of the mockery of Christians today is <u>*not persecution at all*</u>; rather, that common mockery arises every time the World sees <u>*none of the above*</u> in one that calls himself a Christian.

But if we humble ourselves, confessing our sin and renouncing our independence, and *"be converted"* (Acts 3:14-21) we become the Second Mankind (**this** is baptism). We can then step out of our doors to obey Christ as the servant of man, and the Spirit of Christ appears to our awareness (John 14:19, 23) and – as Lake discovered – life becomes a "grand new thing".

Caution: Your "Soul" is Not "You"!

If we have made the trade (of our way for His way; of our will for His will; of our life for His life), then <u>*as a matter of fact*</u> our ***innermost nature*** has changed; Therefore, in speaking these passages, we are speaking of the glories <u>*of the Sons of God*</u>, and we are speaking them of <u>*ourselves*</u>. In other words, you should restate them using "I"! This is hugely important.

In doing so we are drawing the character and nature of God as *"from a well"* that is inside us. We draw this truth up from our spirits and into our souls; we also, by discipline, practice goodness to drive the transformation from the outside-in as well (Rom 8:13; Eph 421-22). We do all these things by an obedient act of the will and by cooperating with the power of God at work in us (Col 1:27-29).

Bible Quotes are Word English Bible (WEB) except where noted.

These truths ignite Hope; Hope produces diligence and perseverance; (Rom 5; 2 Pet 1; Heb 6) and then the faith and love that spring from hope – are ours Col 1:3; Rom 5:5).

Do not be deceived by the enemy's lies, but *stand on the Love and promises of God in Christ*. Our "feelings" will come around soon enough, in a wonderful, beautiful turn.

We are invited to live the very life of Christ. There is no more wonderful thing available to a breathing human being, and that's what the Lord Jesus has purchased for us!

Desperate Times, Desperate Measures?

Is *everything that is good* under assault? You know it is (Romans 1 and 2). "Knowledge shall increase" (Daniel 7, 11). We are drawing near to the end of the Age.

The question for a rebel is, will you neglect the way of escape, before it is too late? If you want "dominion" there is coming One that will judge the living and the dead.

The question for a follower is, what will you do with the presence of God in you, and the time you have?

There are of course in the church many "pockets" of radical Sons of God and <u>followers</u> of Christ in the sense He intended. To be honest, however, *most* members of *most* churches are suffering *routine defeat*; Parents are cut to the heart as they *watch their children turn away*. The leaders of these churches need to embrace – and then demonstrate in truth – and then preach the truth we have just seen; the truth that makes us like the *First*born from the dead.

In case it works for others – and it will – here is the way that I was awakened. First, I stumbled upon the history of John G. Lake. I got very, very hungry as I devoured his autobiography; After a few months I stopped reading only long enough to discover John G. Lake *Ministries* led by Curry R. Blake. I took the two-year Bible School and have been growing up quickly with a wonderful awareness, not only of being reconciled, but of being "alive". I am now connected with a church where dozens of us – nearly 50% men – are growing together "toward the measure of the stature of the fullness of Christ" (Ephesians 4).

I have shared the truth of the Word of God in a manner that would restore the larger themes of the New Covenant back to center-stage of the "Gospel". As these full-gospel themes (restored fellowship, freedom, strength, holiness, righteousness-consciousness, and dominion) make their way back into our sight, hope will arise and will give birth to faith and love (Col 1:3).

The glory of God will cut through the thick darkness that the "forgiveness-only gospel" has put upon the church and through the "just a poor sinner saved by grace" mindset. I lived for 40 years under that deception, and it was being maintained by the church itself more than by any other entity. I myself have seen the principality that commands the Kingdom of "Religion", on the other side of a church banquet table.

But I have also seen the King of Glory that is seated – with me in Him – at the right hand of God, *__far above__* every name that is named in this age or in that which is to come (Eph 1:22).

Please plant yourselves where the whole Truth of the New Covenant is embraced and proclaimed. Plant yourself into Christ; Tend your garden ... and you will grow ... and you will bear acceptable fruit, fruit that abides! Because *He is faithful to do what He has promised*!!

Bible Quotes are Word English Bible (WEB) except where noted.

New Covenant Impacts for Sound Teaching

Those of us that teach will be held to a higher standard; judged more strictly (James 3:1). Therefore, it behooves us teachers to be *extremely* diligent to rightly divide the scriptures! Again, as Albert Einstein has said, "Make it as simple as possible, but no simpler".

This whole book lays out the clarifications that the church needs in order to undo the gross oversimplifications that have been advanced by popular "cultural" Christianity. The only valid basis for going about this correction is to put the Second Mankind – the literal heart of the New Covenant itself – back into our gospel message.

And we *do not have another century* to perpetuate the FOG, the Forgiveness-Only Gospel.

Points Most in Need of Elaborating and Clarifying

This is not a "catechism", but rather a collection of clarifications to help crystallize the passage studies in this book.

First, let's be clear on what the fundamental salvation non-negotiables are: A true salvation is our conversion from the First Mankind to the Second Mankind in our innermost constitution, which is our spirit. It does not occur without a denial of ourselves. It is the ultimate cost, but the exchange literally brings to us the "heart" of the New Covenant (Ezekiel 36:25ff), and there is nothing more important for us to "get right" (Galatians 6:15).

One is reconciled to God when we hear His call in whatever form and respond with *repentance* and faith. Repentance is forsaking all known sin; not just being sorry and believing we need forgiveness to get into Heaven. Faith is not just belief in salvation facts, but is a change of *allegiance*, from self-as-King to Christ-as-King [71], and the practice of a walk of fidelity.

Saving "belief" is "***entrusting ourselves into Christ***" (a precise translation of the phrase in John 3:16 based on its context). When a teacher or student turns this corner, they are on their way to breakthrough.

This is initial salvation, the "setting free" part.

---

[71] In *Gospel Allegiance*, Matthew Bates soundly makes the case for the allegiance aspect of saving faith. Numerous passages make sense only when we replace "faith" with "faithfulness" or "allegiance".

Final Salvation:
By Simply Utilizing the Gift

A true Christian no longer *practices* sin. Its power is broken and we are able to resist it; as a salvation matter, we are to ***persevere*** in actively putting it to death by His *righteousness* in us, not his *forgiveness* in us. But even when we fail in weakness, we have a means of obtaining quick restoration, and we have an Advocate (1 John 1:9-10; 1 John 2:1). The Word of God is clear as day on all of this.

With these basics in place, let's make some connections and distinctions, and watch the scriptures take on their righty-divided consistency.

Pastors, Teachers, and Preachers – if you grasp these critical distinctions and then be true to them, you will find the refreshment of your own souls that you have hungered for, and your ministry will bear fruit that abides (John 15:16).

You will see some of the same truths – and some of the same passages referenced under several points; I do this to show that a small number of missing pieces form the backbone of a coherent gospel (e.g. 2 Pet 1:3-4 and Rom 6:7); When we allow these pieces to rest in our minds in the right place, the grand puzzle gets solved!

In the following I use bold and italics and underline to convey importance and urgency, and in love. If you say these aloud, please emphasize words and phrases accordingly to better see the "operative words".

One Being, Three Persons, Perfectly Agreed

God is one *being* in three persons, in absolute perfect mutual agreement of will, and *that will* is only good. God is ***all-powerful*** – as an ***attribute***; but He "*is*" **_Love_** as His ***essence***. Healing is one of His names (Exodus 15:26). His love is *steadfast*, enduring forever (Exodus 34:7; Ps 136). He is faithful to His promises and keeps His Word; He does not change (Isa 55:11; Malachi 3:6; Hebrews 13:8).

Escaping the Corruption and Its Condemnation

Holiness (Greek Haggios) is the state of "being set apart". In the context of spiritual things, it is being set apart from the unclean things of the World, as in "come out from them and touch no unclean thing" (2 Cor 6:17). If we are still bound to the "system" (cosmos) of this World that is passing away,

Bible Quotes are Word English Bible (WEB) except where noted.
then we will be destroyed with it. We are invited to live the life of God through the ages.

Walking in His Way, by His Righteousness

There is a specific "Way" that God in Christ calls us to (the Isaiah 35 "Highway", the "Way of Holiness"). We are to walk in it as Kings (Rom 5:17) and Priests (ushering others both to victory and to holiness); We enjoy the freedom, the dignity, and the glory – of *holiness* (Isa 40:3-5), because we have been cleansed by God; and *Christ has become our actual righteousness* (Rom 6:1-7; 2 Cor 5:21). **We are finally "okay with"** "Be Holy for I am Holy" (Lev 19; 1 Pet 1:16). Not only are our sins forgiven (clean hands), but our hearts purified (converted! Recreated after the pattern of God Eph 4:24). We are now free to approach the throne of God not as mere servants, or even merely friends (a blood covenant "friend" is a profound bond of glad commitment); but rather we approach as Sons sharing in very His nature ((Jn 1:12; 2 Pet 1:4), all by His Grace (2 Pet 1:3). Summary ... Psalms 24. With clean hands and purified innermost hearts, we say "Lift up your heads, oh gates, that the King of Glory may come in!"

Choosing the Joy of Union Over Selfish Independence

We obtain the righteousness of God not by earning, but by *surrendering out of our prideful independence, into His love* (Mt 16:24), and walking with Him with diligence (2 Pet 1:5) and perseverance in doing good (Rom 2:7), putting off sin and putting on (in our souls) the actual, practical, overcoming holiness of Christ. We do it all in the joy of union as the Bride of Christ (Eph 5). We become like Him and He brings down the proud (Isa 40).

He Became what We Were, and Died as Us

Christ is the Foundation upon which all the blessings of God come to mankind (1 Cor 3:11). In a massive exchange – *everything that was His He gave to us*, and *He took upon himself the consequences of our rebellion* (Isa 53). This is not merely the paying of our debt, though it was that; Going further, He also **"became" Sin, that we might become His righteousness** (2 Cor 5:21). And His yoke, we finally find, **is Easy** (Mt 11:28)! That yoke is "practicing obeying Christ's command to love as He loved, by His own righteousness within us".

Renouncing What We Are, to Become One of Him

Again, it is not merely admitting our sinfulness (though it must start there), but *renouncing what we are* by nature (innermost depravity as some traditions rightly say) to "make the trade" (Mt 16:24; Lk 9:23); *as a matter*

Sown in Weakness and Shame

of exchange, to receive a heart of flesh and the indwelling Spirit of God (Ezekiel 36) and serve God without fear (Rom 8:1-4). He came to **bring many Sons to Glory** (Heb 2).

The Blood of Christ is His Blood of the New Covenant

Fallen man could do nothing to help himself, but Christ as High Priest of the New Covenant[72] provided the sacrifice on "both sides" - both as the ***Son of Man*** and as the ***Son of God***. The New Covenant was ratified – legally put into effect – by the shedding of the innocent Bood of Christ (1 Cor 11:25). **The shedding of His Blood *in and of Itself is not good news*** until we know ***what the Covenant is that it puts into effect*** (1 Cor 6:17; Heb 2:10-14). The New Covenant promise is what we look for. What the early church lived by is the main entrée that Jesus Christ instituted as the New Covenant – It is the provision of the presence of God, not just *upon* us, or *with* us, but "*in* us".

That gift of righteousness (Rom 5:17) could be legally purchased only by innocent Blood. In other words, forgiveness was not the ultimate objective. The ultimate objective was *reunion*, and restored dominion could finally flow from that union. This unlocks the meaning of John 14:12. I fyou set your heart on it and go after it, you will come to minister with power.

Why We Needed a New Covenant

Freedom from *guilt* comes to us when we see that Christ died "for" us, but unless we accept that He died ***"as us"*** *then we sin again and again.* In Forty years of ministry in evangelical churches, my observation is that most "Christians" are *absolutely unaware* of the power of the Romans 6:7 truth. These millions of hurting lives ***are not honoring God***. But Freedom from the *power* of sin – the transition from *shame* to ***dignity*** – comes when we see that Christ died "AS" us. We obtain glorious freedom (Rom 8:21) from the very *consciousness* of sin (Heb 10). God implemented the New Covenant – by placing us (those who surrender into Christ), literally, *into Him* and Christ, *into us*. This is the truth that will make you free, and the enemy knows it and has already stripped it from most church teaching. Weary Pastors and teachers – be sure to get *true rest for yourselves*, and *then* witness of it with boldness, and with authority (Titus 2:11-15!).

---

[72] A Blood covenant includes sacrifices and promises by both parties as they pledge to the benefit of the other; A blood covenant signifies not only union but also the mingling of natures, identities, and sometimes names. The life and nature of a person is in their blood. As mentioned earlier, I very highly recommend *The Blood Covenant* by E.W. Kenyon, and *The Power of the Blood Covenant* by Malcom Smith.

Bible Quotes are Word English Bible (WEB) except where noted.

The Mystery is the Ambush that was Coming

The "Mystery hidden through the ages" (Romans 1-8, 1 Cor 1-3, 1 Cor 2:8, Eph 1-3) is that the Anointed (Appointed) One, anoints (appoints) even the gentiles that will entrust themselves into Him. And Jesus Christ the **Last Adam** (1 Cor 15), is now fruitful and multiplying His own glory – just as the first Adam has been multiplying his own image of weakness and shame (Heb 2:10). In the last days of this age, those that know Him will grow to the measure of His stature (Eph 4).

Renew Our Minds to What We Are

We that are in Christ – *__to the extent that we know__* who we are in Him – and who He is in us[73] – increasingly know the *__joy of victorious battle__* … *__now__* (2 Cor 4; 1 Jn 4:17).

God's Sovereignty? Man's Responsibility? Yes to Both!

God is "sovereign", and He sovereignly assigned the earth to *man* (Gen 1:26; Ps 115:16; Ps 8:6). Furthermore, God has sovereignly chosen to give His grace to those who will humble themselves before him; and he knows in advance who these are. What is the culmination? *__Man__* shall reign both *with* Christ – who is both Son of God and Son of Man (1 Tim 2) – and *under* Christ (Eph 1:19), *forever and ever* (Dan 7:27; Rev 22:5).

A True Christian "was" a Poor Sinner

A "Poor sinner" is only what we were *__before__* we were saved by grace" (Eph 4:24; 2 Cor 5:21) while we were *yet* sinners (Rom 5:6). **Christians are Sons of God**, reigning in the life of God as Kings (Rom 5:17). "Reigning in Life" is the highest "working out" of God's kindness to us.

Restoration of Companionship and Dominion

Under The New Covenant – *__if we will enter into it by the surrendering of our rebellion and the forsaking of sin__* – then God will forgive our sins, evict the intruder, and sprinkle us clean. He will put *His Spirit* into us and give us *new hearts* that desire to do the things He commands; He shall be our God and we shall be His people (Ezekiel 36:24; Jer 31:34; Joel 2:28). That is the Gospel. He who hungers and thirsts for this righteousness receives it (Mt 5:6). What the enemy did not anticipate, was that by this covenant, *millions of sons of God* would appear, with *Christ Himself living His life through them* (1 Cor 2:6). The fact that Christ could not yet divulge this secret until His resurrection explains the odd "difference" between the

---

[73] Marcus Plating summarizes the JGLM "New Man" and "Divine Healing Technician" teachings by Curry R. Blake in this way.

gospels and the Epistles. Christ demonstrated "Dominion in Union with the Father" – it is "that which was lost"; The Epistles writers walked in it and explained it, but they could do so only *after the ambush was complete*.

The Second Mankind is a New Lineage

God was never interested in improving a human. Rather, in Christ – the Last Adam (1 Cor 15) – He instituted the <u>Second Mankind.</u>

There is a lineage of the First Mankind, enslaved in selfish independence; and there is a lineage of the Second Mankind born of God (Romans 5:12-17). Every human in this age is born into the <u>*first*</u> by default (Rom 3:10-12, 23) but all are invited to the second on a trade-in basis. And it's the Gospel. To draw on a current notion – this is the ultimate *identity* politics (Mat 10:34-36). The work of Christ brings the power to choose the Second but does not force us into it (1 Jn 1:12; Rom 5:17; 2 Cor 5:17; Rev 3:20). Those in the Second Mankind are Sons of God – no longer sinners by constitution; by innermost nature (Ezek 36; Eph 4:24). Christ is not ashamed to call us His brothers because we are born of the same Father (Heb 2) by the power of the same Spirit (1 Cor 6:17).

The Mind of Christ

God has, as part of the New Covenant itself, *given us the mind of Christ* (1 Cor 2:16), and he who pursues it *diligently* (that includes you if you got to this point in this book) *receives it*. This "change of thinking" is the literal meaning of Greek word underlying "repentance". The Greek is "metanoia"; "meta" means "**change**" and "noia" (from gnosis) means "**thinking**". We are to live from that mind (Acts 17:28; Gal 2:20). A Christian is not only reconciled to God, but lives in conscious companionship with Him (John 14:19, 23), and this changes everything.

A Christian is Seated both Here and There

We are seated with Christ (Eph 1:19) in the unseen, even as we subdue the enemy on the visible, tangible earth. We haul the Heaven-right version of things onto the earth (Matt 6), sometimes by asking, sometimes by commanding ("Moses" divided the Red Sea after God told Moses to "*stop crying to Him and divide it*" (Exodus 14:19-31). Jesus taught commanding without begging and pleading, because we are to act like the Sons of God that we are. It is war, but victory in this particular war is joy. **Victory and strength bring glory to God. Defeat does not**. The Love and Power of God are the things we are *witnesses* of (Acts 3:11-21) **If there is no strength, there is no witness at all**. Powerless missions do not re-present Christ in the way He intended. Deliverance and healing were not only

Bible Quotes are Word English Bible (WEB) except where noted.

"signs" to unbelievers, but also "demonstrations" in the face of the enemy of the coming of the ultimate "New World Order" (Eph 3; Rev 19, 20, 21, 22).

The Gospel of the Kingdom

In representing the Kingdom of God, we do not downplay or omit the supernatural simply because we haven't yet renewed our minds to believe it and walk in it (1 Jn 4:17, 1 Cor 2:8, John 14:12). Jesus Christ never once ministered in *mere sympathy*, nor taught his disciples to do so, nor commissioned believers to do so. The "Great Commission" in Matthew starts with verse 18. Why do mission organizations start with verse 19? Why do they quote "teach them to obey all that I have commanded you" without even *mentioning **what it is** that He has commanded* them (Matthew 10)? *Heal the Sick, raise the dead, and cast out evil spirits.* It was not just Bible stories and Bible studies.

Military Dominion struck fear into the Kings of the World under Moses and Joshua in and after the Trouncing of Pharoah and Egypt (read Exodus through Joshua). But <u>restored dominion over the power of the enemy</u> – by "us" as "carriers" – is the glorious platter in the middle of the banquet table that God has prepared for us *in the presence of our enemies* (Ps 23). But somehow, the church – ever since the reformation – has settled for "mere amnesty"; nibbling on only the first course of the meal, and *it doesn't satisfy*. Can we admit it? Conversion is a joyful trade-in (Matt 16; Luke 9; Mark 8) for deliverance and power by the Life of God.

The Enemy has Thoroughly Twisted "Grace"

The Good News is that He has given us the **means** *of righteousness*; *not that He has **excused us from the requirement** of it!* We persevere with our merciful High Priest (1 John 2:1). Anyone that reads the New Testament honestly – not through the lens of the forgiveness-only gospel – will see it. But so many millions have been inoculated by bad teaching – exactly as I was – to the point of not seeing it even as we look directly at the scriptures.

I admit the requirement is scary without a ***rebirth into a new nature**, but fortunately a true conversion includes that*! It is there waiting for all of us – as long as we have life and breath, *that* is; We can have it only by trade-in; by the surrender of our self-will followed by the walk of faith in the One that dwells in us.

Sown in Weakness and Shame

Seek Glory, Honor, and Immortality? What?!!!

If you are in your right mind, then you do in fact <u>seek</u> the right kind of "glory" (Greek doxa). It is the dignity of excellence and of defeating the true enemy. Why do so many traditions teach that it is "pride" to seek it?

We are in fact called to seek after glory, honor, and immortality, as these together form the very *definition of eternal life* (Rom 2:7); We are invited, *not to be above Christ, but to live and reign in Him and with Him and through Him* (Eph 1:19; Eph 2:6; Rom 5:17). It is ultimate pride *to* <u>reject</u> such a *great salvation*; as if we could "reign in life" *without* Him as the First Adam did. This "independence" is a pivotal mindset that every single man or woman must tear down; We must do this *ourselves* (2 Cor 10:4).

We're Not "God", but Partaking of His Nature

In a "Blood Covenant" there is a mingling of natures. Fallen man devises ceremonies seeing to obtain the "life" or the "nature" of another. Savages will even eat the hearts of the courageous victims they conquer. But Christ invites us to *partake in the divine nature*, even as He has partaken of the *human nature*.

As Christians we do not "become God" when we are born again; but upon being *born of God*, we have escaped the corruption that is in the world through evil desire, and are *partaking in the divine nature* (2 Pet 1:3-4); It is then our privilege and *responsibility to use this power* (2 Pet 1:5) *to put to death the sin in our souls.* (Rom 6:22; Rom 8:13). There is then no more condemnation for those who do so as a way of life (Rom 8:1-4).

Finally – There is also now no more contradiction!!

Let's see if we can handle this one. A Christian, standing before an unbeliever, could – in perfect truthfulness – say "I am holier than thou". But would also have to say in the same breath: "all the <u>real</u> goodness in me is <u>by the power of Christ living inside me</u>, I am plugged into His life, so I bear good fruit. He invites you to have His life in you too!".

That is the good news; It awakens a hunger for righteousness – and dignity!

Some Readers will Be Set Free Immediately

God is both just and merciful. *People are not punished for the sins of their parents*, but they will reap for the sins they were taught *and that they also practice*. Every man bears his own guilt, and every man has the freedom to surrender their rebellion (Ezekiel 18:20). By the "great exchange" work of Christ (Isa 53; 2 Cor 5:21; John 3:14) we are invited to **transfer out of that**

Bible Quotes are Word English Bible (WEB) except where noted.

entire rebellious lineage. If a family lineage has a curse on it, anyone that is born as a Son of God has left its jurisdiction and is seated far above the enemy (Eph 1:19). Ephesians 2 tells us we were raised and *seated with Him* there. If you are born again, and you see this and act upon it, it becomes true in your experience. You get to live Matthew 10 discipleship; You get to live the great commission of dominion. You are an overcomer, with ***power to become an image-bearer***; and he who overcomes is given the privilege of eating from the tree of Life in the paradise of God (Revelation 3:7), "Overcoming" is a salvation matter, and grace gives us everything we need for it.

Martin Luther indeed confronted a profound corruption in the Roman Church; But Luther's theology was a half-truth. It should be obvious that if forgiveness were all we received, we would go on sinning and come right back into condemnation. In other words, if there is no new creation (the heart of the New Covenant), then *following* would be impossible; Bearing acceptable fruit would be impossible.

Luther may have believed he was resetting Christianity to what the early church believed; but as an *Augustinian monk*, Luther's frame of reference went back only to the fourth century. Augustine himself got his theology from Manichaean Gnosticism (total depravity, unilateral individual predestination, infant baptism). But the *writings of the very early church leaders* – unanimously affirmed human freedom and responsibility.

The "predestination" of the New Testament was rooted in the foreknowledge of God seeing beforehand who would respond to His kindness with humility and repentance.

Augustine, with his faulty *premises*, got stuck; He had to make obedience either optional or automatic. This is how we got where we are.

Follow the Firstborn Step 1: Deny Self

Therefore, if your tradition says you are still a sinner by constitution, then *your tradition is not Christianity*. But there is a new creation (John 3:3; 2 Cor 5:17, 21). We *identify with His death* so that we **can** follow (the most-repeated saying of Christ, Mt 16:24) and fulfill the great commissions (Gen 1:26; Joshua 1; Mark 16; Matthew 10; Matthew 28)! It really is that simple. He whom the Son sets free is free indeed and ***able to overcome***.

Follow the Firstborn Step 2: Put Sin to Death

Once converted; we are commanded to *put on outward behavior that matches our new nature and constitution* (Rom 8; Rom 12:3; Eph 4:22).

Contrary to Augustine, Luther and Calvin, this is *neither optional - or automatic* (Rom 6:22, 8:1,13), but they built their teachings on it nonetheless. But the fullness of God's grace gives us everything we need to put on that holiness (Rom 6:7; 2 Pet 1:3-4). We need only look around to see that Western Christianity looks much like the rest of world. But some are manifesting as Sons of God. And the number is growing.

No Consciousness of Sins

So precious!! ... but you will almost never, ever, hear of it in a church.

Followers of Christ are to live in the **joy of *dignity*** – *carrying no consciousness of sins* (Heb 10:2). We have power over sin (Rom 6:7), no longer sinners by constitution. A true Christian does not practice sin, by definition (He has repented and forsaken sin); Even if we sin in weakness, Christ is our covenant High Priest – and ***advocate*** (1 Jn 1:9; 1 Jn 2:1). He brings the forgiveness of that sin *immediately upon confession*. That confession is a renewed declaration of loyalty.

If we confess immediately and are restored immediately, then we **carry no consciousness** of sins. And the transformation progresses!

About Confession

1. There must be **restitution** when applicable.
2. There is no **human mediator** between God and Man except the Man Jesus Christ – who now remains both Son of God and Son of Man (1 Tim 2:5-6) that we might partake in the divine nature (2 Peter 1:3-4); If we continue to sow to the flesh after we are freed, *then we will reap destruction* (Rom 8:13-16).

What is "In Christ"?

Objectively, if our will is *to do God's will* – instead of living in self-serving independence – then we are "in Christ" (Gal 5:24). **We are Union with both Christ and the Father** because Christ carried us there (John 20:17; Col 3:3); If we have planted the seed and it has germinated, then the fruit of the new tree will emerge in time. This is the bedrock foundation of freedom, joy, dignity, dominion, and inheritance (Rom 5:5).

Furthermore, by mind renewal (knowing) and by discipleship (doing), we make ourselves *intuitively **aware** of that Union, and we joyfully live by it* – and this is faith (Heb 11:1). What's more, this is exactly the basis of the faith of the Centurion – "Greater than any faith in Israel" at the time (Mat 8:5-13).

Bible Quotes are Word English Bible (WEB) except where noted.

What Did Christ Demonstrate, Teach, Train, and Command?

What did Christ demonstrate, teach, train, and command? He most certainly demonstrated and commanded *love and mercy toward fellow man*. But without His abiding presence this is simply impossible.

He demonstrated *dominion* over all the works of the enemy. He also taught it, trained it, and commanded it, and directly commissioned it. As we saw earlier, Gen 1:26 is the first great commission; and it was repeated at the beginning of every age. Nevertheless, all we will hear in most churches is "forgiveness".

But when this forgiveness-only delusion is removed from our eyes, and we see how great is the thing Christ has purchased – for those "In Him", everything changes. John G. Lake discovered Christ's purpose of "making us like Him" in this World – even *after* he escaped the power of sin (Rom 6); even *after* he was baptized in the Holy Spirit (Acts 2), his response was – *"Life became a grand new thing"*. This happened to me in 2018 and I have never been the same since. Supernatural power for restored dominion entered my living. Not over man, but over the work of the true enemy, both inwardly and outwardly.

The Spirit of God brings *Life* and *power* in into our very beings. But only when we see it does everything begin to change. Only when we then step out to actually obey Christ's command to utilize it – to "do" the will of God – do we experience the joy of it. Power enters our witnessing, and witnessing becomes honest and joyful, because we actually do have good news. And it is all borne of the love of God, bought for us by Christ, and living in us by the Spirit.

Of course, I place these assertions onto your "table of consideration"[74]. All the Word of God soundly supports them; You should find a new hope knowing that indeed, God has given you everything you need for life and godliness, and you *are* a witness, and you *have* the "truly good news"!

---

[74] Faith MacMillan describes this "Table of Consideration" approach to scripture interpretation and discussion. Nobody is "required" to believe anything, but are all responsible to support our perspectives from the Word of God. This makes for peace!

Bible Quotes are Word English Bible (WEB) except where noted.

CONCLUSION

Follow the Firstborn has brought out a variety of New Covenant themes and truths that are absolutely wonderful and profoundly powerful, yet most of them are now entirely omitted from most of today's popular teaching and preaching.

We have seen that the love – and "grace" – of God has been demonstrated not only in the sacrifice of His Son as payment for "sins committed beforehand", but also in is giving us "everything we need for life and godliness"; If we can accept it, the scriptures tell plainly that salvation itself works by Christ setting us free from both guilt and shame in our initial salvation, thus making us accountable for whether we will then "walk according to the flesh or according to the Spirit". I have been careful to affirm that when we fail in weakness, we have a merciful advocate, if we only stay the course.

We have seen that the "sown in ... raised in ..." *Hope* pattern applied first in the pioneering work of Christ – consecration and perseverance, driven by *hope,* and *persevering to "glory"*; and He said, "Follow Me". That very same "sown in ... raised in" *Hope* pattern operates in us, inspiring not only our initial salvation event, but also our transformation process as we endure to the end of our natural lives.

We have seen that God has never relented from His true Great Commission in which He commanded (unfallen) man to be fruitful and multiply, and to subdue the Earth – including the creeping things. The fallen man multiplied, and the Second Man is also multiplying now. They need to know what they are, and they need mind renewal, training, and equipping.

We have seen that the mind of Christ is one not merely a personality of kindness, and not just with an isolated outburst against temple moneychangers; Rather, He walks as a joyful soldier of a different Kingdom altogether (remember the Centurion); Mature sons of God will be *like Him* in that respect... in *this* World.

We have seen that the true Gospel is the announcement of the arrival of what was promised by the prophets (esp. Ezekiel 36:25ff). We have also seen that Christ plainly identified Himself as its fulfilment in John 14, but like a hundred other important passages, it is inadmissible in popular Christianity because Christ messed it up by demanding obedience as a salvation matter.

We saw that the "Romans Road" family of Bible tracts are profoundly deceptive in what they make the scriptures out to say. Even Romans 6 – "the" central New Testament chapter on overcoming sin, is effectively discarded in favor of the "forgiveness-only gospel" (FOG).

I have made so many interconnections that I am confident that you, the reader are now seeing that I have told the truth, not overly simplified. The fact is, the invitation to the dignity and strength and hope of the true Gospel – do not need "varnishing".

Gospel grace doesn't need to be "cheap grace" in order to be *absolutely beautiful, desirable* grace. It has to be a call to belonging, rest, dignity, strength, and overcoming.

I wish to now revisit few central themes that point to the main purpose of Christ – to bear His image again.

Bible Quotes are Word English Bible (WEB) except where noted.

See His Glory
And Hunger for Righteousness

If we get a glimpse of the glory of Christ – and if we hear Him calling us to share in His nature, His strength, and His joy, we simply don't need a phony sugar-coated once-and-done, forgiveness-only gospel.

(Ezekiel 36:25-26) I will cleanse you from all your filthiness and from all your idols. I will also give you a new heart, and I will put a new spirit within you; I will take away the stony heart out of your flesh and I will give you a heart of flesh.

(2 Corinthians 5:21 NKJV) For He made Him who knew no sin to be sin for us, that we might become the righteousness of God in Him.

Bear His Image
And Fulfill the Commission

If and only if we lose our lives to find them – not just "get saved", then we will truly be saved. We will then be transformed in a way that the World – at least the humble in the World – can actually see and actually want. This will utterly transform evangelism. Persecutions will of course ramp up because the proud among the first mankind will want to destroy the Second mankind. But God gives vision and joy His people when they need it, in the face of persecution. Matthew 10 explains it all.

We have seen that Christ did not come merely to *excuse sin* (past, present and future) as commonly taught, but to *destroy it* and replace it with *His very own righteousness*, His very *Life*, *living in and through us*. If we will surrender to do His will, and are truly "In Christ"; He is then pleased to dwell in us, and everything changes if we then live by His life. This is how the burden becomes light.

Millions of eternal lives are at stake. We must no longer reduce and distort what the New Covenant actually offers and demands. We have nearly ruined the very reputation of God by a "grace" and a "gospel" almost entirely emptied of its transforming power. What are we witnesses of?!! We sing "To God Be the Glory", but exactly what glory does God get by the chronic sin and destroyed marriages of the people that call themselves God's people?

Let us restore that reputation of God by an honest and true surrender to do the will of God – by *our* obedience to actively walk by the power of His Spirit that is in us. Let us once again bear the image of His righteousness and exercise absolute dominion over the true enemy.

Again, as Lake has said:

> "If a man is in Christ, he is God's son, man's servant, and the devil's master."

If we preach this Gospel *of the Kingdom* as a testimony to all the earth, then and only then shall we hear "well done, good and faithful servant". Then and only then shall people respond with "I want to ***Be THAT***".

> *(2 Corinthians 5:17, 21) Therefore if anyone is in Christ, he is a new creation. The old things have passed away. Behold, all things have become new...*
>
> *For him who knew no sin he made to be sin on our behalf; so that in him we might become the righteousness of God.*

Bible Quotes are Word English Bible (WEB) except where noted.

Narration
Of a Changed Way of Thinking

The Greek word translated "repentance" means "changed thinking". In the following narrative, I speak my thought process as I consider surrendering my life to God and consider the cost of staying surrendered, too.

As we have seen from the scriptures, salvation is a surrender followed by a life of practicing obedience, all to be walked in humility under the mercy of Christ. Our testimony should include the **resulting joy of being changed from the inside out** and *experiencing winning* over the work of the enemy. Here we go:

I believe that Jesus is the innocent Son of God, qualified to pay my ransom. He who said "Follow Me" was raised from the dead into a glorious being and carried to be united with God Almighty, being given all authority in Heaven and Earth.

He calls *me* to reign with and under Him forever… But He tells me I have to abandon my selfish life in order to be born with the desire and power to do what is right. Will I discard this offer, just to protect my standing with my family? I truly do want to be free from the control of the things that control me–

I know He had died not just for me, but as me (Rom 6:1-7; Gal 2:20; Jn 3:14-15; 1 Cor 1:30-31; 2 Cor 5:7-10). This is good because I know the problem is not just <u>what I have done</u>; but what I am! The power to escape sin is not in me. He tells me to lose my life to obtain His.

[I Surrender Here – I am Baptized, symbolizing and declaring my life-exchange and new allegiance].

I embraced His death as my own. As a seed, I am planted, dead, and germinated. The new life is inside me and my *innermost constitution* has changed. I am "***converted***". Not only is my guilt gone, but so is my **shame**. Times of refreshing have arrived (Acts 3, 2 Cor 5:12) and I am free indeed (John 10).

Because I am now a son of God, not only is my guilt gone; So is my shame; Moreover, I have authority to use the family name. All things are new.

Inwardly – I put off everything that belongs to the World that is passing away; I discard the corruption – the lust of the flesh, the lust of the eyes, and the selfish pride of human accomplishment. I can put off these stains only because sin is no longer my nature; The residue in my soul is no longer … *me*.

Healthy Motives
Not Only Allowed, but Required

I am also not ashamed to say that **I am most certainly now seeking glory, honor, and immortality – this is the "Eternal Life"** (Rom 2:7; John 3:16), I chose that life, and I set out to confirm my calling and election (2 Peter 1:10). I am perfectly content to reign *with but under* Christ forever.

Outwardly – I live now as both servant and soldier. Just as the Father gave Jesus His glory and sent Him, so Christ has given me His glory (John 17:22) and sent me (John 20:21). People now plainly see that I have something they need, and I will not hesitate to tell them what it is, and that it is already paid for.

Like Christ, I too have authority over all the power of the enemy; and it is my joy to know that even the demons are subject to me (Lk 10:18-19). And I have "standing orders"; I have my times of doubting and wavering; Nevertheless, the trendline of my character is upward as I work on renewing my mind.

I choose to obey all He has demonstrated, taught, mentored, commanded, and commissioned; I am loving the joy of the increasing rate of victories.

So – *this* is the Gospel of the Kingdom, and this is the Gospel that must be preached to the ends of the Earth (Lk 24:14).

Bible Quotes are Word English Bible (WEB) except where noted.

The True Church
As the Age Draws to a Close

As we approach the end of *this* Age, the World and its rulers will be put on final notice, because God shall have the vengeance that is His alone.

His people – the true church that is outside any ethnic or organizational lines – being confirmed to the image of the firstborn from among the dead – are of the Second Man, the Last Adam (1 Cor 15). Their souls are kernels of wheat that chose to be buried; have germinated; have sprouted; and are bearing the acceptable fruit.

Not only are they no longer sinners by constitution (Eph 4:24); they are also no longer falling short of the glory of God (Rom 3:23). Christ has given them His glory; it is the *fruit of the right tree (Mat 12:33)*. No longer are they servants of sin; they were freed from its corruption and now use their freedom to gladly serve God, without fear.

Having become servants of God, they have their fruit of holiness and its end, Eternal Life (6;21-23). Even if they stumble; the beloved Firstborn is also their Blood Covenant advocate, Jesus Christ the Righteous (1 Jn 2:1). They don't need a bath, just "foot washings" (John 13); By their immediate confession and cleansing, they no longer even carry consciousness of sins (Heb 9).

They are no longer a part of the World that is passing away (1 Jn 2:17). Their hope has not let them down because the unselfish love of the Lord Jesus is alive in them (Rom 5:5); They have no more fear, because even while still in this World, they are becoming like Him (Rom 5:5; 1 Jn 4:17).

There is no more condemnation for them – because in their freedom they walk no longer after the flesh, and they put its deeds to death; The righteous requirement of God is now fulfilled in these ones (Rom 8:1-4,13). The law of sin and death is no longer in operation.

These servants have entrusted their lives to God (repented); they live and walk in allegiance to Him; They boldly confess His Name with their lips (Rom 10:10). They see Christ (John 14, 16); Simultaneously, they are resting seated with Him in the unseen (Eph 2:6-7) as they follow Him in the visible World.

Inwardly, by His divine power, they are free; by His power they partake in His character and nature. Outwardly, they are the Lord's body acting on the Earth.

Sown in Weakness and Shame

Kingdom Demonstrations
With the Enemy on Notice

The Gospel of the Kingdom is certainly good news to those that are weary of seeing evil dominate on the Earth. But our response must not be passivity. The consistent teaching of Christ is that those that truly love Him ... are diligent to obey Him.

That Lord is still a man of war... And He has given them his glory to subdue even the creeping things (the actual 1st great commission).

Christ is bearing His "much grain" He is multiplying and subduing the earth; The Earth itself watches for the glorious revealing of the sons of God (Rom 8). There will be an open widespread spectacle of this (Rev 19), but there is also even now a growing in the ranks of believers that are taking the standing commission – of subduing the enemy.

> *(Mark 16:17-19) These signs will accompany those who believe: in my name they will cast out demons; they will speak with new languages; they will take up serpents; and if they drink any deadly thing, it will in no way hurt them; they will lay hands on the sick, and they will recover."*
>
> *So then the Lord, after he had spoken to them, was received up into heaven, and sat down at the right hand of God.*
>
> *(Matthew 24:14) This Good News of the Kingdom will be preached in the whole world for a testimony to all the nations, and then the end will come.*

This coming King and His Kingdom are already within us His people and operating though them. If you are in fellowship with God and if you see and accept His promises of overcoming **sin within** and overcoming the **enemy without**, then walking in supernatural power is both your privilege and responsibility.

I believe this is what Isaiah saw when he said "He shall see the fruit of the travail of His soul and be satisfied ... and He will divide the spoil with the strong" (Isa 53).

Do Not Bow to Human Tradition

By this point in *Follow the Firstborn* you might be struggling with the tension between what the Word of God clearly says on the one hand, and what you have

Bible Quotes are Word English Bible (WEB) except where noted.

heard as the gospel. We saw the "Romans Road" gospel tract as the prime example of cheap-grace distortion.

For the non-Christian reader, you might now understand how it came to be that the character of God is missing from so many persons that hand out the booklets.

For the Christian reader, you might struggle because this power is denied by the teaching of your church. As I have mentioned, I lived with that tension for decades. But I snapped out of it in a matter of a few months. People snap out of the FOG when they see the power of Christ being lived out through a human being and when they recognize that that power is plainly promised.

So – to the Christian or the non-Christian that is in despair and unbelief – and in the chronic defeat that comes from it, I testify to you that your life can be utterly different if you remove yourself from any society of unbelief and false teaching, and then connect yourself with people that *demonstrate the love, joy, strength, peace – and yes – **power** to overcome the work of the enemy.*

If that strength that you see is not enough to overcome the power of the enemy, then it is not Christ that you are observing. If the one that commands the power is not attributing the power to Jesus Christ, and if they are not exhibiting the love of Christ inviting your reconciliation with God by the blood of Christ, then **move on**.

Supernatural Signs are Increasingly Common

Thousands are coming to discover this very power to walk as Christ walked; to get supernatural results by Christ working through confirming their words as ambassadors. I have had the very clear supernatural power of God move through me very suddenly in response to my words on about thirty occasions. This is a tiny fraction of the times I have ministered, but it is way more than the zero percent that I directly experienced in my decades of standard church teaching before that.

But that power is only for setting the oppressed free, ***not for anybody's personal dominion apart from God***. Part of my problem was retaining an independent untouchable plan for my life. Nevertheless, I also had low incentive to surrender because the "grace" I heard about was just forgiveness – so of course I gladly accepted it and went my way as most do.

Build Your Life on the Word of God

Jesus says, "When he is trained, a student will be like his teacher, and a disciple will be like His master" (Matt 10); "he shall do even greater works" (John 14:12). Does your tradition uphold the Word of God as true? Really? How many of these Follow the Firstborn promise passages – *and their conditions* – have seen the light of day on your church?

Have you experienced the "free indeed? If you haven't, how much is this worth to you? Are you willing to lose some friends? A position of honor in your organization? A job? The wise will obey the Word of the King and enter His Kingdom.

Bible Quotes are Word English Bible (WEB) except where noted.

Full Salvation:
Entering Followed by Abiding

We have seen that God calls us to glory, and we are not converted merely to *grateful **sinners***. If we are truly saved – by life-exchange – then we have been reborn and adopted as His **sons and daughters**, and our spirits are perfected. Knowing the central promise of the New Covenant, we of course ask and are filled with His Spirit to be with us forever, provided we *continue in Him*.

The Unpopular Second Stage of Salvation

We then are not only "free indeed", We are "back to the garden", but now having *everything we need for life and godliness*; We have knowledge of the deceiver and authority over all his power (Luke 10, Mark 16, Eph 1, Rom 16).

We are "back to the garden", but this time we are the Second Mankind, and we are fully accountable for what we do with *so great a salvation*. If we use the power of God to overcome, then we inherit the Life of God through the ages. If we do not, then we will be given over to wrath and darkness.

Ways to Describe the Two Phases

We have now seen the truth of "how salvation works" from various perspectives and with the corroboration of many passages. How to say it? Here are a few, but you will – or perhaps already have – found more ways to say it; but the moment we make it a once-and done "event", it is no longer Biblical Christianity.

- Deny Self and Take up cross … then Follow Christ, compelled by love.
- Sow self-will as a seed … then tend your garden in thankful patience.
- Be grafted into the vine by faith … then remain by obeying
- Trust … then Obey the Law of Christ - to bear one another's burdens.
- Be reborn and adopted as a son for God… then walk as man's servant and the devil's master (John G. Lake).

Finally, The FOG Lifts

The Second stage is unpopular precisely because it does not make room for continuing to live to serve our selfish desires. But if you can accept it – and it is the truth – you will know what Christianity is and is not; and your Bible will now make perfect sense. The FOG will have lifted.

You will feel the dignity of a being loved by God and invited to use your free will to give yourself to Him. If you do, and you continue in the faith then when you have endured, He will, as promised, give you the Kingdom!

Sown in Weakness and Shame

He is Calling;
You'll Be More than Satisfied

To the mere-human Church, God is calling you to truth of the requirement of life-surrender and true repentance.

To the church of the Lord Jesus Christ, God is calling us to wake up, to revive, and to not wait for a "revival" to do it.

We need not just a way of forgiveness, but the *Way of Holiness* – our cleansing from the stain of the World.

Then – and only then – shall we gain not only the "clean hands", but also the "pure heart", and ascend the Hill of the Lord.

We need *The Second Mankind*… Now.

Both have been there waiting for us, like a banquet prepared in the presence of our enemies.

> **Blessed are those who hunger and thirst for righteousness, for they shall be filled" (Matt 5:6).**

Make it Personal

Jesus Christ is calling me to strength, freedom, glory, honor, and dominion!
He is the Firstborn from among the dead.
And He *calls <u>anyone</u> that would* …
<u>to follow Him</u>.
With all my heart, my answer is …

Bible Quotes are Word English Bible (WEB) except where noted.

Questions for Study

Here I am including some questions for study, to help you the reader assess your level of *factual understanding* of how grace (everything we need for life and godliness) works.

To assess "spiritual" understanding, I still encourage all readers (and even church groups) to use the "MRI" method that I described in the introduction. It is also my joy to bring *Follow the Firstborn* to as many possible! For time and logistics, the best use of my years is to present to leaders; The most powerful leaders in the Kingdom of God will be those that are not blinded by FOG glasses. One of my smallest quizes is (a) what are the basic provisions of the New Covenant? And (b) "what is the "FOG"?

To renew our minds (Eph 4:23; Romans 12:3), we must sort out the "traditions of man" (Mark 7:13). In these exercises you will hear me press hard on a few themes here. I press hard only because in America, there are many millions of Christians that have settled for a very small, oversimplified "grace"; even reduced to amnesty for criminals that go their own way the very next day.

Resist Oversimplification

The oversimplification of the terms of salvation has left millions of true Christians in defeat and quiet despair; and many are dangerously living under false assurance.

Very little of the defeat is "persecution". Today it is as if the prophets could say again: "the people perish for lack of vision" or "are destroyed for lack of knowledge". I know from direct personal experience, that it is possible even for a truly surrendered and converted person to live in defeat for years and years; If this is you, then you stand to enjoy the same breakthrough that I experienced when these were cleared up.

Indeed, teachers will be held to a higher standard, but the Word of God is right there for us to see. Let us, and Einstein has said, "Make it as simple as possible, ***but no simpler***". We will then have our breakthrough, and the God of Hope will make all things new. This very thing finally happened to me after decades of "religion".

Your new faith and love will spring from *hope* (Col 1:3). Because we are free, that's how it has to work - or else love couldn't exist.

1. How many stages are there in salvation? Describe them both and then use this to explain John 15:22. Which one is by "grace" (trick question)? By persevering, are we "earning" our entrance into the Kingdom that will never end? If your pastor or teacher never explained the "two phases" of salvation to you except as a matter of "rewards" or as "it's automatic", then ask yourself why the Bible doesn't teach those things. Then please decide whom you shall obey – God or man. The choice is not easy, but it is simple!
2. To Whom has the Earth been assigned? Who was crowned with glory and honor? What was placed under our feet?
3. Why does God think we need His Spirit mingled in ours and a brand-new heart? What have we done as individuals and as a corporate people that makes such drastic measures necessary? (All in Ezekiel 36). For whose reputation does He renew us? His glory or ours? Hint – the scriptures (Rom *2:7* and 1 Cor *2:7*) it's not either-or. Describe godly and ungodly ways to relate to "glory".
4. If you are converted (Acts 3:19), what "were" you? What "are" you?
5. How and where do we find "life"? I'm speaking of the "Zoe" Life of God. Don't just say "Jesus" but explain its characteristics from the Word of God. Start with a one-minute answer drawn from a few of the central panels. Develop your ability to speak it naturally.

Bible Quotes are Word English Bible (WEB) except where noted.

6. As we have seen, believing starts the Do-over; and this Do-over is under the best of possible conditions (Ezek. 36:25, John 14) for anyone that will submit to the Word of God on this matter. Describe what makes the conditions so good that Christ can reasonably make our destiny hinge on what we do with it. Exercise: Lovingly – but by the Word of God – convince a Forgiveness-Only believer that this is how it works. In the very exercise of preparing, your mind will be refreshed in a big way.
7. Christ likened salvation to a bath followed by foot-washings as needed (Jn 17). What is the meaning (1 Jn 1:9)? Is the dirt part of us (Rom 7:7-20)? How does it get onto us? Who removes it (Eph 4:22-24, Jn 3:3)?
8. True or False: Christians are those that always hunger and thirst for more righteousness because they know they are sinners (Jn 4:14; Jn 6; Mt 5; Col 2:9; Eph 4:24).
9. True or False: If we have obtained forgiveness from Christ, then actual righteousness becomes just a rewards issue (Again Rom 2; Rom 6; Rom 8, Heb 10; 2 Pet 1:10). Passivity always leads to defeat. The Second Mankind is "able" to bear acceptable fruit as we surrender daily to follow Him; it is not "automatic". Don't let human *tradition* nullify the Word of God in your life.
10. True or False: God sees our hearts, that we are sorry, and forgives us; then He sovereignly, inilaterally begins to *improve* us.
11. Is a Christian a "Sinner Saved by Grace?" Correct the statement using the words "before", "was", and "but now" (John 1, Heb 2).
12. For whom is there no more condemnation? (Rom 8:1-4) Why? Is it simply for all who were "truly saved"? (verse 1b in some Bibles; but repeated in verse 4 in all Bibles).
13. Who shared the original good news (John 20)? *What was that news*? Who did she say ascended? Why does this matter? Where are you seated? What are the implications for authority?
14. What does it mean to be "In" Christ? How to "get in" (Gal 5:24 Col 3:3: Jn 15:10)?
15. What is the most-repeated saying of Christ (Mt 16:24-29)? What did He mean by it? Have you ever heard it in your church? If not, leave and find a *Christian* church.
16. Why didn't Christ explain "The Second Mankind" during His earthly ministry? (1 Cor 2:8)
17. What is "Grace"? There are many elements in it. In your own words, name and describe five elements other than "forgiveness" and "going to Heaven". In my opinion, the best *starting* point is 2 Peter 1:3-4, but we should be able to expand on it as we renew our minds.

18. Are we to be like Him in this Age, in this World? Or not? Does it really matter for our daily well-being? For eternity? (1 Jn 4; Mt 16:27).
19. How dare Christ demand actual righteousness from us (Rom 2:7-8)? Is He demanding perfection (See Ezek. 36:25-27; Rom 6:7; 1 Jn 2:1)?
20. Exercise: For each of the six passages quoted in all Romans Road Gospel tracts, state how it has either surgically omitted repentance and holiness, or made them out to be "optional" or "automatic". Show how each Romans Road quote violates its immediate context. What would be the effect on the American Christianity of a million of these tracts got around and people accepted them? That happened and that's how we got here.
21. (A big exercise) Read David Bercot's "Will the Theologians Please Sit Down" to fully understand how profoundly dangerous gnostic teaching thrived in Politically powerful Christianity; both in Catholicism and then again in the Reformation itself.
22. What definitions of the Greek words "Pistis" and "Pisteuo" are always used in Bibles? What legitimate definitions for these two words make the entire Bible consistent? Why would translators since the Reformation always go with the "easy" meanings?
23. What is Glory? Is our transformation for *God's* glory, or is it for *our* glory? The answer is a three-letter word starting with "y". It's a false dichotomy; It's not an either-or question!
24. Who is it that gets to go to Heaven (1 Jn 2; Rom 8:1:4)? To him to who simply believes? Trusts? Or to one who *entrusts* his life to God … and is converted, then overcomes by the power of God? Exercise: Be able to state this naturally and easily to anyone at any time.
25. Given any single panel or any single frame, teach it. Be able to say how it connects with each of its progressively larger contexts (panel; surrounding panel; the New Covenant; or the plan of God toward man.
26. In your own words, summarize each of the three central panels in light of the headings (*the hope, the call, sown in…, raised in…*). In particular, describe how faith and love spring from hope (Col 1:3). Be as plain and personal as you can. This is how evangelism used to work, and how it will work again!

Bible Quotes are Word English Bible (WEB) except where noted.

In Closing

In about as concise as I can get - we were alienated from God in our innermost natures, and before we are reborn, we all experience the separation and weakness against the work of the enemy and against our dignity itself.

But God through Christ made a way for us to "get back to the garden"; to get right with God, and then to stay right with Him by His power and His mercy. None of it was automatic according to the scriptures, but He has provided for us everything we need.

Puzzle Completed

If you, the reader, are seeing this clearly for the first time, then you have escaped the strongest single stronghold of Gospel oversimplification in the Church today, worldwide. The puzzle of the Bible will no longer be a puzzle at all, because you have removed the FOG (Forgiveness-Only Gospel) lenses.

I hope and expect that you are now better able to see that you are invited not only to amnesty, but to unspeakable dignity! You are called to BOTH - to the glory of God. You are now falling in love with Jesus Christ because He is good enough to have raised you up and carried you to the throne room with Him at the right hand of God, and you need not settle for defeat.

Your newfound clarity will very quickly and naturally bring you a boldness that will astonish you. And you will be truly falling in love with God in a way that will transform you. Now, why would you ever leave Him? Once-saved always-saved is not the issue. Knowing and loving God is the issue.

What you have found will astonish all who know you, and they will want it. That's how the gospel spread like wildfire in the early church!

Bible Quotes are Word English Bible (WEB) except where noted.

ABOUT THE AUTHOR

By "wiring", Jon is an artist (musician), analyst (obsessively solving complexity) and a teacher.
By formal training, Jon is an aerospace engineer and large-systems analyst. But by "calling", Jon is a Bible teacher, writer, and Gospel preacher, sent to *ignite faith* – or to "jump start" through the restoration of hope grounded in the true and full promises of God.
Jon is ordained by John G. Lake Ministries and is a ministry elder and teacher at Bethel City Church in Morrisville, North Carolina.
Jon and his wife Mary live near Raleigh, North Carolina.